UTOPIAS ELSEWHERE

UTOPIAS ELSEWHERE

Journeys in a Vanishing World

ANTHONY DANIELS

CROWN PUBLISHERS, INC.

NEW YORK

Published by Crown Publishers, Inc.,
201 East 50th Street, New York, New York 10022.
Member of the Crown Publishing Group.

Published in Great Britain by Random Century Group Ltd. in 1991
as *The Wilder Shores of Marx*

CROWN is a trademark of Crown Publishers, Inc.

Manufactured in the United States of America

Library of Congress Cataloging in Publication Data

Daniels, Anthony.
    Utopias elsewhere / Anthony Daniels.
        p.   cm.
    Includes index.
    1. Communism—1945—Case studies.   2. Communist countries—Description and
    travel.   I. Title.
    HX44.D26412   1991
    335.43'09172'4—dc20   71702
                                                                                        91-13505
                                                                                          CIP

ISBN 0-517-58548-0

10   9   8   7   6   5   4   3   2   1

First American Edition

CONTENTS

ACKNOWLEDGMENTS

I should like to thank all those people in the countries I visited who spoke to me, sometimes at considerable risk to themselves. I should also like to thank Mr Charles Moore, Editor of the *Spectator*, Mr John O'Sullivan, Editor of the *National Review*, Mr Alexander Chancellor, Editor of the *Independent* Magazine, and Mr Nicholas Shakespeare, Literary Editor of the *Daily Telegraph*, in whose journals some of the material in this book has appeared. I am grateful to Mr Mark Almond, for his advice about Romania and to Mrs Jessica Douglas-Holme of the Eminescu Trust for her help. I should also like to thank Mr Taylor of Regent Tours Limited, Bristol, for his help and advice, my Editor Ms Kate Mosse, and my Literary agent Mr Bill Hamilton for their patient and sensible counsel. Finally I am grateful to my friends, Drs Richard and Frances Latchman and Mr Ingo and Dr Helen Evers for their hospitality to me while I was writing this book.

Needless to say all the views expressed in this book are my responsibility.

INTRODUCTION

I have long been fascinated by the passing of ways of life. In 1975, shortly after I qualified as a doctor, I went for a few months to work in Rhodesia, as it was then still called. I wanted to witness the last gasp of the colonial world before it passed into an oblivion from which it would be rescued only by vilification.

Scarcely fourteen years later, at the beginning of 1989, another way of life, which had then seemed entrenched and solid enough to endure a millennium, was under threat: communism. Its failure in the land which had first adopted it was evident for all to see, and denied by practically no one. There was ferment in communism's empire: the spectre of liberty was haunting Eastern Europe. I knew I had to hurry if ever I were to experience the full flavour of communist autocracy.

Fortunately for me, though not for the millions of people who had to live in them, there remained on the periphery of the communist world a handful of states whose leaders refused to read the writing on the wall, and who were dedicated to the petrification of their own absolute power. It was to those countries, starting with Albania in April 1989, and ending with Cuba in January 1990, that I bent my steps. My visits were short and hence my experience of each country, however intense, was necessarily limited; but because the countries were of such diverse cultures, the common effects wrought by communism stood out all the more clearly, and gave to my journeys a comparative perspective that a more prolonged sojourn in any one of them could not have given. Individually unimportant as the countries might be in world history, collectively they tell us much about one of the central political currents of the twentieth century.

I do not claim I approached my travels with my mind a *tabula rasa* as far as communism was concerned. Only an anchorite who had spent the last half century in a cave or a fool could have done that. In 1988, I had visited the Baltic Republics, which were just emerging from five decades of coma punctuated by nightmare. Everyone I met there had terrible stories to tell. A professor of chemistry recalled his schooldays under Stalin when he would emerge from school to find trucks parked outside with parents crowded inside. If yours were among them you climbed aboard and were deported to Siberia, never to be heard of again. A woman of my own age remembered, as a child, sitting up till three o'clock in the morning for several months in all the clothes she possessed, because the secret police might call at any hour up till then to deport the entire family, giving it no time to prepare. Such experiences were not those of isolated, disaffected individuals, but of entire nations: not of a few score, but of scores of millions of people.

Nor were these atrocities unconnected with the doctrine in whose name they were committed. In my youth, as a student, I read a fair bit of Marx and Lenin, and shared a house with an unreconstructed Marxist-Leninist who believed that the organisation of which he was the General Secretary – which had one other member – was the only genuinely Marxist-Leninist organisation in the world. He read the speeches of Enver Hoxha and Leonid Brezhnev as others read murder mysteries; he preferred nylon shirts to all others not because they were comfortable or aesthetically pleasing, but because they represented a Triumph of Man over Nature. No beautiful landscape was complete for him without a factory with smoking chimneys, because there was no smoke without proletarians, and no proletarians without Revolution. It didn't take me long to conclude that communism was dismal, and that the words of Marx and Lenin betrayed an infinite contempt for men as they were, for their aspirations, their joys and sorrows, their inconsistencies, their innermost feelings, their achievements and failings. Below the surface of their compassion for the poor seethed the molten lava of their hatred, which they had not enough self-knowledge to recognise.

I make no claim, therefore, to have travelled in a neutral frame of mind. But neutrality is not a precondition of truth, which itself is not necessarily the mean between two extremes. One does not expect neutrality of someone investigating Nazism, and would be appalled if he affected it; why, then, expect it of someone investigating a different, but longer-lasting, evil?

ALBANIA

Where religion is compulsory, I am an atheist; but where religion is forbidden, I am a believer. All public worship ceased in Albania in 1967, nearly a quarter of a century after the communists took power, when Albanian youth decided – spontaneously and with revolutionary enthusiasm, according to the official explanation – permanently to close the churches and mosques. What a wealth of thuggery and intimidation lies hidden behind this bland explanation!

I arrived in Tirana one morning in spring, 1989, wearing my protest against such intolerance. It was a sweatshirt with a picture on the chest of a toucan sitting amidst tropical foliage. Above the picture were the words *South American Handbook*; below it, the Spanish words *Vaya con Dios*, Go with God. In the circumstances, the sweatshirt might have been considered subversive, an attempt at religious propaganda. But no one at the airport understood Spanish, despite the presence on the bookshelves of the airport's VIP lounge of Enver Hoxha's *Selected Works* in Spanish translation. In any case, sweatshirts did not undergo the same degree of censorship on entry into Albania as more conventional forms of literature, and I was thus left in peace to enjoy my little private joke throughout the country.

Some might say that the violent suppression of religion (and who can doubt that after a millennium of profound social and cultural influence, the suppression must have been violent?) had nothing to do with Marxism-Leninism, having been rather the whim of an ideological pervert, a chance despot. Yet the scriptures provide ample justification for such action, whether or not it was the real motive for it in Albania. Before the days when Marxists and Christians discovered supposedly mutual ground, Marx wrote of the post-revolutionary era to come:

> When the [revolutionary] political state . . . comes violently into being . . . [it] can and must proceed to the *abolition of religion*, to the *destruction* of religion.

And this was because:

> . . . to abolish religion as the illusory happiness of the people is to demand their real happiness; the demand to give up illusions about the existing state of affairs is the demand to give up a state of affairs that needs illusions.

As for the Lenin's opinion of religion, it was, if anything, rather less favourable than that of Marx:

> . . . any religious idea, any idea of god at all, any flirtation even with a god, is the most unutterable foulness . . . It is the most dangerous foulness, the most shameful 'infection'.

When a man compares religion with venereal disease, it is scarcely surprising that those who claim to be his followers close churches and mosques.

At Tirana Airport one leaves a continent and several decades behind. No businessmen bustle self-importantly here, no one rushes to buy a watch or a camera he does not need simply because there are a few francs or marks or pounds to be saved. People move slowly, almost with reluctance. The aircraft in which one lands stands in solitary glory on the tarmac (apart from the few ancient and probably flightless MiG fighters half-hidden behind the bushes, procured from the Soviet Union or China many years ago, before those countries were declared Antimarx by Albania's absolute dictator for forty-two years, Enver Hoxha). One walks to the terminal through a pleasantly seedy garden with spiky grass and stunted palm trees, and notices there is no smell of aviation fuel in the air, as at other airports, and recalls the paeans of praise Albania once earned from enthusiasts for its freedom from pollution. Before the entry formalities are completed, the aircraft has taken off for its return to the other world, and suddenly the reality of Albania's terrible isolation is revealed to the tourist. If he contracts appendicitis now, he will have to submit to an Albanian appendectomy.

Foreign visitors can enter Albania only in an officially supervised group, unless the Albanian government extends a special invitation to them: an unlikely eventuality in my case, since I had never acted as an apologist for the regime. Few groups are allowed in each year; they are escorted everywhere, but then even Albanians are not permitted to leave their home district without permission from the authorities. While we filled in our declaration forms, listing the narcotics, explosives and books we had brought with us, and waited for the customs and immigration officials to compose themselves in preparation for their inspection of us and our forms, I cast my eye over my companions of the next twelve days. I had hoped for a rich crop of eccentrics among them, such as I had encountered at the annual general meeting of the Anglo- Albanian Society in London a month previously. The secretary of the society was a retired optician from Ilford who had discovered the Balkan paradise late in life and learnt its language; the rank and file of the society seemed either elderly revolutionaries of the upper classes, who knew the key to world history yet somehow had never learnt how to do up their shirt buttons properly, or lonely, embittered proletarian autodidacts, who dreamed of vengeance upon the world and called it love of humanity.

I scanned the group in vain for believers in Tirana as the New Jerusalem. The nearest I came to finding them were a retired architect and his wife from Hampstead who were so appalled at Thatcher's Britain that they wanted to examine other possibilities for themselves. ('One is always looking for an alternative to our ghastly predicament,' said the architect.) But it didn't take them very long to realise that, bad as things were at home, the little Balkan state provided few solutions. Our drive to Tirana from the airport was sufficient to prove it.

Tirana is in one of the few fertile valleys of an exceedingly mountainous country. It is important, therefore, that these valleys should yield as much produce as possible, especially as the government is determined for political reasons that Albania should be self-sufficient in food, as in everything else. Certainly, every inch of land appears to be cultivated; but the statistical claims made by the government about the mechanisation of Albanian agriculture seem, at least to the casual observer on his way from Tirana Airport to Tirana, to be – well, exaggerated. It is true there are tractors to be seen, but of a vintage that any visitor will not have encountered outside a museum, and in such a state of battered disrepair that, belching thick black smoke in protest, they move scarcely faster than the oxcarts that still trundle the tracks and roads of Albania in greater numbers than the generally limping motor vehicles. The utility of these tractors must surely be limited. And in many of the fields there are still to be seen large groups of peasants, mainly kerchiefed women, tilling the soil with handhoes and weeding by hand. Were it not that the fields are vast in extent, thus proclaiming themselves part of state farms, the scene might be immemorial.

There is one further feature of the landscape, however, that an Albanian peasant, returning from another age, would not recognise. At frequent intervals as far as the eye can see, on every hillock and in every declivity, are rows of flattish concrete domes (I counted thirty-two in one field alone), a succession of tiny Santa Sophias, each with a gaping black slit in its walls. These are defensive gun emplacements, patiently awaiting an invasion of Albania to find their use. Here is the first intimation the visitor receives of that wild nationalism and xenophobia that has so completely isolated Albania from the rest of the world for nearly half a century. Of the military worth of these artillery emplacements I cannot speak; I do not know whether Albania has sufficient men or arms to defend them, or indeed whether they are defensible against modern weaponry. But as a constant message to the peasants in the fields that foreigners are enemies, to be guarded against at all costs, the gun emplacements are unrivalled. And in hillier areas, where there are vineyards, the message is reinforced by the iron spikes that are set in the tops of each of the posts supporting the vines, to spear enemy paratroops as they land.

Where does this insane xenophobia come from? After all, human behaviour has an explanation, if not a justification. And it isn't long before your guides in Albania (there are always two of them, one to watch the behaviour of the other) recite the list of invaders and occupiers of their country: Roman, Bulgarian, Serbian, Byzantine, Turkish, Italian, Austrian, French, German, and Anglo-American. Thus the Albanians have learnt the harsh lesson of history: unfortunately, the wrong one.

It began to rain as we approached the city. The approaches to very few cities are edifying, especially in the rain, but Tirana was particularly dispiriting in this respect. First came a few factories, draped with red banners proclaiming glory to the Albanian Party of Labour, and then apartment blocks, built of rough red bricks, all of them in a little sea of mud, and finished to a standard that would have disgraced Calcutta.

'Look at that!' exclaimed William, a psychiatric social worker. 'It's awful.'

He was perfectly right, of course, it *was* awful, but William's furrowed brow and the dying fall of his voice told us that this was the opening shot in a campaign of continuous complaint, for William would have found Lausanne no less intolerable than Tirana.

There was no traffic in Tirana and no commercial life. The disfiguring vulgarity of modern advertising has often been remarked upon: the dreariness of its replacement by political slogans rather less often. As for the people who trudged along the pavements, they too were clad in dreariness. Their clothes were of man-made fibre, of colours with which they used to paint the corridors of mental hospitals, chocolate brown and a shade of dark and dirty orange particularly prominent among them.

After forty minutes, we reached Skanderbeg Square, in the very heart of the city. It was named after the Albanian national hero who raised the standard of revolt against the Turks in 1443 and won every battle against them except his last in 1468. In modern Albanian historiography, Skanderbeg was unequivocally a Good Thing, a forerunner in fact of Enver Hoxha and the Albanian Party of Labour. As is usual in the extreme nationalist version of history, inconvenient facts are overlooked: that the people Skanderbeg fought against were mainly Albanians led by other Albanians, that Turkish suzerainty was by no means a chapter of horrors and nothing else, that Albanians were privileged within the Ottoman empire and more than thirty of them became viziers, that Albanian troops were used by the Turks to put down Greek rebellions, etc.

In any case, it is not Skanderbeg whose huge statue is at the centre of this vast square so devoid of traffic that people stroll across it without having to look: it is Enver Hoxha, plump, avuncular and metallic in his heavy bronze overcoat.

We stayed in the Hotel Tirana overlooking the square. It is the city's only real tower block, and from its upper floors you can look down the Boulevard of Martyrs to the green hills beyond the Enver Hoxha University. I found myself sharing a room with a member of our group, Albert, an incessant chatterer who was as little able to resist filling silences with verbigeration as a glutton can resist emptying boxes of chocolates. The banality of his conversation drove me to the brink of despair, and I understood at last Sartre's remark that hell was other people. That Albert was kindly and well-meaning made it worse, not better. Just occasionally, however, he said something interesting. He had been to Albania before but unlike most people who have been more than once was not an apologist of the regime. In addition to snapshots of the high street of his south London suburb with which he hoped to increase disaffection among the citizens of Albania, he brought photographs of the guides on his previous tour of the country, and showed them to our present guides. One of the photographed guides had in the interval managed to defect while acting as an interpreter in western Europe. Our present guides suggested that, as a traitor, his face be ceremonially scratched from the photograph.

Although it was raining, I went out at once for a walk, glancing behind me at intervals to see whether I was tailed. I wasn't, and I felt mildly put out at being so unimportant. I took shelter for a time under the colonnade of the Palace of Culture, a marble-faced building that ran along one side of the square. The marble columns of the colonnade were rectangular, with ninety degree corners on which one might cut oneself. Why was it, I wondered, that both fascist and communist architects were so drawn to columns of this type? Was it because they embodied power, naked and unadorned? I couldn't think of a style of architecture more completely antithetical to culture than that of the Palace of Culture.

A few bedraggled Albanians also took shelter there. They looked at me with as much curiosity as I looked at them. Their language was radically incomprehensible to me, the only surviving descendent of ancient Illyrian and quite unlike any other European language, even Hungarian. A question and answer from *Twelfth Night* ran through my head over and over again, like a fragment of a melody that won't go away, or a record stuck in a groove: What country, friends, is this? Illyria, lady. What country, friends, is this? Illyria, lady.

I had to move away to escape the repetition of these pointless phrases. New impressions would drive them from my mind, I hoped. And sure enough, I was soon intrigued by the little eighteenth century mosque across the road from the Palace of Culture. It had a single minaret and was decorated with a charmingly naive floral frieze. The iron gates, however, were padlocked, and my attempts to see in at the windows of the mosque were observed somewhat nervously by the few passers-by. A new question entered my mind: did Albanians, in the privacy of their homes, offer up illicit prayers to the deity? After all, 70 per cent of them had once been Moslem (though not devoutly so), and the rest Christian. Official historiography explained the mass conversion of Albanians to Islam after the Turkish conquest by the lower taxes paid by Moslems. This sounded to me not implausible: having witnessed mass conversions elsewhere, I doubted their spirituality. But official historiography was itself less interested in truth than in self-validation. If peasants converted to Islam because of tax advantages, it made religion – with all its supposed otherworldliness – look sordid and hypocritical. And it helped support the Marxist contention that, *au fond*, all human activity is motivated by economic considerations. It was ironic, then, that the leader of the new godless Albania should have been called Hoxha, which is Turkish for religious teacher. Some might say, of course, that it wasn't ironic at all: he merely replaced one religion with another, a religion even less squeamish about forced conversion than Islam in Asia or Christianity in the New World.

With these thoughts in mind, it seemed only right that I should make for the Boulevard of Martyrs. This was reached via a little circus of yellow stucco buildings which were ministries: one could tell by the chauffered new black Mercedes with grey curtains in the rear windows that waited at the entrances. On the walls of the ministries were moulded plaster decorations in the Stalinist baroque style: sheaves of wheat and bunches of grapes.

There were a couple of sets of traffic lights in the vicinity, the only ones in the whole of Albania, which were of recent installation. It is said there are but five hundred cars in the country, and Tirana being a city of wide streets and boulevards, it has an atmosphere of calm that is at first deeply refreshing, at least to those who are used to the frantic, choking cities of Europe, but which – after no great length of time – becomes rather sinister. It is the silence, interrupted only rarely by a distant rumble over the cobbles of an approaching vehicle, that disturbs. Cities were not made for silence. For whom, then, or for what were these wide streets constructed, if not for traffic? For military parades, to prevent barricades from ever being erected across them, to overawe pedestrians? Or were they made like this simply because grandiosity is the nature of tyrants?

I reached the Boulevard of Martyrs, pausing before the statue of Stalin, one hand held Napoleonically in his military greatcoat, opposite the art gallery. Six months previously in the Soviet Union I had read in the *Moscow News* of the discovery of a mass grave in Byelorussia containing at least 102,000 bodies, a mass murder freely attributed to Stalin, who was acknowledged as one of the greatest criminals in history. This was scarcely news outside the Soviet Union, of course; but the final acceptance of this truth in the land of his crimes made the presence of a statue to him anywhere else all the more shocking. Yet at the same time I was aware of a strange ambivalence in my reaction: admiration of, even affection for, the dottiness of a tiny nation that had set its face against the accepted truths of the rest of the world. If Albania did not exist, it would be necessary perhaps to invent it. But my ambivalence was essentially self-indulgent. The eccentricity of believing in Stalin was not that of a private person, but of a state and a government; nor was it harmless, like believing the earth was flat or the future was decipherable in tea leaves, but vicious and nasty, like anti-Semitism or religious fanaticism.

Because of the rain, the Boulevard was almost deserted. I entered the only other hotel for foreigners in Tirana, the Dajti, reserved for diplomats and visitors of consequence. The enormous entrance hall was empty: but a black and white television in the corner was broadcasting an English lesson from the sixties into the void, given by comically prim English actors:

Repeat Walter's reply to Connie's question.
Connie: Have you enough money?
Walter: I think so, thank you.

How English, I thought, that Walter should reply *I think so* rather then *Yes* or *No*: it is scarcely any wonder that Albion is regarded as diabolically perfidious when often she is only mealy-mouthed.

I drank some coffee – the best I had in Albania – and ate a cake of astonishing sweetness which somehow left a chemical aftertaste, as though an unpleasant medicine had been insinuated into it in an attempt to get by stealth a difficult patient to take his afternoon dose. I left the Dajti with Connie and Walter still enunciating away, their words clearer than their meanings, and continued down the Boulevard of Martyrs.

I crossed the road but was soon waved back by soldiers with stubby automatic weapons at the ready. They wore drab uniforms of Soviet inspiration and long olive green waterproof capes. The building from which they waved me away was clearly important: Party Headquarters or the like. There was tension here which had been absent from the ministries, and the building itself was severe, massive and grey.

I reached the end of the Boulevard. By now it had stopped raining and there were some students and soldiers around. The main building of Enver Hoxha University was much smaller and less impressive close to than when seen from the other end of the long, wide Boulevard. Its rough-hewn grey granite facing was positively ugly. To the left of the Enver Hoxha University was the Enver Hoxha football stadium, reached across a wide expanse of white stone. Here there was another colonnade of square pillars, under which was an outdoor café where – to my astonishment – people were actually being served drinks by waiters in white jackets and black bow ties. As I approached, two young men (there were no women to be seen) motioned me to sit at their table, and I accepted their invitation.

The young men – hardly more than youths – were thin and wiry, as though they had spent time in the mountains as goatherds, and their hair was cropped very short. Their faces, scalps and arms were scarred by old cuts, and their eyes had that strange limpidity that people with olive complexions sometimes have. They were amiable, but I should not have underestimated their toughness.

We had no language in common, but one of them knew a little Italian, which he spoke slowly and badly enough for me to understand. They were army conscripts on leave, and I was surprised that they showed no fear of speaking to me. They had already had a few drinks and insisted that I joined them in a cognac. Since I dislike all cognac, I cannot comment on the Albanian variety: but it certainly seemed no worse to me than many others I have tried.

The two conscripts – who hated the army – asked me, like Daniel come to cast judgment, to settle a dispute between them. The first of them maintained there were three important things in life, while the second maintained there was only one. The three things were sex, whisky and music; while the one thing was sport. Ideology, patriotism and the rest were obviously of no account to them. The one who favoured music, among other things, recited the names of pop groups with the same expression as a mystic reciting the many names of God. 'Dire Straits', he said, and repeated it many times. 'Gary Lineker', countered the other.

'Is it true that Michael Jackson has AIDS?' asked the first.

To his evident disappointment, I had no special information on the subject. He found my lack of interest in it strange: to be free, and yet to know nothing of Michael Jackson!

A friends of theirs came to sit with us. He was taller than they, with pretensions to charm and elegance, a coat draped over his shoulders somewhat in the manner of Prince Yakimov in *The Balkan Trilogy*. His shabby moulded plastic shoes let him down, however. He managed to convey that it was only by accident that he found himself in Tirana: spiritually, he was more at home in Paris or New York. And he let it be known also that he was by no means a drone of the socialist state: he was a dealer in dollars, in watches and in Walkmen.

There followed an ominous inspection of my watch, which I knew from experience would lead to urgent and heartrending requests that I should part with it, on the most advantageous terms to me, of course. The deal would be presented as though the future of the whole world depended upon it, and it was a last chance. I would need all my minimal strength to resist the arguments of the aspiring purchaser. And then the subject would switch to dollars, failing agreement on which I should be expected at least to exchange my shoes for his, since the purchase of new ones would be 'no problem for me'.

The three of them followed me back down the Boulevard of Martyrs, increasingly desperate for some tangible memento of our meeting. Then suddenly they melted away, as though they had remembered other urgent business: I surmised that it wasn't safe to be too long in the company of foreigners, especially in the centre of the city.

Back in the hotel, at seven o'clock, it was time for dinner. One of the strangest things about group holidays is the eagerness with which everyone, hungry or not, rushes to the dining room three times a day, as if afraid that a moment's delay will cause the food to disappear. I felt this anxiety myself, very acutely. Of course, by the standards of Albanians, for whom everything was, is and will continue to be severely rationed, and very few of whom are fat, we ate enormously, even obscenely. The Albanians did everything they could to please us, but neither their efforts nor our situation of extreme privilege inhibited some of our number from complaining vociferously about the staleness of the bread, the smallness of the portions of butter etc. At such moments, I wished for a chasm to open up and swallow me.

After dinner, I went for a walk in night-time Tirana. Not even the firmest of Enver Hoxha's partisans would maintain that Tirana is an exciting or vibrant city, but it is safe, and though the streets are only half-lit by lamps of feeble power, whose principal effect is to cast deep shadows without illuminating anything, one senses at once that muggings and robberies do not happen here. In a country with an immemorial tradition of banditry, and a world in which it is ever less safe to venture out of one's room after dark, this is no mean achievement, a triumph, one might almost say, for personal liberty. But liberty to do what, except stroll? No village in Wales on a wet Sunday afternoon is more dead than Tirana after dark.

Eventually, however, I found a bar. It was down a long, wide street with apartment windows, but almost all were sealed off from view by dark curtains of rough material, and those that were not were illuminated by too dim a light – a yellowing gloom of forty watts or less – to see much beyond the general dinginess within.

The bar was large and bare, with an iron-railed gallery above. There were about twenty white-topped tables, stained with the evaporated slops of beer and spirits. Only three of the tables were occupied, for it was late: nine-thirty. The other drinkers, all unshaven men in workaday clothes, scarcely looked up when I entered: the table tops seeming to exert for them a deep, if melancholy, fascination. They did not ask me to join them: indeed, they hardly communicated among themselves. I ordered a *raki*, a viscous clear spirit of considerable strength. The waiter let it be known it was near to closing time by removing his white jacket as soon as he had brought me my glass. I drank the *raki* and returned to the hotel, the waiter locking the bar door behind me as I left.

By this time, the sound of folk music was issuing from the subterranean taverna under the hotel lobby. I went down to investigate. The taverna had been badly damaged only a few weeks before by English football hooligans, in Albania for an international match, who had got drunk, stripped naked and given Nazi salutes, than which nothing would be better calculated to insult and enrage the Albanians. Folk dancers in colourful traditional Albanian costumes were performing on the dance floor, but because the audience was sparse and consisted entirely of foreigners, for whom the dancers might as well have been sea-lions, the gaiety of the dances was forced and without meaning, lifeless and dishonest. I fled from this ghostly charade to my room.

Albert was there, bursting with platitudes. But I have to admit he was very well prepared for the trip: not only had he brought ample supplies of chewing gum and pens for the children that he assured me would pester us later on, but he had a light plastic mackintosh against the squally showers that were seasonal elsewhere in the country, dozens of rolls of film and a bag of tiny chocolate bars for when lunch or dinner was unavoidably delayed, to say nothing of a travelling electric teapot with adaptors for use in all electric points of the world. More importantly, he possessed a guidebook to Albania written by the secretary of the Anglo-Albanian Society and an Albanian phrasebook not easily come by. While he poured details of the new compact disc player he had just bought at home into my ear, I read these volumes, so full of strange and mysterious information.

What, for example, was one to make of the guidebook's statement that there was one shop in Albania for every 268 people? Was it a complaint or a boast? What did they sell, these shops for 268 people? And where did one go to taste the 'popular' Albanian cocktail, the *Lumumba*, which is made of *raki* and cocoa? And where did one obtain a copy of the town of Fier's twice weekly newspaper, *The Sweat of the Peasant*?

With non-ferrous metals one was on firmer ground. The output of chromium in Albania since 1938 had increased 256 times, that of copper since 1946, 617 times. Ah, I thought, if only happiness could be measured in the same way! That would soon put a finish to all those endless ideological disputes and settle matters once and for all. The output of happiness in Albania between 1938 and 1980 rose 479 times, while that of Belgium rose in the same period only 4.7 times, *ergo* . . .

I turned to the phrasebook. I learnt that the Albanian for perhaps was the same as for probably: an explanation for Albanian production statistics, perhaps – or probably. And the phrasebook reminded me of my time in Somalia in 1986 when, in the midst of a cholera epidemic, I was equipped by a Somali phrasebook, compiled during the period of Soviet influence, with such useful phrases as 'Hand me the opera glasses, please'. I repeated to myself in Albanian: 'Industrial production has increased ninety-seven fold as against 1938.' The only authentic phrase appeared in the *At the hospital* section: 'I am feeling worse.' The section on polite greetings and valedictions, by contrast, betrayed the heavy hand of the ideologist. I attempted to commit to memory the Albanian for 'We must live and work as under a siege', but the effort proved too great, and I was overcome by sleep.

The next morning, after a breakfast whose coffee not even the most accommodating of guests could have called good, or even coffee, it was time to commence our visits. For some reason the Albanian tourist authorities were convinced that museums were what we had come to Albania to see: at any rate, that was what they were going to show us. Thenceforth, we were taken to see three museums a day, until the very idea of a museum induced in me a faint sensation of nausea – still I cannot enter one without being overcome momentarily by a feeling of profound gloom. Halfway through the tour, I thought we must surely by now have exhausted the museums of Albania: it is, after all, a very small country, only the size of Wales, with about the same population. In this I was sadly mistaken, for according to *40 Years of Socialist Albania* the number of museums in Albania has risen from seven in 1950 to 2034 in 1983. It would therefore have taken a tour of approximately two years to exhaust them. A tour of only twelve days exhausted me.

The museum that evidently required the most urgent visit was called Albania Today, an exhibition of socialist Albania's achievements. Unfortunately, when we arrived Albania Today was closed. Our guides attempted to find out why, but were given a dusty answer by the doorman: Albania Today would be open tomorrow, perhaps or probably.

By way of compensation for our disappointment, we were taken instead to the Enver Hoxha Museum in the Boulevard of Martyrs. This is the metropolitan cathedral of the new Albanian religion. The building itself is hi-tech, startlingly so in a capital where the construction of even quite large apartment blocks seems hardly above the mud hut level. It is in the style of modern cathedrals, as built by atheist architects: a shining white pyramid with a translucent red star set horizontally as a window at its apex. It does not lack devotees, of course, for a prolonged communion there is an important part of every schoolchild's education. One enters reverently.

From the entrance run two red carpets (upon which one may not step) up to a large and dazzling white statue of Hoxha, seated Pharaonically on what one suspects is an armchair. The statue has red gladioli at its base and is situated exactly at the centre of an expanse of white stone. I wanted to laugh.

The galleries depicting his life and work run round the inside of the pyramid, rather as in the Guggenheim. The exhibits start with his childhood and progress upwards to his death. Throughout there are glass reliquaries, containing his hat, his pen, his revolver, his shirts (minus their foreign labels), and his sunglasses. The photographs are mainly in the Soviet style, with that peculiar grainy fuzziness unknown outside the communist world which presumably makes it easy to add or subtract people whenever ideologically necessary. Looking at these semi-sepia photographs one feels not that the camera cannot lie, but that it cannot tell the truth.

There are pictures of Enver Hoxha as a youth. To emphasise the quasi-miraculous nature of his intellectual powers, it has been found advantageous to assert that his revolutionary ideas came to him very young, and that he never subsequently deviated from them. This version of his biography not only proves the precocity of his genius, but demonstrates the extraordinary fidelity of his character. If, in ordinary conversation, we said of a man that he had not changed his ideas since the age of fifteen, it would not be taken as a compliment; but conversations about Enver Hoxha were never intended to be ordinary.

It is clear from the photographs of Hoxha as a youth that in one respect the otherwise preposterously hagiographic account of his life is perfectly correct: his will was always indomitable. The handsome and intelligent youth who stares out at the camera, dandyishly adorned in a bow tie, his head inclined at a disdainful angle, is at once proud, scornful, arrogant, rebellious and self-possessed, already aware of a

special historical destiny. I should not care to have been his teacher at
school. As to the ultimate source of his infinite self-assurance, it must
remain a mystery; a throw of the genes, perhaps, or an over-indulgent
mother. But whatever explanation is proposed, the effect was disproportionate to the cause. One thing seems certain: he had a predis-
position to rebellion against any authority but his own, for which, by
contrast, he conceived an immediate and infinite respect. And in the
particular historical conditions in which he grew up, these unpleasantly
adolescent traits, which in other circumstances he would have had to
subdue, were a positive advantage.

One spirals upwards towards his death, or what would have been his
death were he not immortal. He was a student (on an Albanian
government stipend) in Montpellier in the early thirties until he was
expelled for subversive behaviour. He spent some time in Paris before
becoming personal secretary to the Albanian consul in Belgium. In
1938, he returned to Albania as a teacher at the French *lycée* in Korce,
never for a moment letting up on subversion.

At all times in his life he was a leader: in the whole of the museum he
is never portrayed in a position of subordination to anyone. And it was
the war that gave him his chance. Without it, he might have remained
an autodidact Marxist *enragé* for the rest of his life; but the foreign
occupation of his country, so ideally suited geographically and
culturally to guerrilla warfare, gave him the opportunity, which he
exploited brilliantly, to become an autodidact Marxist dictator for the
remainder of his life instead.

During the war, Hoxha was a guerrilla leader of great prowess.
According to the official version of history now peddled *ad nauseam*
everywhere and on all possible occasions, it was Hoxha and his
partisans who were responsible for the defeat of the Nazis in Albania.
Throughout the whole of the country, in hundreds of monuments and
posters, I never once saw an allusion to the wider context of the war
years. One might have supposed that Albania stood alone against the
Nazis.

The truth was somewhat more complex than the official version,
though since its accession to power the Albanian leadership has been
able to put into practice the incantation theory of historical truth: that
something becomes true by constant reiteration. In fact, the withdrawal
of the Nazis from Albania was part of their general retreat in the face of
the onslaught of the Russians and the Americans, compared with which
the Albanian partisans were able to administer no more than pinpricks.

It is no disgrace to a tiny and backward nation that it should have been unable, by its own unaided efforts, to rid itself of occupation by one of the most powerful military machines of all time; but it is a disgrace that its leaders should have misrepresented the past so consistently and self-glorifyingly for four and a half decades, with the sole purpose of maintaining themselves in power.

Actually, Hoxha and his partisans had other fish to fry than the Nazis. Realising that the Nazi withdrawal was in any case inevitable, the partisans strove as much to secure their own future position inside the country as to expel the Nazi invaders. A considerable proportion of their military activity was directed not against the Germans but against other, non-communist, Albanian armed groups, which wished to restore the *status quo ante*. In this sense, the partisans *were* wholly successful: by the time the Nazis left Albania, they were the only ones who could fill the power vacuum.

Another interesting aspect of Albania's modern history that somehow escapes memorialisation in Albania is the strange alliance between Enver Hoxha and certain members of the British upper-middle classes. Indeed, it would hardly be too much to say that Hoxha owed his power to this unholy alliance, and thus the Albanian people had it to thank for forty years of Hoxha's rule. It was not Stalin who supplied the partisans with the arms that helped them defeat their Albanian enemies, but the British, who did so on the recommendation of their Balkan intelligence network, which – it transpires – was riddled with upper class communists and fellow-travellers. And it was Kim Philby who ensured the failure of Anglo-American attempts to overthrow Hoxha after the war by revealing the plans in advance to the Russians and Albanians. Probably the attempts would have failed anyway; whether they deserved to is another question about which much could be argued. When Albanians are free to erect statues to whomsoever they please, we shall see whether they erect any to Philby.

The photographs in the museum show Hoxha emerging from the war surprisingly sleek, indeed fat. Addressing the microphone during the proclamation of the new republic in Tirana in 1944, he reminded me very powerfully of another leader: Franco. So alike were they physically that, were it not for the star on Hoxha's military beret, this photograph of him could be inserted in a biography of Franco, and not more than one in a hundred readers notice the substitution. Shortly afterwards, fatter still, he developed a taste for Soviet marshals' uniforms, with much gold braid and a gold belt that kept his expanding paunch under control as he bent over to pat children on the head. An extract from a speech in French that he gave during his gold braid period is played over and over again, hour after hour, day after day. *Nous rejetons avec mépris . . . Nous rejetons avec mépris . . .* I never quite caught what it was that he rejected with such contumely, but the tone of his surprisingly squeaky voice was full of that unthinking self-righteousness and injured innocence that allows a man to justify to himself the vilest crimes (such as the execution of his erstwhile colleagues, a particular forte of Hoxha's) and then to sleep easily.

He soon abandoned magniloquent uniforms for grey suits. We hear him next addressing a party congress: his speech is greeted by applause rising to (in the Stalinist terminology) a thunderous ovation. And we see a film of the congress delegates getting to their feet and clapping frantically. Did they really clap like this, or has the film been speeded up? And were the delegates afraid to be the first to stop clapping, lest they be thought traitors? The applause continues, day in, day out, with only the briefest of interludes for the voice of Hoxha himself.

As he ages, he mellows; he becomes slimmer and his suits are a lighter shade of grey. He is seen now with his new best friend (having shot the previous one or driven him to suicide), his disciple and successor, Ramiz Alia, a man to all intents and purposes without a personality. Hoxha spends more of his time on park benches surrounded by adoring children; he goes for walks in private gardens with his wife (also, as it happens, a member of the Politburo). And we see him in his study, quietly working on state papers.

Towards the end of his life he becomes doddery, and has the haggard look caused by spreading cancer. There is a memorable video of him taken, I should imagine, not long before he died. He is filmed approaching the bookcase in his study. He looks the books up and down, evidently searching for something good to read. Finally, after some considerable thought, he alights on something suitable: Volume Six of his own *Collected Works*. He settles down contentedly to read it.

Enver Hoxha's library is preserved in the museum. The books are mainly in French, a few in Albanian and Italian. There are perhaps five hundred of them, a number to overawe a barely literate peasant or to impress the inhabitants of a country where the only choice in the ubiquitous bookshops is between different *ersatz* bindings (usually wine-coloured) of the *Collected Works*. The books in Hoxha's library demonstrate a wide, if superficial, interest in archaeology and the visual arts, with a smattering of history: in short, a typical autodidact's library. Most of his books, of course, would have been forbidden his subjects, contaminated as they were by bourgeois idealism against whose blandishments only the ideologically fortified, such as himself, were proof.

I examined the library carefully, supposing that a man's books proclaimed the man, and I came to a somewhat disdainful conclusion concerning Enver Hoxha. In this, of course, I made the same mistake the Bolshevik intellectuals made about Stalin: that someone who was pedantic, bureaucratic and without originality could not also be formidable. But the twentieth century has seen the creation of societies in which precisely such faceless qualities are the *sine qua non* of success and survival: and despite the thousands of photographs, the relics of his life, the speeches and videos, Hoxha remains faceless, the object of a personality cult without a personality. As presented in the museum, he lived only in the sense that a Haitian zombie lives; he spoke a form of language not used by any but the undead. In *40 Years of Socialist Albania*, for example, each section is headed by quotations from him, a few of which I here take at random:

A broad system of transport . . . has been created. This system has strengthened the unified character of the economy and greatly enlivened the economic and social life of the country.

The increased level of knowledge and culture of the people represents a great potential for the realisation of the current and future plans, for the advance of technical and scientific progress to new heights.

The Party has shown constant care that culture, literature and arts develop in a pure and sound atmosphere, that they follow the revolutionary transformations of the country step by step and steadily strengthen their socialist content, their militant character, their popular spirit and their national features.

I shall spare the reader more (the *Collected Works* are sixty volumes long), but he or she might like to ponder the consequences, both for individuals and for a country, of the forcible imposition of this style of public expression to the exclusion of all others, not for ten minutes or a week, but for forty-five years: in other words, for nearly three generations of adults. A drowsy numbness pains my sense as though of hemlock I had drunk . . .

I looked at some middle-aged Albanians as they peered without curiosity into the glass case containing condolences on Hoxha's death from all over the world. Considering how many people enter the museum, very few survive to its final stages. And did those hardy few who reached the condolences realise that the telegram sent by Hardial Bains, First Secretary of the Central Committee of the Communist Party (Marxist-Leninist) of Canada, did not exactly express the sentiments of the whole Canadian people, if indeed it could be said to express any sentiments at all?

> The path which has been proven to be invincible by the life and work of Comrade Enver Hoxha, who led his party and people in their most militant and uncompromising struggle against imperialism, social imperialism, the bourgeoisie and all reaction and revisionism and opportunism of all hues in their service and who has left an indelible mark on history . . .

Mercifully for the reader of English, the rest of Hardial Bains' message is covered by a telegram from Thomas Sankara, soon to be murdered by his best friend but who was then President of the country he renamed Burkina Faso, Land of Incorruptible People, telling of his profound *sympathie émue*.

I left the museum, this cathedral of untruth, with a strange knot in my stomach. The idea that Hoxha should have gone to his grave triumphant filled me with rage. I felt I should have screamed 'Lies, lies, lies!' and trampled on the red carpet leading to his statue, just to let everyone know that I, at any rate, did not acquiesce in this elevation of mendacity to the status of religion. But of course I was silent, like everyone else, and my silence demeaned me and turned me into an accomplice. I wondered what went on in Albanian minds behind those impassive, weatherbeaten peasant faces. Had lies become truth simply through repetition? Or did they not impinge on consciousness at all, acceptance of them having become part of every citizen's repertoire of automatic behaviour, like walking or climbing stairs? One cannot, after all, be angered by the same lies year after year. But what effect, if any, did passive acceptance of systematic untruth have on the human pysche? Would the effect disappear with the regime that produced it? Albania was an experimental laboratory of the human soul in which, however, it was forbidden to ask questions.

In between visits to museums, our guides granted us what they called 'free time', never long enough to wander far. It was like being back at school. They suggested that we might like to use this time to do shopping, though what they thought we should buy is a mystery. Even the most inveterate of shoppers – amongst whom I am not one – would have found Albanian shops unenticing, poorly stocked as they were with those ill-designed, shoddy, unmistakably communist goods that are saleable only in conditions of shortage and monopoly, and sometimes not even then.

What, I wondered, is the defining characteristic of communist shoddiness? It certainly exists, for it is instantly recognisable among all the other possible forms of shoddiness. What have the tubes of Bulgarian toothpaste on sale in kiosks in Tirana in common with the packets of Czechoslovak soap or East German buttons also on sale there? How would one know, beyond any possibility of doubt, that Albania was communist merely by looking at a bottle of its brandy or a jar of its bottled fruit?

In the latter cases, of course, the labels would not be stuck on straight. One speculates as to whether this endemic crookedness represents revolt on the part of the bottle-labellers, or subtle satire. For if the labels were pasted on only *carelessly* – the result of drunkenness, say – one would expect that, now and again, a label would be pasted on straight. But this never happens: I examined the bottles in several stores to check the veracity of this peculiar observation.

Furthermore, where there are tins and metal tops, the rust gives them away as being of communist manufacture. And even this rust is of a special kind, being not just the result of time and oxidation, but of a fusion with the contents of the container that have somehow managed to seep outwards and mix with the rust, leaving a dark brown sticky mess that repels any but the most desperate customer.

However, it is the printing and design of packaging that is most thoroughly characteristic – pathognomonic, as doctors put it – of communist manufacture. The paper or cardboard is always rough and absorbent, so that ink often sends little spidery strands through it; the calligraphy is crude and inelegant. The labels bear as little information as possible: *toothpaste*, they say, or *soap*, and nothing else. This is because the alternatives to *toothpaste* and *soap* are not other brands, but no toothpaste at all and no soap. This is not to say that the information on a label that a bottle contains plums is entirely useless: it isn't, because in the bottling process the plums have been rendered revoltingly indistinguishable from cherries, olives, apricots, green-gages, peppers or tomatoes bottled by the same process: that is to say, they are all roundish objects of a faeculant brown colour. But since any product's competition is only a blank space, an absence, there is no need to dress it up attractively. Besides, it is in no one's interest that products should be sold rather than stored or even thrown away. Under socialism, production is not for profit, but it is not for use either; it is divorced from all human purposes whatsoever.

Does it matter, though, that the everyday objects of life should be so profoundly unattractive? Does it matter that clothes should be of dirty colours, that shops should be as inviting as empty morgues? How many times have we heard of the meretriciousness of commerical culture, of the essential unimportance of having a choice of breakfast cereals in the morning, of the waste involved in elaborate packaging that is designed to sell unnecessary or worthless products? There is so much in our lives that is trivial, that inhibits us from considering what is truly important in our existence, that to be freed from the complusion to possess goods ever remoter from our natural needs sometimes seems to us highly desirable. But there is a world of difference between voluntary renunciation of what is available and embittered resignation in the face of permanent shortage. And it is only by visiting countries that are relentlessly serious and puritanical ('We must live and work as under a siege') that one appreciates – within a very short time – the vital importance of frivolity.

The lack of aesthetic feeling in everyday objects is not compensated for in Tirana by the beauty of public works, though the city is clean and no one drops litter (possibly there is little to drop – only once in twelve days did I see a man reading a newspaper, and that was while he waited for a haircut). There are pleasant enough boulevards, if you can ignore the tendency to grandiosity, and Tirana is uncrowded: it is a city of only 200,000 inhabitants, a vast metropolis by the standards of most of Man's history, but now considered scarcely more than a town. There are a few corners where the old Turko-Parisian style persists: individual houses with crumbling yellow stucco, shutters and ornate ironwork, with small front gardens where vines grow in profusion. These houses were made for a languid life, for endless conversations over coffee or *raki*, for gossip and intrigue. But most of Tirana is given over to apartment blocks built by men for whom life is reducible to statistics, for whom quantity exists because it is an arithmetical expression, but for whom quality is too intangible a concept to have any reality.

Off the main boulevards, the apartment blocks are not faced with stucco or stone but left permanently unfinished, their breezeblock masonry and rough cementwork exposed, the walls so poorly constructed and carelessly aligned that it seems any minor vibration in the ground must shake them to rubble. Furthermore, the ground around them has not been cleared, still less landscaped: it remains scarred and scoured, like on a building site, turning to mud in the rain and dust in the sun. Piles of unused building materials or rusting equipment take the place of trees; the roads to the apartment blocks are no more than tracks strewn with rubble – along which people cannot walk but only trudge. After passing through acres of such 'scenery', one suddenly realises that this bureaucratic architecture is without precedent in the whole of human history: that never before has mankind constructed homes for himself which are so utterly devoid of decoration, which are so exhaustively constituted by a roof and four walls. The effect is dreary beyond the imagining of even the most advanced British architects.

On clement evenings, however, the centre of Tirana has (briefly) the feel almost of a normal, even happy city. The Boulevard of Martyrs is given over to the *volta*, the Mediterranean evening stroll, when everyone walks out to see and be seen. Young men walk to and fro past girls who pretend to ignore them, and old men link arms as they reminisce for the thousandth time. The two distinguishable ranks of the Albanian army – soldier and officer – mingle with the crowds, acknowledging greetings and exchanging jokes. The absence of traffic at such a time is a delight. During the *volta*, one might believe all that the regime says of itself.

This moment soon passes, though; at about seven o'clock, the crowds melt quickly away, like dusk in the tropics, and there are no cafés for the more garrulous of intellectuals to repair to, only a few bars where men go to forget. A darkness falls that is pierced by no garish neon proclaiming vulgar entertainments. People in Tirana go home early, the better to build socialism on the morrow.

My infuriating but generous room companion was once more useful to me. So possessed was he of the desire to talk that he would approach complete strangers to engage them in conversation without fear of rebuff, which occurred more frequently than not. Having a skin thicker than a pachyderm's, however, he would eventually find people willing to speak, and on our second day in Tirana had come across a couple of students of engineering who positively longed to speak – but only after dark, and in the shadows.

We met in the Boulevard of Martyrs but moved into the pitch darkness of a side street. Was this melodrama or sensible precaution? Whenever the nearby headlights of a car cleaved the darkness and seemed to approach us, the students grew nervous and asked us either to move further into the blackness of shadows or to walk away from them until the car was no longer visible. They said that every car in Albania belonged to someone of political consequence, loyal servants of the regime, by definition therefore informers and spies.

They told us of the material deprivations of Albanian life, of the overcrowded apartments, the shared kitchens and bathrooms, the vigils against interruption that have to be posted while young people attempt to make love, the bad plumbing and universal delapidation, the 'voluntary' work days at weekends (the guidebook written by Bill Bland, secretary of the Anglo-Albanian Society, says of the 273 miles of railway track in Albania 'All the lines have been built by youth volunteers under professional supervision'), the food rationing which in winter frequently includes bread made of rough fibrous flour of unrecognisable provenance, the meat ration (a kilo per family per week) that is mainly gristle and bone, the absence of sugar and other simple commodities that everywhere else have been taken for granted for centuries and the general unremitting struggle for a meagre subsistence that leaves everyone halfway between hunger and satiety.

Yet they said that all this might have been bearable had it not been for two things: the knowledge that essentially nothing will change, and the triumphalist lies which everyone must not only hear and see, but learn by heart and repeat.

Then why, one asks naively, do not more people attempt to escape? After all, Albania is a small enough country with long borders to Greece and Yugoslavia . . .

This question alone proves that one comes from another planet entirely, that one knows nothing of life here, that one has lived in a comfortable cocoon.

In the first place, the borders are heavily guarded. Anyone caught trying to leave the Brave New Albania is shot. Sometimes people try to swim the Corfu Channel, which at it narrowest is only two or three miles wide. Many of them drown; others are caught by patrol boats and ploughed under into the sea. Besides, as we saw when we stayed the night at the Channel port of Saranda, a searchlight sometimes scans the coast, and it is assuredly not searching for Greeks desperate to reach Albania. Along many miles of Albania's Adriatic coast we saw not a single small boat, such as one would expect to see along a coast of such beauty (which, admittedly, the xenophobia of the government in-advertently did much to preserve). Even the fishing trawlers of Saranda did not leave port singly, but only in convoy, each acting as guard on the other. As for the two large lakes on the Yugoslav border, the Albanians permit no boats on them either, and this shoreline inactivity gives the lakes a sinister, almost poisonous deadness.

But it is not the physical obstacles to escape that prevent larger numbers of Albanians from fleeing; rather, it is the consequences of doing so for relatives and friends. For, as the students informed us, there is no concept of individual responsibility in Albania. If a man deserts his homeland, his family and some of his friends will be held responsible. They will be sent down mines under conditions that will make it unlikely they will ever return; at best, they will live in perpetual internal exile, half-starved and with no rights. They, the students, knew people to whom this had happened.

In my mind's ear, I could hear at once the justifications that western sympathisers might compose for this system of 'justice'. Man is a social animal, they would say; no man is an island, entire of itself. A man's values and aspirations are formed not abstractly or in isolation, but socially, from his family, his friends, his workplace. If a man were a traitor, then, if he reverted to bourgeois individualism by escaping to the outside world, there must have been something unhealthy about his upbringing, his social milieu. It was only right, therefore, that those around him should be punished.

But what, I wondered, does this system of collective responsibility do to personal relations? If you are held responsible for what I do and I am held responsible for what you do, does that make us not friends but mutual spies? Normal human bonds are dissolved by collective responsibility, to be replaced by distrust, fear, dissembling and withdrawal. Surely it requires no great effort of imagination to see that this is – must be – so, yet how many western intellectuals over the last half century or more have constructed ingenious arguments to deny it?

I should have liked to correspond with the Albanian students, but it would have been impossible. According to them, if an Albanian should receive a letter from abroad whose contents appear suspect to the police in the slightest respect (naturally, they read all letters from abroad, and almost all are suspect), it will not be delivered in the normal way, but the addressee will be called to the police station and asked whether he wants to receive the letter. Sometimes the police even offer to read it out rather than hand it over. It is not difficult in such circumstances to guess the 'right' answer to their question; those who fail this test are likely – as happened to one of their friends – to be exiled to the mines.

As for their aspirations, the students looked blank. When they completed their courses, the government would send them wherever they were needed, a decision against which there was no appeal. Personal aspirations were not for young Albanians; everything was decided for them. In a certain sense, they had achieved that liberation from desire which Buddhists seek.

'We are already dead,' one of them said, and we parted. There was no possibility of our ever meeting again.

After two days in Tirana, we set out on our journey round the country. We spent most of our time south of the River Shkumbi, which divides the Albanian population into two great branches, the Gegs to the north and the Tosks to the south. The Gegs, who were once Moslems with a Catholic minority, lived in isolated homesteads in the highlands, their social organisation based on clans between whom blood feuds passed from generation to generation, and as late as 1920 it was estimated that a fifth of Geg men died while pursuing them. The heads of the clans were absolute patriarchs. The Tosks, by contrast, lived in villages or towns and were mainly subsistence peasants or landless labourers working on the estates of the Beys, Moslem landlords. In the days before the abolition of religion, the Tosks were also Moslem, with an Orthodox Christian minority.

Enver Hoxha was a Tosk, the son of a Moslem landlord. No doubt he would furiously have denied that ancient considerations of regional and family allegiance played any part in the new proletarian world which he ruled purely in accordance with the dictates of dialectical reason. Yet there were few proletarians or Gegs in the leadership of the Albanian party (and those few usually ended up in front of a firing squad), and of the sixty-one members of the central committee in 1960, twenty were related to each other as first cousins or as father and son-in-law, while there were also five married couples. Some families had as many as seven representatives on the committee. Thus the leadership was united not only by complicity in the same crimes (the political ambience of Albania can be judged by the fact that of the thirty-one members of the original central committee established in 1948, fourteen were 'liquidated', while three interior ministers died of unnatural causes), but by traditional ties of family and clan.

Perhaps it is in the nature of conducted tours that they should so overwhelm the tourist with sights and visits and compulsory entertainments that his memory of that period, even of the day before, soon becomes a kind of purée with a few undigested lumps. In the case of tours to countries like Albania, however, there is an additional and deliberate effect: to keep the tourist so busy that he should not see the general conditions of the country, nor make contact with any of its people. The tourist should be worn out, exhausted, so that he has neither physical nor mental energy to make enquiries of his own; above all, he should be accompanied everywhere and treated with the most flattering politeness.

Nevertheless, it is impossible to travel through a landscape and observe nothing; and even the most stilted of official commentaries is revealing, though not of its ostensible subject matter. We had with us a professor of classics at Oxford who came to Albania in the hope of examining the inscriptions at the famous ruins of Butrint, near the southern port of Saranda. The official guide to the ruins asked the professor the language of the inscriptions. It came to him as a complete surprise that they were in Greek: he had been told they were in ancient Illyrian and in his exposition of the ruins he had completely omitted to mention that they were Greek, talking only of the Illyrians who built them. Thus is the extreme nationalist view of history projected backwards two and a half millennia; and ancient stones are put into the service of modern lies.

Some things it was impossible to disguise from us. Descending from mountains into the valley of the River Shkumbi, we saw a pall of smoke hang over it the like of which none of us had ever seen before. The smoke was of various colours: grey, carmine, mauve, black and sandy red. It issued from a vast steel complex, built by the Chinese with whom (said our guide) a political quarrel had broken out before they could fix the filter equipment to the smokestacks. Most people accepted this explanation; all I can say is that similar political quarrels must break out with monotonous regularity all over the communist world just before the installation of such filters.

As we approached Elbasan and as we left, I noticed that for several miles the leaves of the crops were grey, covered by a deposit of soot. And the air was almost thick with filth. It would have been interesting to know the prevalence of lung conditions there.

Nevertheless, the landscape as seen from the top of the pass through the mountains conformed well to communist iconography: a large expanse of fertile agricultural land in the midst of which chimneys, representing industry, belched forth good, proletarian smoke.

We stopped for a short time in Elbasan ('You have forty-five minutes'). I dived at once from the main road into the back streets, narrow, cobbled and ancient. Two young men approached me and beckoned me to follow them. It was clear they wanted to show me something. We wound our way through more narrow lanes and arrived at an ancient stone church. It was closed, of course, but the two young men knew the keeper of the key and the church was soon opened. Inside, it was undergoing restoration in a desultory kind of way, though not for the purposes of worship. My two companions took me behind the iconostasis. There was a wooden chest, carelessly stuffed with ecclesiastical robes, as at a bankrupt theatrical costumier's. They looked vainglorious, even silly, these robes woven with gold and silver thread, now dulled by age and neglect (they must have been there for over twenty years).

The young men pointed to a cupboard and opened it. I was unsure from their manner whether they were enthusiastic atheists exulting in their triumph or clandestine religionists seeking to engage my sympathy. A book fell out from the cupboard in a cloud of dust, an early nineteenth century Greek bible printed in Alexandria. Its leather covers had been torn from it, its pages were dogeared by the way it had been thrown into the cupboard with other books and objects.

No doubt Christianity has much to answer for in its long history, but the sight of an age-long tradition treated in this way filled me with disgust. It is one thing for traditions to die out of themselves; it is quite another for them to be killed by men who think they know everything, by men whose vengeance extends even to the past, even to the dead. In Albania, crosses have been removed from cemeteries; now when people die they are interred in identical tombs, centrally designed. And dates are no longer AD and BC; they are *Our Era* and *Before Our Era*, a piece of petty dogmatism the Albanians shared with the Cubans and – as I recalled from my recent residence in Guatemala – with Guatemalan historians of Marxist persuasion.

Our forty-five minutes in Elbasan were over. We had to reach the little town of Pogradec, on the shores of Lake Okhrida, in time for lunch. For everything had been arranged in advance. Two thirds of the lakeshore belonged to Yugoslavia, as a consequence of which not a single boat was to be seen on its Albanian shore, lest it be used to escape from purist paradise to revisionist hell. Fully 40 per cent of Albanians live in Yugoslavia, in Kossovo, and have not been well-treated there, to put it no higher. It is eloquent testimony, therefore, that precautions of the utmost vigilance had to be taken not to prevent Albanians fleeing Yugoslavia, but to prevent them from escaping Albania. National persecution in Yugoslavia was more of a temptation than national freedom in Albania.

The waterfront of Pogradec was of an extraordinary deadness, with none of the bustle that one might have expected from its position: no fishermen, no boatrides, no cafés, no crowds. Nothing was for sale, all was silent, and even one's footfall on the promenade died immediately. Somehow the deadness seemed to communicate itself to the very waters of the lake and the surrounding mountains, as if Nature herself were under strict ideological control. But the lunch was good, and under the influence of the professor of classics, I soon formed the habit of having a *raki* before lunch and three glasses of red wine (by no means bad) with it.

We went on to Korce, an important town and one of the centres of the Hoxha cult. The future leader was sent to the French *lycée* there, where he also taught French on his return from Brussels in 1938. Later, on the steps of the hotel in Berat, as I took the evening air, I met a man in his late sixties who told me, in French, that he had once been a pupil of Hoxha's at the *lycée*.

'And what was he like?' I asked, somewhat fatuously.

'He was a great man,' was the reply. 'He knew everything, science, engineering, languages, art, everything.'

Everything? My informant appeared to believe it. He spoke with the undimmed faith of a man whose brother had been killed fighting for the partisans, and who himself had spent six years in Kharkov, starting in 1940, before the Albanian party even existed. Perhaps at that time it was possible, in Albania, to believe that one man could know everything; a misconception which Hoxha did nothing in his forty years of absolute power to dispel.

In Korce we encountered beggars for the first time, ragged children with no shoes who wanted 'cheeklets'. They pursued us for some distance, until shooed away by citizens (and soldiers) zealous for the good name of their city.

Opposite the hotel was a large and fairly modern library. In a moment of 'free time' I slipped across the road to examine this cultural monument in a little greater depth. In King Zog's time, more than four fifths of the population of Albania was illiterate; now the literacy rate was probably higher than Britain's. The entrance hall contained a glass case with a few volumes of the *Collected Works* – I don't have to say whose. I went upstairs to the two large halls that constituted the bulk of the building. There were bookshelves but no books. This was not a temporary absence: everything had clearly been like this for years.

A question arose in my mind, to which the answer was not clear, as to whether it was better to be illiterate with something to read, or literate with nothing to read.

The next day, we were taken to the famous *lycée*. Off the main hall was a shrine, a chapel draped in red cloth, dedicated to Hoxha, with photographs that were by now thoroughly familiar to us, since they appeared also in a corner of the lobby of all our hotels and indeed in almost all institutions. The headmistress gave us a brief and flat history of his connection with the school. I was told by someone who had visited Albania while Hoxha was still alive that his cult was considerably less extravagant now than then, though it seemed stifling enough to me even four years after his death. On many of the mountainsides of Albania, a single word was spelt out in white stones: ENVER. Even more obsequious, a date was similarly inscribed on yet other mountainsides: 1908, the year of his birth.

Strangely enough, Hoxha was able to see and despise the cults of other communist leaders. Of Mao's cult he had especially harsh things to say:

> Marx condemned the cult of the individual as something sickening. The individual plays a role in history, sometimes indeed a very important one, but for us Marxists this role is a minor one compared with the role of the popular masses [and] . . . also in comparison with the major role of the communist party, which stands at the head of the masses and leads them.
>   . . . the Chinese comrades have set out on a wrong anti-Marxist course. In reality they are turning the cult of Mao almost into a religion, exalting him in a sickening way . . .

Why did Mao's cult so sicken Hoxha that he used the word twice in a very short passage? It is difficult not to conclude that the real objection of this invincibly and viciously self-righteous man to the cult of Mao was that it had two or three hundred times more followers than his own, that while Mao was worshipped by a quarter of mankind he – whose ego was wider than the sky – was worshipped by less than two thirds of a tiny nation in the obscurest corner of Europe.

We were taken to see the classrooms of the school, in one of which an English lesson was taking place. The children were neat and obedient; I doubt that the teacher had many discipline problems. They were well-trained, and stood up and applauded when we entered. One of them, a handsome girl with dark eyes, stood up and recited a poem, her eyes flashing with thespian fury, about the fascist hyena and the Albanian eagle. Her too-burning sincerity contrasted very strongly with the apathy of British youth, but pleased me no more than that apathy: for it represented a centralised attempt by authority to fossilise thought, to set it motionless in amber.

I was not surprised at the choice of authors extracted for the textbook. They were precisely the authors who would have appeared in a Russian textbook of English forty years ago: Dickens, Jack London and Galsworthy, each of them demonstrating the rottenness of capitalism. Interspersed among them were translations of Albanian verse, so extreme in their patriotism and self-worship that, just as communist iconography eventually induced an insensate hatred of white doves and even flowers, I came to detest for a time *all* patriotic sentiment, however expressed. Months later, I still could not hear a patriot speak without feeling sickened.

Also in Korce we performed other touristic duties known only in socialist countries. We visited a 'knitting combine', a precision instrument factory and a state farm (named after Enver Hoxha, oddly enough). The conditions in the knitting combine appalled most of our party, who had never been inside a factory before. Outside were loudspeakers relaying martial music:

KNITTERS OF THE WORLD UNITE! YOU HAVE NOTHING TO DROP BUT YOUR STITCHES!

The work was all peformed by women, sitting at tiny tables close together with Chinese sewing machines, in rooms fifty yards long. It was like a sweatshop where the conditions were neither terrible nor good. Above the workers hung single light bulbs at the end of a flex – there were fitments for strip lighting, but no flourescent tubes, the supply of which presumably came to an end after the quarrel with China.

One the walls were slogans painted on red banners:

THE DATE OF THE 16TH IS THE DATE OF ENVER'S BIRTH

The knitting combine, too, had its shrine to Hoxha, and on another wall were pictures of workers who had overfulfilled their quota by 102 per cent. (Did this mean they had produced more than twice their qutoa, or merely a fiftieth more than their quota? The guide did not know, and neither did anyone else.) In any case, I found the figure suspiciously precise: the factory did not seem to me well enough organised to measure anything this exactly. The pace of work was scarcely feverish, some of the women doing nothing all the time we were there. Some stared at us, others averted their gaze. I had the slightly unpleasant sensation of being a voyeur. The garments under manufacture were the usual terrible colours, neither pastel shades nor primary hues, but dull brown, burnt orange and dark green, as though for camouflage rather than fashion.

The precision instrument factory turned out mainly micrometer screw guages, measuring calipers and slide rules. The director spoke with what seemed like genuine pride of Albania's achievement in producing these instruments that, in the nineteenth century, would have been considered marvels of engineering. In King Zog's time, there was almost no industry: Albania had had to start from scratch.

Even I, who knew nothing about such things, could see that the factory was crude and primitive. The machine tools were either Polish or Chinese; the metal stamping was, in industrial terms, prehistoric. A machine moulded the white hot metal into the shape of a micrometer handle, which then slithered while still red hot down towards a worker who caught it in a pair of tongs and placed it under another stamp. If this worker were inattentive, or turned to speak to a colleague, the red hot micrometer handle would land in his lap, there being absolutely no protection for him. We also noticed that welders did not use goggles of any kind. When one of our party drew attention to the lack of safety precautions, the director said that the workers refused to take them.

A country that was able to suppress religion entirely and executed dissenters on the merest suspicion was unable to get welders to wear goggles.

At the state farm we re-enacted a charming little pastoral scene traditional ever since land was first forcibly collectivised: the duping of the foreigners. We were taken to a 'peasant's' house, a suitable compromise between simplicity and comfort, a vine twining itself about its pleasant verandah, and were sat round a low table in the living room where we were plied with drink and statistics. How demurely the peasant's wife brought in the tray, how modest her smile! How golden the life conveyed in the statistics! After a few drinks, all men were brothers and we felt we had really penetrated the soul of Albania, having stripped away the thin veneer of politics that divided us. With what bitter contempt they must have witnessed our happy, contented smiles and our cheery waves as we drove away!

We went to Gjirokastra, the Bethlehem of Albania, where Enver was born. It is a very pleasant town (apart, as usual, from the modern additions), with whitewashed walls and narrow cobbled lanes. At the brow of one of the hills not far from the centre was a large statue of Enver Hoxha, seated in a forties-style armchair at the centre of an area of cobbles patterned, appropriately enough, like a spider's web. Nearby was the Veterans' Club, where old men, presumably former partisans, went in the evenings to have a chat, to drink and eat olives. I hung about a little, in the hope that one of them would invite me in and tell me stories of the war; probably they thought I was a spy.

Next day, we were taken to the house where Enver Hoxha was born. We also went to the town's castle, to be shown the cells in which partisans had been tortured, their graffiti preserved on the walls. The partisans were extremely brave, and two sisters who had gone to their deaths rather than betray their comrades were commemorated there; but I should have found the commemoration of these sisters less equivocal in the emotions it evoked had I not known of the fate of two leading women partisans, Liri Gega and Liri Belishova, both one-time members of the Politburo, the former shot while pregnant in 1956 as a 'Titoist agent', the latter, who had had her eye gouged out by the fascists while in captivity, strangled in 1960 for being a 'Khrushchevite agent' at the time of Albania's break with the Soviet Union. Incidentally, Belishova's husband, Nako Spiru, another wartime leader, committed suicide in 1947 (and was later denounced as a traitor – suicide is regarded in Hoxha's memoirs as the *petit bourgeois* way out) when it appeared he was losing an argument with another member of the Politburo, Koci Xoxe, over Albanian policy towards Yugoslavia. Xoxe was strangled two years later by yet another member of the Politburo, Mehmet Shehu, who was denounced by Hoxha in 1981 as a multiple foreign agent and committed suicide – or was 'suicided', a fitting end to a man who said 'For those who stand in the way of unity, a spit in the face, a sock on the jaw, and, if necessary, a bullet in the head'. As our guide expatiated on the horrors endured by the partisans, I swallowed back several pertinent but impolitic questions.

There were also one or two mysteries attached to Hoxha's birthplace. The holiest of the rooms, of course, was that in which he first saw the light of day, a room treated with all appropriate respect, and in which voices were hushed as if by mystical force. But earlier the guide had told us that the present house was not the original, which had burnt down in 1936. So how could this be the room in which Hoxha was born? One of our party annoyed the guide by remarking that in any case the house appeared far from poor, indeed quite the contrary. Since we were in his alleged birthplace, complete with bed, the guide could scracely point out again that the building was not original; instead, she remarked that though the house was larger, it had been home to many people, who therefore lived poorly. This answer, naturally, did not satisfy the member of our party who had made the remark and who, not realising that the purpose of public utterance in countries such as Albania is to express not truth but power, persisted for a time, like a terrier with a rat, in trying to unravel the mystery of a *post facto* birthplace.

From Gjirokastra we drove to the coast, to the little port of Saranda. Our hotel overlooked the Corfu Channel, three miles wide, where in 1946 two British warships were damaged by mines with the loss of forty lives. The British claimed the waters were mined by the Albanians; the Albanians said they were mined by the British themselves, for the Albanians did not possess the capacity to lay such mines. The case went to the International Court of Justice, which found for the British and awarded compensation; but the Albanians did not accept the judgment and refused to pay. The British thereupon declined to return the Abanian gold (now worth $80,000,000) looted from Albania by the Italians and Germans, which then found its way to London. The dispute has prevented the establishment of diplomatic relations ever since, Britain demanding its compensation and Albania its gold.

We drank wine on the verandah and contemplated Corfu – which the professor of classics knew intimately – across the Channel. It was near but as inaccessible as the moon. Boats from the Greek side were fired upon if they strayed too near Albania (a fact known to yachtsmen all over the world); there were no boats on the Albanian side.

The coast was beautiful and the sea wine dark, but Saranda was dead. It reminded me strongly of a fresco in a Catholic church on the tiny coral atoll of Abemama in the Gilbert Islands. On Christ's left hand was Hell, full of orange flames stoked by black demons who also found time to poke screaming sinners with their tridents; on Christ's right hand was Heaven, a kind of Mediterranean resort on a rugged shore with cypresses in the background, a single figure in a pale linen suit and a Panama hat wandering through the streets between white stuccoed buildings as though waiting for the heavenly *table d'hôte*.

The discouragement of tourism had at least preserved a coast that otherwise might have been turned into an Adriatic Costa del Sol.

Our breakneck progress – we had now been a week in Albania –

through the country continued to Berat, another ancient town whose old quarter was as beautiful as its modern part was ugly. There the mosque had been converted into a community centre and a shop. We were taken to the Onufri Museum, Onufri having been a famous painter of icons in the Orthodox tradition who worked five centuries ago in Berat. A shade of blue, found in his paintings but nowhere else, was named after him. Even I, no connoisseur of Greek Orthodox icons, could tell that his were of a very superior kind; but I thought the guide was moved by patriotic pride to flights of exaggeration. And even Onufri, a monk, could not escape the dead hand of ideology. He was a progressive, we were told, because all the angels that he painted had their feet planted firmly on the ground, while other icon painters had them flying through the air. This implied that Onufri thought heaven should be created on earth, not in the hereafter; if he were alive today, he would be painting children offering up flowers to Enver Hoxha and his wife Nexhmije.

The only northern town to which we went was Shkodra, once known as Scutari. The north-east of the country was entirely closed to us, and it is there that the forced labour camps and mines are said to be situated. When Albania rejoins the rest of the world, there will be some terrible revelations.

Shkodra, now entirely peaceful, was at the beginning of the century a hotbed of intrigue fomented by the consuls of various powers, jockeying for position and influence in a country with indeterminate political status but of strategic importance. The intrigue extended even to the orthography of the Albanian language, the Austrians introducing a new system into their sponsored schools further to divide the already fractious Albanians.

The town still had a slight Austro-Hungarian atmosphere, thanks to its architecture, with pastel facades and moulded plaster decorations. As people took the evening *volta*, one forgot the town was on a lake bordering Yugoslavia, to cross into which was a capital offence.

Across from our hotel was a building that had once served as the British Council. It was now the Museum of Atheism, but it was closed – not just for the afternoon, but with the kind of finality that complete desertion brings. I have always been amused by the idea of exhibits devoted to non-existence and was sad to miss them. If the Albanian Museum of Atheism followed its Soviet prototype, the exhibits would have traced the ascent of Man from amoebae to Enver Hoxha.

We returned next day to Tirana and, with some time to spare before our departure, were taken to the exhibition called Albania Today, which at last had opened. Inside an enormous hall were glass cases containing samples of everything that the country produced, from bottled plums to electrocardiographs, from the *Collected Works* of Enver Hoxha to antibiotics, from farm machinery to lavatory paper. I suspected that certain of these items were more readily available than others. Even at their best, most things looked shoddy, produced by factories either whose mastery of technique was marginal, or by workers with no incentive to produce anything better. Nevertheless, several members of our party were impressed: for Albania, it seemed, produced a wide range of goods. It never occurred to them that only a country with a great deal to hide would produce such an exhibition; or that almost any country, if it chose to do so, could fill many such halls with exhibits of its products. It was the choice to do so that was significant, not the things displayed.

All the same, there is no doubt that Albania has developed enormously in the last forty-five years. For example, it now has railways where it had none before. Even if the statistics are not wholly reliable, Albania is not as backward as it once was. But then, which country is? The whole world has moved on, not only Albania. Its development, furthermore, has been far less autochthonous than it sometimes likes to claim. In the years immediately after the war, Yugoslavia paid 40 per cent of Albania's government expenditure (as Italy had paid 40 per cent during Zog's time). Then, after the break with Tito, the Soviet Union took over, until it, too, was cast into outer revisionist darkness by Hoxha. China provided aid on a similar scale (though never large enough for Hoxha), until it, too, fell by the ideological wayside.

Moreover, at least twice in those forty-five years Hoxha brought his country to the brink of starvation, and even now during winter food is scarce (it is never plentiful). Production statistics cannot in any case convey the atmosphere of a country. According to the preface to *40 Years of Socialist Albania*:

> Study of this statistical year-book in close connection with the materials of the Party and Comrade Enver Hoxha helps to understand the glorious road of our country, the difficulties that have been overcome in the different stages of socialist construction, the efforts made to smash imperialist-revisionist blockades and the anti-Albanian activity of internal and external enemies, as well as the majestic victories achieved for the formation and tempering of the new man with the features of communist morality.

This single sentecne says as much as all those sharply upward lines on graphs which, no matter how high they climb, never seem to assure an adequate supply of bread or vegetables. Plenty of glory, plenty of victories over enemies, but never enough cooking oil.

Albania Today has a book in which visitors write down their impressions. J. Hurtado of Ecuador wrote in Spanish but also in the purest *langue de bois*, that extraordinary lifeless syntax and restricted vocabulary that has been adopted the world over by communists, and is the same whatever the ostensible language:

> In this display is demonstrated the superiority of the the socialist system. Albania is the best example to teach how, by applying principles, the greatest advances can be made.
>   Glory to Marxism-Leninism!

Our tour was over. As the Swissair plane landed at Tirana I suddenly realised how caught up in the Albanian world I had been. For twelve days nowhere else had existed for me. Yet in only a couple of hours we were flying over that other small, mountainous and fiercely independent country. I looked down, and seeing the marvellous orderliness of Switzerland, the industrious harmony of its landscape, I felt an immediate pang of nostalgia for the imperfections of Albania. A self-indulgent pang, of course, the pang of a man who could choose. A few months later, a small article appeared in the *Independent* newspaper with the headline *Albania liberalises its criminal code*:

> . . . agitation and propaganda against the state will now draw 5 to 25 years in jail instead of death . . . The power of local authorities to deport whole families to another region by simple administrative decision has been scrapped. Only a court can order a removal, and then only of the guilty party, not the whole family . . .

NORTH KOREA

Approximately every four years since the end of the Second World War, the Soviet Union has subsidised a World Festival of Youth and Students. Thousands of young people (many of them young only in the communist-youth-movement sense of the word) gather from every corner of the world in the capital of a communist country to dance, sing and denounce the United States. The festivals, which last two weeks, are the Olympics of propaganda.

The 1989 festival was in Pyongyang, capital of the Democratic People's Republic of Korea. The British 'delegation' was fixed at 100 and I was accepted as a member because, though neither a youth nor a student, I was a doctor who had practised in Tanzania, a country whose first president, Julius Nyerere, was a close friend and admirer of Kim Il Sung, Great Leader of the DPRK (as the country is known to cognoscenti). It was therefore assumed I was in sympathy with what was sometimes called, rather vaguely, 'the movement'.

I first met my fellow delegates in Islington, a couple of weeks before our departure, in one of those dingy public meeting halls that reek of resentment and frustration as strongly as men's changing rooms reek of sweat. I soon found myself having to explain, somewhat shamefacedly, that I represented no one but myself: to be a mere individual when everyone else represented, or claimed to represent, the downtrodden, the disadvantaged or the dispossessed, was tantamount to class treachery. In the hall, the pleasures of grievance, past, present and to come, flourished abundantly. The members of the British delegation who had foreign passports – Turkish, Jamaican, Cypriot, Indian, Iraqi – asked what harassment they might expect from immigration officials when they returned from North Korea, and were told that an immigration lawyer would be on hand to help them. A member of the Broadwater Farm Defence Campaign, who called the recent riot there 'the Uprising', spoke against the western conception of human rights. He had become a professional proletarian (I was later told) on leaving Cambridge, adopting a cockney accent of considerable strength. He also assumed a roughness of manner that indicated his conception of the class he wished to join – and lead – was not an entirely flattering one. Like most socialists, he wanted to rid the world of all egotism and selfishness, yet he had no hesitation in putting his feet up on the public seats at Moscow airport. Indeed, he appeared to think it his proletarian duty to do so. His closest associate on the delegation was a young Jewish activist from Hackney who was so intemperately anti-Zionist that even the Palestinians in Pyongyang, so I was told, began to give him a wide berth, no doubt suspecting he was a Mossad agent.

Our journey to Pyongyang, of necessity via Moscow, was uneventful, though even by the time we reached Moscow airport a certain strain had begun to make itself felt. A temporary but enforced association of left-wing activists, each with his or her own cause to promote, and each utterly convinced of his or her own righteousness, is not necessarily a recipe for social cohesion. The blacks had brought a ghetto-blaster, and the question of whether everyone wished to listen to (or at least hear) reggae music all the way from London to Pyongyang was not one to whose answer they gave deep thought: and such is the moral terror that the accusation of racism now exerts among all right-thinking people that no one dared to tackle them about it. To be the member of a victimised group was a vocation and destiny that obviated the need for consideration of others. Persecution, real or imagined, was sufficient warrant for the rightness of their behaviour. The trouble was, of course, that the majority of the delegates considered themselves persecuted, whether as women, members of splinter communist parties, vegetarians, homosexuals, Irish by descent, proletarians, immigrants, or any combination of these. Hence almost everyone acted more-persecuted-than-thou. By contrast, I was the very epitome of bourgeois contentment. No stranger in my youth to the sterile joys of resentment, by means of which one ascribes all one's failures and failings to circumstance, I had become convinced over the years that men are sometimes masters of their fate, and that – to an extent – they make themselves. Naturally, these were not sentiments I dared utter in my present company, especially as I should have had to deliver them with my unmistakeably bourgeois diction.

Tired as I was after dozing only fitfully across the several time zones of Siberia, our arrival on a cool morning in a new and exotic land with a reputation for extreme xenophobia acted like a drug coursing through my veins, causing an almost febrile hyperalertness. Not that Pyongyang airport assaults the senses in the way that Indian or African airports do, with their pullulating chaos of officialdom, passengers, relatives, touts, idlers and general agents of uncertain employment. On the contrary, there is no bustle at all; only a large concrete apron dotted with expressionless guards in ill-fitting drab green uniforms and an airport terminal with a huge portrait of Kim Il Sung slanted at a backward angle on its roof. When the jet engines are turned off, an almost monastic silence reigns.

We were treated with consideration by the Korean officials, for we were honoured guests. We were put aboard brand-new airconditioned coaches (imported especially from Japan) and were soon speeding along the six lane highway towards the city, a police car with blue flashing lights and a siren preceding us. This was not strictly necessary for there was absolutely no traffic in either direction, except once for a cavalcade of Mercedes saloons and police outriders, with a Mercedes as long as a city block at its centre which bore Yasser Arafat, Palestinian guerrilla leader and building tycoon, back to the airport after yet another fraternal visit to the Great Leader of People's Korea.

The police escort was not entirely without purpose, however. At a stroke, it transformed a group of unimportant young discontents into people of consequence. This form of flattery exactly suited the psychology of at least some of them, convinced as they were that the country from which they had come unjustly failed to recognise and reward their manifest talents.

The countryside through which the highway made its eerie way was the brilliant green of fresh young rice shoots. The fields were beautifully neat and demarcated with geometric precision, in contrast to the scratched and haphazard appearance of the Russian soil, where everything Man has done still seems impermanent and at the mercy of Nature. Could it be, I wondered, that here in Korea there existed a culture that accorded well with the tenets of a planned economy?

We reached the city. Pyongyang was almost completely destroyed during the Korean War, with hardly a building left standing. It is one of those places with the distinction of having received more bombs than were dropped on Germany during the Second World War. Even accounting for the aid received from Korea's great neighbours, the Soviet Union and China (which was never as much as requested), the reconstruction of Pyongyang was a phenomenal achievement. It is now a modern city, with public parks and gardens, huge monuments and buildings, and a Swiss standard of cleanliness. It created a fine impression on those of us who had come to worship at the shrine of Korean socalism, and even those less reverentially inclined admitted it was beyond anything they had expected. Coming as we did from a country whose cities seem endlessly in decay, whose streets are disfigured by garishness and strewn with litter, and millions of whose citizens live in neighbourhoods that seem to be the graveyard of hope and ambition, the scrubbed and scoured orderliness of Pyongyang was momentarily invigorating and even refreshing. The monumentality of the city seemed to indicate a pride in the present and a faith in the future. Here indeed was a change from our tired – no, exhausted – civilisation.

And yet I soon found the city profoundly disturbing, even sinister. No one can remain immune to the effect of size; but size in architecture is often a quality that speaks more of folly or megalomania than of genuine achievement. In the centre of Pyongyang rose something that looked like a great concrete rocket, the shape of a spaceship from the comics of my youth, a thousand feet high with row on row of portholes. Atop the 105th storey fluttered a huge red flag; at the bottom, a large poster depicted the completed structure, the concrete walls to be faced with shiny blue tiles. This would-be wonder of the world is to become a hotel with 3000 bedrooms. Since the existing luxury hotels of Pyongyang are seldom more than a tenth full, why this colossus of hospitality? The answer is simple, and mad: the South Koreans, the ideological enemy *par excellence*, were awarded a contract in Singapore to build a hotel of 103 storeys.

The streets in Pyongyang are never less than four lanes wide, usually with a special additional lane for the sole use of a certain well-known person, and are usually very much wider. Pedestrians must take underpasses: they may not cross the street above ground. At many intersections stand traffic police, young women in light blue skirts and white socks who perform an elaborate, slightly robotic dance on pedestals, swivelling round smartly with their batons every few seconds, hour in, hour out, directing traffic – that is not there. Are these vast boulevards, then, a miracle of foresight, a preparation for the inevitable day of universal prosperity when every North Korean will own a car? (At present, they are not permitted to own even a bicycle, in case they use it to attend subversive gatherings.) Or does the width of the streets serve the same function as in Tirana, as a deterrent to insurrection? Or is it merely part of the grandiosity that inspired Kim Il Sung to erect a triumphal arch one metre higher than the Arc de Triomphe, and a stone tower one metre higher than the Washington Monument (the tallest free-standing stone structure in the world), to commemorate his own seventieth birthday?

No visitor to Pyongyang escapes a visit to the Juche Tower, nor should he. The tower is built in segments, seventeen up two sides, eighteen up the remaining two, making seventy in all, each segment symbolising a year in the Great Leader's life. On the top of the tower is a large red flame, constructed of glass, illuminated at night. The tower is called Juche after the Great Leader's philosophy of Juche, which is described as a brilliant extension, deepening and completion of Marxism-Leninism, a synthesis of all human experience hitherto. At the base of the tower is a little grotto whose walls are covered with marble plaques attesting to the appreciation by foreign disciples of the 'Juche Idea'. In design, the plaques are exactly like those one finds at the tomb of a miracle-working Catholic saint. I looked up, half-expecting to see crutches hung as trophies, testimony to the success of Juche in curing paralysis. The largest, most prominent plaque belonged to the Portuguese Committee for the Study of Kimilsungism; but there were also plaques from India and Senegal, Paraguay and New Zealand, indeed from every country in the world.

What exactly is this Juche, the idea that replaces and renders redundant all previous ideas? Insofar as it means anything intelligible at all, it seems to mean self-reliance, particularly Korean self-reliance. The Great Leader's son and probable successor if the army doesn't kill him first, Kim Jong Il, known as the Dear Leader, is an exponent of the Juche Idea. Though I tried harder and persisted longer than most, I found his writing – even allowing for deficiencies of translation – radically unreadable, its only claim to originality being a peculiar combination of opacity and banality. Each participant in the Festival of Youth and Students was presented with a booklet by him, entitled *On the Juche Idea: Treatise Sent to the National Seminar on the Juche Idea Held to Mark the 70th Birthday of the Great Leader Kim Il Sung March 31 1982*. It had a grey cover with gold lettering. Inside, protected by a leaf of tissue paper, was a photograph of the Dear Leader, looking exactly as rumour holds him to be: a plump, humourless, cruel, spoilt, but possibly intelligent, prig. Here are a few of his reflections on Juche:

As the Leader [ie Dad] said, the Juche idea is based on the philosophical principle that man is the master of everything and decides everything. The Juche idea raised the fundamental question of philosophy by regarding men as the main factor, and elucidated the philosophical principle that man is the master of everything and decides everything.

That man is the master of everything means that he is the master of the world and of his own destiny; that man decides everything means that he plays the decisive role in transforming the world and in shaping his destiny.

The philosophical principle of the Juche idea is the principle of man-centred philosophy which explains man's position and role in the world.

The Leader made it clear that man is a social being with Chajusong, creativity and consciousness. Man holds a special position and plays a special role as master of the world because he is a social being with Chajusong, creativity and consciousness.

The leader gave a new philosophical conception of man by defining Chajusong, creativity and consciousness, as the essential features of man, the social being.

Chajusong, creativity and consciousness are man's social qualities which take shape and develop socially and develop historically. Man alone in the world lives and conducts activity in social relationship. He maintains his existence and achieves his aim only socially. Chajusong, creativity and consciousness are peculiar to man, the social being.

Man is a being with Chajusong, that is, an independent social being.

I have quoted the Dear Leader at such length not to amuse, but to *bore* the reader, to give him some idea, however faint, of what it must be like to live in a country where passages such as the above must not only be read but committed to memory, publicly regurgitated and applauded as brilliant beyond precedence; where all printed matter is in the same style, no other style being permitted; where the eye is constantly assaulted by slogans and the ear by speeches (there are inextinguishable loudspeakers in the carriages of the trains, in the escalators down to the subway, in the factories, in the housing estates and even in apartments). Imagine further that this state of affairs had existed not for an hour or a week or a month, but for forty-five years as in Albania: and you begin to grasp what it is to live in North Korea.

One of the only two spontaneous, non-official conversations – as intense as they were brief – I had with Koreans during my two weeks in North Korea occurred a few days after our arrival in the country outside the Grand People's Study House, a vast building that is half pagoda, half fascist mausoleum. Quite unexpectedly, a young man asked me as I walked by whether I spoke English.

'Yes,' I replied.

'Do you mind if we speak?' he asked. 'I like to hear standard English spoken. It is a great pleasure for me.'

He was a student of English at the Foreign Languages Institute where, as in every educational establishment, Marxism-Leninism and the Juche Idea were taught – *ad nauseam*. Suddenly he said:

'My only happiness is to read English literature. When I read Shakespeare and Dickens I feel a joy that is so great I cannot express it.'

Was this a form of flattery? I do not think so: his speech and emotion were unmistakeably sincere.

As I walked away – we could not tarry long, we should have been noticed – I pondered why Shakespeare and Dickens meant so inexpressibly much to him. I found the answer in Kim Jong Il:

> The Leader put forward the idea of revolutionising, working-classing and intellectualising all members of society and thus transforming them into communist men of a Juche type, as a major revolutionary task in modelling the whole society on the Juche idea . . . Thoughts define men's worth and quality and, accordingly, ideological remodelling is of the utmost importance in the transformation of man.

Who would not turn with relief (too weak a word) from that to this:

> For God's sake, let us sit upon the ground
> And tell sad stories of the death of kings:
> How some have been depos'd, some slain in war,
> Some haunted by the ghosts they have depos'd,
> Some poison'd by their wives, some sleeping kill'd;
> All murder'd: for within the hollow crown
> That rounds the mortal temple of a king
> Keeps Death his court, and there the antick sits,
> Scoffing his state and grinning at his pomp;
> Allowing him a breath, a little scene
> To monarchize, be fear'd, and kill with looks,
> Infusing him with self and vain conceit
> As if this flesh with walls about our life
> Were brass impregnable; and humour'd thus
> Comes at the last, and with a little pin
> Bores through his castle wall, and farewell king!

Was subversion ever sweeter?

As for Dickens, he was no doubt taught to demonstrate the horrors of capitalism, but lessons taught and lessons learnt are not necessarily the same. For the fact is that every character in Dickens, however ill-used or wicked, speaks at least with his own voice and in his own words, and therefore is more human than North Koreans are allowed or supposed to be.

Pausing after parting from the student of English, I gazed at the townscape in front of the Grand People's Study House. What exactly was wrong with it? In some ways so impressive, why did it send such shivers down one's spine? I cast around for the explanation, which eluded me but which was long on the edge of my consciousness.

Broad steps led from the Study House across the wide street to a square full of fountains, shrubs, concrete terraces, waterfalls, open spaces and an enormous group sculpture of dancing women, throwing concrete scarves up in the air to form arches. Then came some ministry buildings, with the colossal rectangular grandeur that the Chinese once favoured when building railway terminals in Africa. In the distance, up a gently sloping hill paved with concrete, with an arm stretched out in a Nazi-like salute, was a giant bronze statue, sixty feet high, of the Great Leader. Apparently, when Enver Hoxha died he bequeathed his overcoat to Kim Il Sung, for it was the same one that Enver wore on his statue in Tirana.

People moved about silently, insignificant as ants on a runway. At last I grasped what troubled me about this scene, apart from its bad taste: Pyongyang was *langue de bois* made stone.

We were put up in a vast new complex of apartments in Kwangbok Street, which itself was thirteen lanes wide (the thirteenth, central lane solely for the sole use of the GL). The complex had been built in the expectation that North Korea would be host to some of the events of the 1988 Olympics, but when it failed in its effort to attract any such events, the history of Kwangbok Street was changed, and it was decided that it was built not as an Olympic village but specially for the World Festival of Youth and Students. This illustrates the way North Korea lives in triumph and avoids humiliation. No historical event is too insignificant to be re-written.

The apartments were well-constructed, a long series of towers on both sides of the street that might have reminded me of Miami had there been any neon. There were five of us to each apartment; I noticed that the blacks and whites, except for a charming young physics student of Nigerian descent who was as interested in fun as in politics, stayed as separate as if there had been a law against fraternisation. We were given coupons for all our meals, which we ate in a canteen looking out on Kwangbok Street. The Korean waitresses who served us had enchanting smiles and moved with a natural grace that made our movements appear gross and clumsy.

At our first meal a young woman of clearly middle class origin, who wore only black shapeless clothes and had owlish round spectacles, startled everyone by announcing that she was always shocked how left-wing people, who called themselves caring, could eat meat. She was a person of very definite opinions, including a rather poor one of the male sex in general: when she signed her name, she appended a cross to the *o* it contained, to turn it into the biological symbol for female. Her reproach was of limited effect, though; for many of our 'delegation' were not the kind of people to wax sentimental over the fate of dumb beasts. They were hard-faced communists, who dressed tough and cut their hair short so that their heads should appear as bony as possible. I overheard one of them describing a demonstration he had attended in England, in which there had also been a member of Amnesty International with a placard.

'I went up to him and said "I don't believe in that bourgeois shit", and he said "Do you think political prisoners should be tortured and killed, then?" "Too fucking right, I do" I said.'

The person to whom he related this charming little exchange laughed. What I found frightening about the pair of them was that their faces were contorted with hatred even as they laughed, and when they talked of killing political prisoners they meant it. They were members of a little communist groupuscule for whom Stalin was a god, not in spite of his crimes but because of them. I wondered what life experience, what temperament, could have given rise to such venom. What splendid torturers and concentration camp commandants they would have made, had they only been given the opportunity.

If they had heard, as I did from diplomats in Pyongyang, that the World Festival of Youth and Students had caused food shortages throughout North Korea for several months in advance, they would not have believed it, or if they believed it, would have dismissed it as unimportant. Nor would they have thought significant the seemingly casual remark made to me by a North Korean lady that she and her twelve-year-old son had for many months spent their evenings and weekends in 'voluntary' construction work on Kwangbok Street and its associated complex of arenas and sports halls. They would simply have praised the Stakhanovite spirit of the Korean people. If they had heard the end of my conversation with the student from the Foreign Languages Institute, they would have dismissed him as a 'remnant' of the old order, though he was born a quarter of a century after communism was established in North Korea.

'Is it correct in English to use idioms?' he asked me.

'Of course,' I replied. 'We use them all the time.'

'Would it be correct, then, to say "This festival is as welcome as a snowstorm before the harvest"?'

I replied that he was in a better position to know than I.

What importance would my hard-faced communists have attached to the answer that one of the North Korean guides gave in reply to a question about the handicapped and war-wounded people of North Korea (only people without physical blemish are permitted to live in Pyongyang)?

'That,' he said, 'is a problem we have solved.'

Of course, they would have attached no importance to it at all. What is a little eugenics measured against the March of History? For myself, I rapidly became convinced – absolutely and unshakeably convinced – that one day stories would emerge from North Korea that would stun the world, of cruelties equal to or surpassing those of Kolyma and the White Sea Canal in Stalin's time.

The leader of our delegation was a journalist on a radical Asian affairs magazine who devoted much of his life to Anglo-North Korean relations which were, of course, of an entirely unofficial nature. Kim Il Sung and Nicolae Ceausescu (not yet fallen from grace) were two of his heroes. A graduate of the School of Oriental and African Studies, he was socially inept. His clothes, like those of many intellectuals, were shabby, and he always looked as if he had just been struck by a whirlwind; but unlike some of the communists on the delegation, he was a kind man, incapable of deliberately giving personal offence. Yet for all his kindness, knowledge and intelligence, he had hitched his political wagon to a regime of unspeakable tyranny. During our two weeks in North Korea, he approached one of the women on the delegation and said 'I've been informed by Korean comrades that you were out all last night'. Having transformed himself into the instrument of spies and informers, he was genuinely surprised at the outraged reaction this remark called forth. He used the words 'Korean comrades' without irony; he was a true innocent abroad.

Of course, the Koreans treated him – as they treated all other heads of delegation – with great consideration. He was provided with a new Mercedes car and a driver; he was invited to attend meetings that seemed of great moment. He was a genuine idealist, materially unambitious, but still the contrast between the attention he was paid in North Korea and the disregard with which he was treated at home must have impressed itself upon him. What saddened me was the near certainty that in their hearts (and minds) the Koreans would have nothing but contempt for him, using him as a willing dupe and thinking of him as one of Lenin's 'useful idiots'. His naivety was appalling, but as a man he was not contemptible. One day he would be ashamed of his attachment to North Korea.

We arrived some days before the opening of the festival and were taken on tours of the city. As our bus passed through the streets of Pyongyang, the pedestrians stood still and waved to us, and the faithful waved back happily, thinking they were expressing international proletarian solidarity. But for those who cared to observe, the waving of the pedestrians had an odd quality to it, like a smile of the mouth without a shine in the eyes. They waved stiffly, like automata; as soon as the bus had passed, their upraised arms dropped like stones to their sides and they walked on. This was friendliness by decree, militarised hospitality.

We were taken to the History Museum and the Martyrs' Cemetery. The exhibits in the History Museum were largely photographs to prove how Kim Il Sung had liberated Korea from Japanese colonial rule, something which it required every class of historical falsification and photographic forgery to prove, since in fact he had very little to do with the liberation of Korea in 1945. It was the Russians in the north and the Americans in the south who defeated the Japanese. While it seems to be true – every fact of modern Korean history is a minefield, figuratively speaking – that the Great-Leader-to-be once led a small detachment of anti-Japanese guerrillas and displayed bravery in incredibly hard conditions, he fled (sensibly enough) to the Soviet Union. There he spent most of the war years once he realised the unaided Korean cause was hopeless, returning to Korea only with the Red Army which established a communist state north of the 38th parallel.

Foreign armies did not get a mention in the History Museum; the part played by the United States in the defeat of Japan was not emphasised. But we learnt that Kim was, like Hoxha, a precocious revolutionary, beginning his anti-imperialist career even earlier, at the age of twelve. And as in the Hoxha museum in Tirana, the photographs in the Pyongyang museum were blurred and grainy, ready for subtraction or addition of personnel as political circumstance demanded.

Outside the museum was the giant copper-coloured statue of Kim looking humourless and bloated as a toad. I stood under it and laughed. But I also found myself wondering about the psychology of men like

Kim Il Sung and Enver Hoxha. Did they come to believe in their own infallibility, or were they out and out cynics? What does a man think who sees his own statue, his own picture, his own words everywhere? If anyone holds the comforting belief that a man's crimes eventually find him out, let him reflect on the fact that Enver Hoxha died peacefully in bed after forty years of triumphant psychopathy, and that Kim Il Sung could well beat this record.

As for the Martyrs' Cemetery, high above the city, it was a fine example of the genre, somewhat more elaborate than the Albanian equivalent, as one might have expected from a nation seven times larger. Soft organ music emerged from speakers hidden in the clipped shrubs, which reminded me rather of the days when a Wurlitzer used to rise up from the orchestra pit in cinemas between films. The cemetery was terraced, with symmetrical rows of graves and a bust of each martyr on a white pedestal. This was not a place of mourning, still less of remembrance (to possess a memory being a crime in North Korea); it was just another propaganda tableau, and the busts almost certainly bore no relation to interred martyrs – if any were in fact interred there.

We were also taken on visits to schools and hospitals. The Secondary School Number 1 was the institution of its kind that visitors are always taken to see: when I mentioned to a diplomat that I had visited such a school, he said wearily, 'Ah yes, Secondary School Number 1'. Its entrance hall is built of marble, the whole building is immaculate and a perfect silence reigns. We were told by the guide that the school was historic because the Great Leader had visited it twice. We were then shown classrooms whose tidiness was almost supernatural, with not so much as a piece of chalk out of place. The blackboards had never been written upon and the blackboard dusters never used (for once used, a blackboard and its duster cannot recover their pristine condition). We were shown laboratories with magnificent new equipment, again never used. Such children as there were in the school – few, considering the size of the building – were elsewhere. The computer laboratory was equipped with the latest Japanese models, but neither the machines themselves nor the furniture showed the slightest sign of use.

'Only socialism can do this,' said one of our party with face aglow, a man who worked for the Soviet news agency in London and was, despite the revelations of *glasnost*, still a believer. His voice had the catch of religious hysteria in it.

He did not wish to understand the significance of the unused blackboards, of the tidiness that would have satisfied the most obsessional of housewives, of the fact that it took 45 minutes to reach the school via a circuitous route but only 5 minutes to return by the direct route. He did not ask whether the school, even if real, was typical, though if he were shown anything good in his own country would immediately retort that it was exceptional, resorting to a barrage of statistics to prove it. Here critical thought dissolved at the first sight of a marble entrance hall; far from unintelligent, he was a true political pilgrim, precisely the type of willing dupe for whom this preposterous charade was staged. Perhaps in the 1930s there was some slight excuse for intellectuals who were taken in by such a performance, inasmuch as it was then something the world had never previously experienced. But what excuse was there nearly 60 years later for such a fatuous response?

We went into the language laboratory (as I had been in the language laboratory in the school in Korce in Albania). I asked to see the English textbook, but had little time with it. One of the stories was about a hedgehog whose prickles repelled a tiger, and just in case the pupil failed to understand the moral it was pointed out to him; North Korea was the hedghog, the United States was the tiger. There was poetry in the textbook as well: an ode by the Dear Leader, Kim Jong Il, on the joy of entering university named, as it happened, after Dad, Kim Il Sung.

One of our party asked about sex education in the school. The girls, we were told, learn about menstruation when they are 12 years old. And the boys?

'They are learning engineering.'

The hospital in Pyongyang that foreigners ineluctably visit is the Maternity Hospital. This was said to be the Dear Leader's pet project, indeed his personal gift to the nation, though how he was in a position to make such a gift is not a question prudent to ask in North Korea's present climate of opinion. The Dear Leader, as well as being the 'genius of the arts' and a great musician (he has written a piano concerto, no doubt in the 'correct' musical style) is said also to be an authority on obstetrics.

The entrance hall is more like the foyer of an opera house than the reception area of a hospital. The Dear Leader, who is credited with having designed the hospital himself, is said to have exclaimed 'You have built a palace, not a hospital!' when he saw it for the first time. The multicoloured marble floor and the marble walls and columns reflect the light cast by the central chandelier. On the far wall is the inevitable mural of the Great Leader. Every public building has one of these paintings, thirty feet wide, portraying the GL standing alone on a mountain top wearing a dark blue gaberdine raincoat and cloth cap among the pink cherry blossom, with a vast landscape at his feet, or with a crowd of lesser mortals – workers, soldiers, children, intellectuals, farm labourers – around the base of the pedestal on which he stands, their arms stretching up towards him as though his touch cured the king's evil.

We donned snowy white gowns and put on overshoes: a hygienic proceeding that impressed the faithful deeply. We walked through laboratory after laboratory, facility after facility, with no sign of current use. I have seen a good many laboratories in my medical career, but the calm of the Pyongyang Maternity Hospital laboratories I had encountered previously only in mortuaries. In the radioisotope laboratory I noticed a small pile of liver scans. The last had been performed more than six months earlier, and they were few and far between. No patients, no staff, no trolleys cluttered the corridors, which echoed to no sound except that of our praises.

A few of the faithful were anxious to hear my opinion of the hospital, another achievement of socialism which brought the light of ecstasy to their eyes. Was not a hospital like this possible only under socialism, they asked? I replied that it was, though perhaps I did not mean it in quite the same sense as they.

Shortly afterwards, we met a charming and intelligent young Russian called Boris, a linguist who was fluent in French, English and Japanese. In the company of a young communist on the British delegation – of the naive rather than the hard-faced variety – I described to Boris our visits to the school and hospital. He laughed, for he remembered having taken part in precisely the same kind of visits as a guide and interpreter in the Soviet Union before the advent of Mr Gorbachev. Foreigners were solemnly taken to institutions of improbable perfection. The purpose was to dupe them: a process that required their willing co-operation.

'Thank god we are past that stage now,' said Boris.

This was too much for the young communist; he fled the table so as to hear no more.

In the evening, Kwangbok Street came alive. Korean women who lived in Japan had been allowed to return to their ancestral home to set up stalls selling food and drink to the thousands of delegates. There were several temporary cafés run by a Japanese company whose staff wore American-style sun shades and who hoped every time we bought something from them that we would have a nice day. Many of the delegations had brought public address systems, causing the concrete of Kwangbok Street to vibrate with rock music. The Latin Americans had bands of their own and congregated to dance and sing until late into the night. The few Koreans who witnessed this Latin exuberance stood gazing as if they were creatures from outer space. The Latin Americans tried to get the Koreans to join in: but the depths of cultural difference, to say nothing of the political dangers, could scarcely have been greater, and the Koreans remained passive observers.

Diplomats posted to Pyongyang were astonished at the transformation of Kwangbok Street. They had seen nothing like its liveliness in all their time in the city. (Normally, they told me, even *they* lived in fear of the security apparatus; and one of them told me that the North Koreans killed foreign diplomats whenever they felt like it, though he was in such a state of abject terror that I did not know whether he was realistic or a psychiatric case – or both). But of course Kwangbok Street was sealed off from the rest of the city, as if plague raged there. At a curve in the single road that led to the centre of Pyongyang, the police had set up a huge spotlight to dazzle oncoming vehicles so that they slowed for the police to take pictures. In any case, it was unlikely that unauthorised Koreans would attempt to reach Kwangbok Street, North Korea not encouraging quixotic private initiative.

In any case, they would not have been able to buy anything there with their money. There were three kinds of currency in North Korea: 'blue' money, exchanged for hard currency, 'red' money, exchanged for socialist currencies, and 'white' money, in which Koreans were paid and which foreigners were not permitted to hold. Of course, blue money bought the most; prices in red money were at a premium; but only white money was accepted for train or bus fares, creating an additional problem for foreigners who wished to travel within the country.

There was very little for North Koreans to buy; they depend on rations (rationing is the essence of 'actually existing' socialism). I was told by a diplomat that on national holidays – when no special influx of foreigners was expected – the shops were filled with fruit. Not, of course, *real* fruit, but the plastic variety, so much more advanced technologically. Thus comes true the Marxist dream of Man's domination of Nature; no longer dependent on seasons, Man becomes truly Man for the first time in his history, for the decision as to when to festoon the shops with plastic fruit is one that depends upon his consciousness and nothing else.

I went several times during the festival to Pyongyang Department Store Number 1. This is in the very centre of the city. Its shelves and counters were groaning with locally produced goods, piled into impressive pyramids or in fan-like displays, perfectly arranged, throughout the several floors of the building. On the ground floor was a wide variety of tinned foods, hardware and alcoholic drinks, including a strong Korean liqueur with a whole snake pickled or marinated in the bottle, presumably as an aphrodisiac. Everything glittered with perfection, the tidiness was remarkable.

It didn't take long to discover that this was no ordinary department store. It was filled with thousands of people, going up and down the escalators, standing at the corners, going in and out of the front entrance in a constant stream both ways – yet nothing was being bought or sold. I checked this by standing at the entrance for half an hour. The people coming out were carrying no more than the people entering. Their shopping bags contained as much, or as little, when they left as when they entered. In some cases, I recognised people coming out as those who had gone in a few minutes before, only to see them re-entering the store almost immediately. And I watched a hardware counter for fifteen minutes. There were perhaps twenty people standing at it; there were two assistants behind the counter, but they paid no attention to the 'customers'. The latter and the assistants stared past each other in a straight line, neither moving nor speaking.

Eventually, they grew uncomfortably aware that they were under my observation. They began to shuffle their feet and wriggle, as if my regard pinned them like live insects to a board. The assistants too became restless and began to wonder what to do in these unforeseen circumstances. They decided that there was nothing for it but to distribute something under the eyes of this inquisitive foreigner. And so, all of a sudden, they started to hand out plastic wash bowls to the twenty 'customers', who took them (without any pretence of payment). Was it their good luck, then? Had they received something for nothing? No, their problems had just begun. What were they to do with their plastic wash bowls? (All of them were brown incidentally, for the assistants did not have sufficient initiative to distribute a variety of goods to give verisimilitude to the performance, not even to the extent of giving out differently coloured bowls.)

They milled around the counter in a bewildered fashion, clutching their bowls in one hand as if they were hats they had just doffed in the presence of a master. Some took them to the counter opposite to hand them in; some just waited until I had gone away. I would have taken a photograph, but I remembered just in time that these people were not participating in this charade from choice, that they were victims, and that – despite their expressionless faces and lack of animation – they were men with *chajusong*, that is to say creativity and consciousness, and to have photographed them would only have added to their degradation. I left the hardware counter, but returned briefly a little later: the same people were standing at it, *sans* brown plastic bowls, which were neatly re-piled on the shelf.

I also followed a few people around at random, as discreetly as I could. Some were occupied in ceaselessly going up and down the escalators; others wandered from counter to counter, spending a few minutes at each before moving on. They did not inspect the merchandise; they moved as listlessly as illiterates might, condemned to spend the day among the shelves of a library. I did not know whether to laugh or explode with anger or weep. But I knew I was seeing one of the most extraordinary sights of the twentieth century.

I decided to buy something – a fountain pen. I went to the counter where pens were displayed like the fan of a peacock's tail. They were no more for sale than the Eiffel Tower. As I handed over my money, a crowd gathered round, for once showing signs of animation. I knew, of course, that I could not be refused: if I were, the game would be given away completely. And so the crowd watched goggle-eyed and disbelieving as this astonishing transaction took place: I gave the assistant a piece of paper and she gave me a pen.

The pen, as it transpired, was of the very worst quality. Its rubber for the ink was so thin that it would have perished immediately on contact with ink. The metal plunger was already rusted; the plastic casing was so brittle that the slightest pressure cracked it. And the box in which it came was of absorbent cardboard, through whose fibres the ink of the printing ran like capillaries on the cheeks of a drunk.

At just before four o'clock, on two occasions, I witnessed the payment of the shoppers. An enormous queue formed at the cosmetics and toiletries counter and there everyone, man and woman, received the same little palette of rouge, despite the great variety of goods on display. Many of them walked away somewhat bemused, examining the rouge uncomprehendingly. At another counter I saw a similar queue receiving a pair of socks, all brown like the plastic bowls. The socks, however, were for keeps. After payment, a new shift of Potemkin shoppers arrived.

The Department Store Number 1 was so extraordinary that I had to talk to someone about it. But the young communist from Glasgow to whom I described it simply exclaimed: 'So what! Plenty of people go to Harrods without buying anything, just to look.' Nevertheless, I returned twice to Department Store Number 1 because, in my opinion, it had as many layers of meaning as a great novel, and every time one visited it one realised – as on re-reading Dickens or Tolstoy – that one had missed something from the time before.

Department Store Number 1 was a tacit admission of the desirability of an abundance of material goods, consumption of which was very much a proper goal of mankind. Such an admission of the obvious would not have been in any way remarkable were it not that socialists so frequently deny it, criticising liberal capitalist democracy because of its wastefulness and its inculcation of artificial desires in its citizens, thereby obscuring their 'true' interests. By stocking Department Store Number 1 with as many goods as they could find, in order to impress foreign visitors, the North Koreans admitted that material plenty was morally preferable to shortage, and that scarcity was not a sign of abstemious virtue; rather it was proof of economic inefficiency. Choice, even in small matters, gives meaning to life. However well fed, however comfortable modern man might be without it, he demands choice as a right, not because it is economically superior, but as an end in itself. By pretending to offer it, the North Koreans acknowledged as much; and in going so, recognised that they were consciously committed to the denial of what everyone wants.

But the most sombre reflection occasioned by Department Store Number 1 is that concerning the nature of the power that can command thousands of citizens to take part in a huge and deceitful performance, not once but day after day, without any of the performers ever indicating by even the faintest sign that he is aware of its deceitfulness, though it is impossible that he should not be aware of it. One might almost ascribe a macabre and sadistic sense of humour to the power, insofar as the performance it commands bears the maximum dissimilarity to the real experience and conditions of life of the performers. It is as if the director of a leper colony commanded the enactment of a beauty contest – something one might expect to see in, say, a psychologically depraved surrealist film. But this is no joke, and the humiliation it visits upon the people who take part in it, far from being a drawback, is an essential benefit to the power; for slaves who must participate in their own enslavement by signalling to others the happiness of their condition are so humiliated that they are unlikely to rebel.

My companions who were duped by this vast simulacrum of a city and a country did not pause to wonder why or how it was that every person in North Korea without exception wore a badge with a portrait of the Great Leader. If they had considered it at all, they would have said it was simply because of his popularity. The badges came in several designs, each apparently indicating the wearer's place in the political hierarchy. No foreigner, however, had ever succeeded in breaking the code embodied in the badges: the world will probably have to wait for the death of the GL for the solution to this enigma.

A diplomat told me that in the competition to prove loyalty to Kim Il Sung, men used to have the date of their admission into the Party tattooed on their arms. And the annual induction of children into the Young Pioneers is a ceremony of mass hysteria, emotions rising steadily for several days beforehand, culminating in a 15 minute invocation to Kim Il Sung at the end of which the new Young Pioneers are declared true sons and daughters of Kim. The girls break down into sobs at the mention of the name of the Great Leader. I was reminded a little of Maupassant's story *La Maison Tellier*, in which a group of prostitutes find themselves at first communion, during which a wave of profound religious emotion sweeps over them (without, of course, ultimately changing their mode of life). And I was reminded also of the way news of Stalin's death was received in Russia, with the sobs of the terrorised.

The festival was opened a few days after our arrival, at a ceremony in the huge stadium that had been built for the Olympics but had never witnessed an Olympic event. Attendance at the opening ceremony, we were several times reminded, was compulsory. We had each received official invitation cards, but *RSVP* was not written on them. Moreover, each delegation was to wear its 'uniform'. In our case, a special shirt had been designed, and by happy coincidence it was coloured storm-trooper brown. About half of us were to take part in the march past Kim Il Sung, and the idea of doing so appealed to me immensely: I should relish relating how I marched past Kim in twenty years' time. Alas, I was not selected as a marcher.

The ceremony was prepared with military precision. The buses taking the delegations to the stadium left at thirty second intervals, an impressive organisational feat. We arrived in the stadium two hours before the Great Leader was due to make his entry, leaving plenty of time for tension to mount: a technique well developed by another great leader, Adolf Hilter.

On the far side of the stadium were 20,000 children, each with a series of coloured cards which, by means of instantaneous and co-ordinated changes, produced patterns, portraits, landscapes, and slogans (the latter in English, French, Spanish, Russian, Arabic and Korean). At the very moment the children changed the colours of the cards they exposed to view, they let out a high-pitched yell which pierced the sky. The effect was undoubtedly impressive because of its scale and the perfection of its timing; but it made one's blood run cold.

Even had I not heard from a diplomat that these children were rehearsing for the opening ceremony for five or six months beforehand; that during that time they did not go to school; that often during that period they were to be seen being driven home in army trucks after rehearsals at two and three o'clock in the morning; that such parades and ceremonies were a constant feature of North Korean life; even had I heard none of these things, I should still have concluded from the spectacle itself that its production involved terrible sacrifices. Here was a perfect demonstration of Man as a means and not an end; of people as tiny cogs in an all-embracing machine. I think it true to say that even if there had been a machine available to do the work of those 20,000 children, the regime would still have chosen the children to do it: for what better training could there be for a life of personal insignificance and subordination to orders than participation in such a spectacle?

The stadium held 150,000 people, of whom only 15,000 were foreigners attending the festival. The rest were North Koreans. As we awaited the arrival of the GL, storms of applause, obviously co-ordinated, would start in the Korean sections of the crowd, and waves of people would stand up and throw their arms in the air, with an effect like wind rushing through wheat. To my horror, the people around me joined in this mindless activity (mindless, but not purposeless). What were they cheering, what were they celebrating, what emotion, or rather pseudo-emotion, were they feeling? I recalled a passage from Vaclav Havel:

> Each person somehow succumbs to a profane trivialisation of his or her inherent humanity . . . In everyone there is some willingness to merge with the anoymous crowd and to flow comfortably along with it down the river of pseudo-life. This is much more than a simple conflict between two identities. It is something far worse: it is a challenge to the very notion of identity itself.

How right Havel was! There was no external compulsion for these
people to behave as they did, to abandon their critical faculties, to lose
their identity, to be united in a pseudo-mystical communion with a
hundred thousand people of whom they knew nothing, absolutely
nothing. Yet they could not wait to do so; in fact they rejoiced in doing
it, and they felt fulfilled afterwards. Here was a profound rejection of
individual freedom by people who were free, and who gratefully
rejected freedom's corollary: individual responsibility, with all its
uncertainties and torments.

It would have been easy to stand and wave and shout hurrah when the
tide of ersatz joy reached our part of the stadium. After all, what was
really at stake? Did it matter whether or not I joined in? Well, it
mattered to me and that was enough: I remained seated.

From time to time before the arrival of the GL, members of a
delegation would take to the running track with their national flag and
sprint round the stadium to the thunderous applause of the crowd. This
was international friendship and solidarity in action, according to the
lights of the North Korean government (for whom friendship is nothing
personal). The first delegation to take to the track was that of the
Palestine Liberation Organisation, followed not long afterwards by the
Iraqis, bearing a portrait of that great friend of humanity and expert on
chemical warfare, Saddam Hussein. The Palestinians received the kind
of adulation normally reserved for pop stars; the Jewish activist from
Hackney nearly swooned. And whenever an African delegation took to
the running track, the blacks in the British delegation, one of them with
Rastafarian dreadlocks and wearing a woollen cap in the colours of the
Ethiopian flag, accorded them a strange tribute, making ape-like
grunting noises in unison, apparently under the impression that this
reversion to the jungle was somehow pan-African. At first I was
embarrassed, and then inclined to laughter; but in the last resort, I
found it melancholy, because these young people wanted desperately to
identify with cultures and people of whom they were deeply ignorant,
simply because they were of the same – or similar – racial origin.

The playing field area began to fill with what our programme called
'performers'. There were to be 50,000 of them, in addition to the 20,000
children with coloured cards. As an organisational feat, it was
stupendous; as an artistic one, it was of course infinitely less than one
violinist playing a Bach partita.

Some of the performers were dressed in blue and white gymnasts' kit;
they goose-stepped and gave the special fascist-style Kim Il Sung

salute. They kept up the goose-stepping until *my* legs grew weary: they were the embodiment of Strength Through Joy, or Strength Through Fear, which of course amounts to the same thing. But they were only a small contingent compared with the dancers. I use the words 'dancers' because the English language, fortunately, has no word that more accurately conveys the nature of these untold thousands of people. Can robots dance? For this was no mere *corps de ballet*. The 'dances' were military manoeuvres performed to music (3000 musicians, naturally), by male and female soldiers in a variety of garish nylon costumes.

The 'dances' they performed bore titles such as *Let's check and frustrate the imperialist moves towards aggression and nuclear war!* and *Fly, doves of peace!* – the latter with the following programme note:

> Doves of peace, fly high up into the blue sky that is clear of the nuclear clouds. Thousands of doves dance as if to cover the sky of the whole world.

The 50,000 performers carried pompoms and scarves, and by a manoeuvre of the utmost precision managed to turn themselves collectively into a representation of a flower. Personally, I did not think this was a fit thing for 50,000 people, with 50,000 personalities and 50,000 aspirations, to do. Only later was I told the true significance of the flower: it was a variety known as *kimilsungia*. The artistic inspiration (if artistic is quite the word) for this dreadful spectacle, it seemed to me, derived in equal measure from Busby Berkeley and Dr Goebbels.

With everyone in place, the moment arrived for which we had all been waiting – the entry of the Great Leader. It was an impossibility that everyone in the huge stadium saw this momentous event; yet a kind of controlled pandemonium broke out instantaneously all around the stadium. The 50,000 performers on the pitch threw up their hands in a gesture of true subservience before their Pharaoh, and the Korean spectators did likewise. They roared and howled in unison, and jumped up and down collectively for minutes on end; the foreigners, caught up in the atmosphere of hysterical self-abasement, stood up and applauded as if to save their lives.

I am not by nature brave, or even unconventional, yet in the moment of Kim Il Sung's entry I decided that I would not stand, not if everyone in the stadium should hurl abuse at me, not even if I were to be threatened with torture or death itself. I was so appalled by the sight and sound of 200,000 men and women worshipping a fellow mortal, totally abdicating their humanity, that I do not think I am exaggerating when I say I should rather have died than assent to this monstrous evil by standing (my mother was a refugee from Nazi Germany). There I sat; I could do no other.

The terrible obedience of the crowd, uncoerced at least in the immediate sense, indicated the power of the regime, a power that seemed absolute and limitless, that had entered the very recesses of minds, that had eradicated any countervailing force. Yet the power that was so strong was also brittle. It would only have taken 10,000 people not to have stood up for Kim Il Sung when he entered the stadium – the omission of one small act of obedience – and his power and mystique would have snapped like a twig, to remain broken and irrecoverable. My refusal to stand was but a feeble, isolated gesture; but a tiny crystal thrown into a sea of saturated solution can cause an immense precipitate, and one day such a thing will happen in North Korea and everyone, wise after the event, will marvel that it didn't happen sooner.

I wondered once again what it must be like to receive such adulation, calmly to watch 200,000 people worshipping oneself. After many years of it, does one become blasé? Does one come to believe that the tribute is merited, or worse still, that it is freely offered and expresses some real emotion? It would have been interesting to have a chat with Kim Il Sung. I recalled the only object of a political personality cult whom I had ever met, some two years previously: Jonas Savimbi. In his 'Free Land of Angola', that part of Angola where his forces held sway, there was a cult as grotesque as any. His picture and words were everywhere; his was the only poetry permitted; and when his name was mentioned in a private conversation, the speaker had to stand up while saying it. I asked Savimbi about his cult (he was claiming at the time to be a liberal democrat). 'If the people love me,' he answered, 'how can I stop them?'

The adulation of the Great Leader ceased as suddenly as it had started, as if on a hidden signal, as if a certain precise length of time had been set aside for it. Then came the march past of the delegations, 140 of them. It was a tedious procession, but the tedium was not pointless. The Koreans, who were not allowed so much as to draw breath without the permission of their government, must have concluded that these delegations were in some way official, and that therefore their country, North Korea, was presently the centre of world attention. Not surprisingly, the delegations from Guatemala and El Salvador were from the URNG and FMLN respectively, that is to say the guerrilla coalitions. At that time the Iraqis still had to be kept away from the Iranians, and the Scandinavians, to my great admiration, unfurled two banners, one asking why Amnesty International was not permitted to investigate conditions in North Korea (not a difficult question to answer), and another expressing solidarity with the Chinese pro-democracy students who had not long before been massacred in Tiananmen Square. Later, when the Scandinavian marchers returned to the body of the stadium, scuffles broke out as security men tried to wrest the banners away. A few of the Scandinavians were punched and kicked (Sweden used to have a diplomatic representative in Pyongyang, but he was withdrawn when the North Koreans refused to pay for some new Volvos which they had ordered and received).

When these scuffles broke out, I overheard some of my fellow delegates, the hard-faced communists, express a willingness, indeed an anxiety, to join in – on the side of the North Koreans, 'to beat the shit out of them'. Discussing among themselves the famous scene when the single student (since executed) stood in front of the column of tanks in Peking and held them up by moral force alone, one of them remarked that if he had been the tank driver he would have driven 'straight over the bastard and squashed him'. And his face showed that he meant what he said.

There were only two delegations that did not carry their national flags with them: the Japanese, who might have thought the omission tactful considering Japan's colonial record in Korea, and the British, for whom the Union flag was the object of concentrated hatred, especially, of course, amongst those of Irish descent.

When all the delegations had marched past, a girl from South Korea entered the stadium, to the great and genuine excitement of the crowd. Against South Korean law, she had come to the North, taking a circuitous route (and when she returned to the South she received a very long prison sentence). All Koreans are agreed that their peninsula is one country, artificially divided at the end of the war. But if Korea is one, the question is, which one? The answer, except to the eccentric and brave girl from the South, is obvious: the North is doomed. Not only is its population half that of the South, but its stagnant *per capita* gross national product is less than a fourth that of the South, its foreign trade less than a fifteenth of the South's, its foreign debt, though small, unpayable. The South, on the other hand, is destined in the not too distant future to overtake many countries in western Europe; and while far from a haven of freedom and democracy, it allows a liberty in everyday life unthinkable in the North. The communists on our delegation saw the constant student riots in Seoul as a sign of weakness;

I saw them rather as a sign of strength, for they have become ritualised and do not threaten the economic order of the country. It is countries with no dissent, which live in the quiet of the grave, that are vulnerable and fragile.

It was time for the Great Leader's speech. The whole ceremony up till now had been so Hitlerian, so megalomanic, that I assumed the Great Leader was a fiery orator, a man able to rouse his listeners to a frenzy of indignation and other enjoyable emotions. I could not have been more mistaken. He spoke like a retired bank manager recalling cheques he had been obliged to bounce. His voice was monotonous, without modulation or intonation: a real bureaucrat's voice. It was impossible to make out the content of his speech, which was translated simultaneously into English and broadcast over an echoing public address system. I am unable, therefore, to comment on its other qualities, except to say that it seemed not to be a model of concision.

The rapture with which the GL's speech was received had nothing to do with what was said: only with who had said it. If he had recited the Pyongyang telephone directory – assuming such a subversive volume exists – the crowd would still have applauded with tears in its eyes. The contrast between the banality of his delivery and the ecstasy of the response was terrifying.

It was now time for the guest of honour, Comrade Robert Mugabe, to speak. Part of his Zimbabwean army, the brigade used to terrify the Matabele, was trained by the North Koreans. The public address system, which relayed his speech almost simultaneously in English and Korean, rendered it virtually incomprehensible, but such snatches as were heard were purest platitude – education was a good thing, the future of the world belonged to the youth etc. Of course, the fact that he had nothing to say did not prevent him from speaking for a long time. The twentieth century belongs to windbags.

The applause he received at the end of his speech was polite but without enthusiasm. I suspect that the Great Leader thinks that a clap for somebody else is one less clap for him.

There was more military dancing, then some lighting effects and fireworks. It was tedious – kitsch on an unimaginable scale. The departure of the Great Leader was accompanied by the same pandemonium as his arrival, and it continued for several minutes after his motorcade must have sped away.

As we left the stadium, one of the naive communists asked me what I had thought of the opening ceremony.

'To tell you the truth,' I said, 'I've never been very keen on fascism.'

So now the festival was open. There were hundreds of 'events' every day: for example, solidarity rallies with the various peoples of the world who were suffering the effects of imperialist intervention. They were held outside public buildings and with the exception of a small contingent of nationals from the country with which solidarity was being expressed, the crowds were entirely Korean, brought in for the occasion by military vehicles.

I attended several of these rallies, which had an air of complete otherworldliness about them. What answer should I have received if I had been able to ask the Koreans at the rally in solidarity with the Guatemalan people where Guatemala was? Members or supporters of the URNG (*Unión Revolucionaria Nacional Guatemalteca*) made emphatic if not eloquent speeches in Spanish which were applauded from time to time by the Koreans, acting on instructions, who had understood not a word of them and who for the most part stood around in a state of bleary and exhausted indifference. Towards the back of the crowd a few of the women surreptitiously chatted during the speeches and even while they applauded. Men held upright banners inscribed with slogans in Spanish, in precisely the same style of lettering as the banners of all the other rallies (except for those in Amharic and Arabic). Their faces betrayed no thoughts. As soon as the rally was over, the Koreans trooped back to the military trucks to be taken home, or possibly to attend another rally in solidarity with another oppressed people.

Alas, the Guatemalans were so wrapped up in their own cause, so assured of its justice, that they were blind to the indifference of others towards it. They did not notice that the people at the 'rally' were there compulsorily; they preferred to believe that the Korean people supported them, and in thus deceiving themselves when the truth was so plainly before them, proved that they were unfitted for power.

The rally in support of the African people was, of course, in the same mould. By coincidence, shortly afterwards I met some African medical students who had nearly completed their studies in North Korea. They were drawn to Kwangbok Street during the festival as moths to light: here was proof that there was life after death.

We had a chat and my admiration for them grew apace. They had come to Korea without knowing anything about it, having answered advertisements in the newspaper. They had failed to gain entry into medical school in their own country and Korea appeared to give them a second chance. Of those who had arrived with them seven years ago nearly half had had to return, unable to tolerate Korean conditions. As soon as they arrived they were told that they were to listen on their radios neither to the BBC nor to the Voice of America; they were not permitted to play foreign music even in the privacy of their own rooms; they were not to visit Koreans in their homes, nor were Koreans to visit them in their quarters; and that if ever they were found with a Korean woman, they would be sent home *and the woman would be killed.*

Was this for political reasons, I asked, or for racial ones? Both, they replied; but the prohibition reflected the strong racial prejudices of the majority of Koreans. Nevertheless, the students were able sometimes to make friends with Korean women, by bribing guards and officials to look the other way.

And in the privacy of their beds, I asked, did the women express unbounded love for Kim Il Sung? They laughed. The women spoke – in whispers – of their bitterness and hatred for the regime.

These students had travelled throughout the country. There was great poverty there, they said; malnutrition still existed and tuber-culosis had not been eradicated as the government claimed, quite the reverse. People were not allowed to travel away from their homes without permission, which was rarely given; Pyongyang was a completely closed city, its inhabitants vastly privileged by the standards of the rest of the country. The students knew of surgeons and physicians in the provinces who had never been allowed to Pyongyang, not even for a brief visit. But bad as things were now, they had been worse a few years ago: there were faint signs of relaxation, and it was no longer the case that everyone was obliged to wear the same clothes. Some variety and colour were now permitted.

One of the Africans, a man with a more melancholy air than the others, said that he had come to realise Man's desperate need for something that went beyond himself, some form of transcendence. Religion gave to human life a significance which no social doctrine could ever give it. He wanted to write a book about his experiences in North Korea, and I encouraged him. In fact, I said it was his *duty* to do so.

We parted, and in the afternoon I attended one of the round table meetings with Boris, the charming and formidably intelligent Russian. The subject of the meeting was religion, in which Boris was particularly interested. It was held in a giant conference hall, with simultaneous translations of the speeches into English, French, Spanish, Russian,

Korean and Arabic. It seemed to me an effort of considerable magnitude designed to persuade the gullible that North Korea was a tolerant state with regard to religion; but residents had told me that religious belief was ruthlessly repressed throughout the country, though a Catholic cathedral still functioned in the capital to dupe foreigners. Once again, in paying lip service to tolerance, the North Koreans were admitting that they had chosen a path they knew to be wrong. At least the Albanians had the courage of their persecutions.

The session opened with a statement by the Korean chairman, to the effect that the fundamental concern of all religions was justice. No one leapt up to deny it; and the hidden implication of his remark, that between religion and Marixsm-Leninism, which was also concerned with justice, there was no real disagreement (until, that is, the Marxist-Leninists achieve full state power), went uncontradicted.

The first speech from the floor was distinctly odd. For some reason, a brochure from the Afghan National Tourist Agency, encouraging people to visit Afghanistan and assuring them of a warm welcome, had been distributed to every desk in the conference hall. The Afghani representative stood up to explain that it was an old brochure, and the name of His Majesty King Zahir Shah, exiled in Rome some 14 years earlier, should be deleted from it, as Afghanistan was now a democratic republic. What, then, was one to make of the picture of the *Bazkashi*, the great ceremony held in honour of the king's birthday in which thousands of horsemen chased after a headless goat dragged along from another horse? In whose honour did they perform the *Bazkashi* now? Were there any goats left in Afghanistan, headless or otherwise? Alas, these questions were never asked, let alone answered, but several of the delegates did dutifully expunge the erstwhile king's name from the brochure, thus helping to build the future by altering the past.

Several speeches followed, all delivered in a determined monotone, and each like a molecule spinning in a vacuum, having no connection with what went before or what came after. It was as if Harold Pinter had written a play about religious fanatics cooped up for a weekend in a country house. Boris, sensitised by years of tedious and meaningless Brezhnevite verbiage, went mad with boredom almost at once, for he had hoped for real discussion. I, on the other hand, had brought a book and was therefore able to laugh. A Colombian in a yellow baseball cap declared himself in favour of human rights. A Sudanese in long robes declared that Islam was the only clear and just religion. A Korean Catholic thanked Christians all round the world for helping to defeat the demoniacal manoeuvres of the imperialists. An Afghani said that Islam demanded that Moslems be good. A Nigerian declared that 'there can only be peace if there is no war'. Boris had to make a dash for the exit, as if in the grip of colic.

In the evening, I nearly attended a semi-clandestine meeting arranged by the Scandinavians behind one of the tower blocks in Kwangbok Street to express solidarity with the pro-democracy students of Tiananmen Square. But before I went, I had a beer with Mr Kim, one of our minders, a man of great charm and kindness. It was impossible not to like him: I could hardly believe he was in favour of all this nastiness. I mentioned where I was bound, and Mr. Kim looked alarmed.

'Please do not go to this meeting,' he said. 'Please do not go.'

'Why not?' I asked.

'It will not be good for me if you go. I ask you as a favour to me not to go.'

Was he serious? He certainly looked it. Later I met a West German businessman, a general agent who dealt in almost everything and who knew North Korea intimately, to whom I recounted this story, and he said that Mr Kim was only playing a part, appealing to my bourgeois sentimentality to help keep down the numbers of people attending a meeting inconvenient for the authorities. The West German business-man, so worldly wise, so evidently successful from the material point of view, made my decision to comply with Mr Kim's request seem naive and foolish. And yet I also felt that if there had been only a thousandth chance that Mr Kim would suffer as a result of my attendance, my decision was correct. At any rate, when I said I would have another (Japanese) beer instead of going to the meeting, Mr Kim seemed deeply relieved. He praised what he called the discipline of the British delegation, so different from the unruliness of the Scandinavians.

Ah, if only Mr Kim had known about the comic opera politicking that went on behind the scenes, the coups and countercoups among the various factions (each believing itself to represent the Absolute Marxist Truth), the clandestine meetings during which a clique would compose a document claiming to represent 'British policy', as if the delegation were a government-in-exile, and the Lilliputian fury such presumption would produce among the other cliques. Mr Kim had heard that the British were unruly (the fame of our football hooligans had reached even North Korea), but he now realised that this was a misconception. On the contrary, he repeated, we were most disciplined. I wanted the praise of a man who, probably through no fault of his own, worked for the North Korean security apparatus.

Once in Pyongyang I glimpsed the terror that underscores the tombstone orderliness of North Korea. I was in a taxi, specially available for the festival, with a fellow delegate. As we were returning to Kwangbok Street, we had to pull over to the side of the road because an official motorcade was going by. My fellow delegate extracted his camera from his bag to take a photograph. In that instant, the taxi driver's face contorted into a grimace of fear reminiscent of the photograph of the little girl fleeing down the road in Vietnam: his arms waved in panic as he tried to push the camera below the window level. My companion took the hint: but one could see that the driver's pulse was racing for a considerable time after the camera was safely back in the bag. As for the motorcade, it did not pass us directly, but only at an intersection far ahead.

A week into the festival I went to the Students' and Children's Palace to attend an international meeting about literature. The building, despite its name, made no concessions to children: there were no pictures of little furry animals, no toys, no games and, at least while I was there, no children, except on the mural in the marble entrance hall where, with shining and adoring faces turned upwards, they mobbed the Great Leader. How Great Leaders love children! How children love Great Leaders!

I was taken to the top floor of the Children's Palace in a lift operated by a lady whose job, I felt as she eyed me discreetly but with care, was as much to observe as to press the buttons. Her memory would not have been taxed by the number of clients: the Palace was empty and no hermit in a desert cave could have desired more complete peace.

I was met by a member of the Writers' Union, who took me down the corridor to the room in which the meeting was held. On either side of the corridor were doors marked *Literature Creating Rooms*, and naturally I was curious to see inside. The member of the Writers' Union opened the door to one of them: a bare room with five desks lined up in a row like a guard of honour, each with a typewriter (three in Latin script, one in Cyrillic and one in Arabic) with a sheet of paper ready inserted and a little pile of paper beside. In short, everything possible had been done to extinguish even the faintest spark of literary inspiration.

The meeting was held in a long rectangular room with an opening to another room of similar dimensions. From both ends portraits of the Great Leader and Dear Leader gazed down on us with the lugubrious omniscience that derives from omnipresence. Around the walls of the room were placed heavy square armchairs upholstered in deep green, each with a frilly lace antimacassar. The taste in furniture was Maoist: and Mao, of course, had an aesthetic fixation with the petit bourgeois style of the thirties.

The meeting was principally between North Korean and Ghanaian writers, but for some reason the General Secretary of the Ethiopian Writers' Union was there, as was a lone American, a radical poet who wore two badges – *Free South Africa* and *Health Care is a Right Not a Privilege* – and who dressed as for an anti-Vietnam War rally. I introduced myself as a doctor who liked literature, not as a writer, and the chief of the Korean poets present said it did not matter that I was not a writer because we were all engineers – doctors were engineers of the body, writers of the soul.

The 'discussion' consisted largely of the Korean poets describing the enviable conditions under which they worked. Writers in Korea were paid a salary equal to a vice-minister's or even a minister's. There were 500 professional writers in Korea, 50 of whom were women, and all belonged to the union. They were trained to be writers at the Kim Il Sung University. There was no problem with publication in North Korea (the Ghanaian writers had complained of the difficulties in finding publishers in Ghana) and one of the poets was able to quote the production statistics for last year:

Novels – 50 pieces
Short stories – 600 pieces
Poems – 1000 pieces

The Ghanaians were impressed. The problem with Ghanaian literature, they said, was that it was not planned. Writers like them had to fend for themselves, there was no state support. Most of them had to work at other jobs to support themselves. The Korean poets shook their heads at such intolerable conditions.

They chain-smoked throughout the meeting. They were intelligent and cultured men, who knew Byron and Shakespeare and Walt Whitman, and who would have quoted French and German poets had there been French or Germans present. Was I imagining it when I detected that under their official optimism there was a profound, unspeakable despair, a sense of total personal defeat and surrender, and a complete absence of self-respect? I asked to see some of their work and one of them said he would bring me translations of his work the following day.

I returned to the Students' and Children's Palace as arranged and the poet, still smoking, gave me a sheaf of poems, one of which I transcribed:

The Sun of Mankind

Comrade Kim Il Sung the Great Leader –
He was awaited for ages
With great anxiety in every heart.
He soared high
To meet their ardent wishes.

The long history that had flowed by
And all the ages to come
Joined hands
To put him high up in the sky of the 20th century.

Comrade Kim Il Sung the Great Leader –
He
Found the beautiful gems of truth
Sought in vain for centuries
Amidst the downtrodden masses
And spread them over the world
In billows of beams of light.

etc, etc.

This is less than a quarter of the poem, in the rest of which the Great Leader, *inter alia*, embraces the people groaning in chains and shackles, stands them on the spring fields of the green hills of bliss which undulate far and wide, dignifies them and gives them the wings of freedom for which they shed so much blood, draws the image of a new world that has been in chaos for so many centuries and gives an immortal banner to the Grand March of History.

North Korea was not so much a factory of flattery as a forced labour camp for it. The only genre for a true poet there was silence, and perhaps even that was dangerous once a man had declared himself a writer. No opportunity was lost to further the cult. Here are a few lines from a Korean phrasebook for English speakers:

His Excellency Kim Il Sung is the greatest genius of present times.
President Kim Il Sung is the sun of mankind.
Marshal Kim Il Sung is the miracle-maker, peerless patriot, and a giant of
history.

On the way to the hotel, according to the phrasebook, one might
exclaim 'Let's mutilate US imperialism!' to which the reply might be
'In our country, 60 is the prime of youth, and 90 the beginning of old
age'.

I leave it to the reader to guess the age of the Great Leader when the
phrasebook was published.

I should have gone on a pilgrimage to the Bethlehem of North Korea,
the village of Magyongdae where the Great Leader was born in a
humble home. It was not far from Kwangbok Street, and I knew that if
I failed to visit it I should regret it immediately I left the country. But
even in that knowledge I could not bring myself to go.

Nor could I bring myself to attend the revolutionary opera, *Song of
Joy* (the 'people's prize laureate work', with 5000 artists). A glance
through the programme of the opera was enough to convince me not to
go:

Prologue: Song of Joy Dedicated to the Leader.
Act I: Happiness Blossoms from Great Love.
  Number: Treasures Shine in the Loving Sunlight.
  Number: We Owe the Bumper Crop to the Leader.
Act II: We Are Happy Loved By the Leader.
Act III: The Sunlit People's Paradise.
  Children's Dance: We Are the Happiest in the World.
  Folk Song and Dance: My Country Is a People's Paradise.
Act IV: Following the Leader and the Party.
  Dance and Chorus: Following the Leader and Party For Ever.
Finale: Song of Long Life and Good Health to the Leader.

One might have supposed that exposure to this kind of 'art' would
immunise people against it forever. Far from it. At the Students' and
Children's Palace there was a collection of poems written by participants during the festival. A lecturer in English Literature from India
had written *A Poem for the 13th WFYS, Pyongyang*:

The atmosphere is joyful
The buildings are so grand

Those who host the festival
Are people of great land

Under the brilliant leadership
Of Comrade Kim Il Sung
A new sun shines in Korea
And every flower blooms

Korea DPR

is a song
the song of mighty
delicate people
bigger than the earth

And one of the Ghanaians, who lamented the lack of outlets for writers in his native land, contributed *Pyongyang, A City of Brilliance*:

How beautiful it is,
How wonderful the works
Structured under the noble guide
Of our dear comerade [sic] Kim Il Sung . . .
Pyongyang, we admire your zeal
In hosting this festival
Indeed you are a city of brilliance.

In these poems is revealed one of the attractions of Marxism-Leninism for certain frustrated intellectuals: it is the revenge of the untalented upon the world. Only in the most absolute tyranny could the authors of these poems live as poets.

With only two days left in Korea, it was time to go on a visit to a Korean family – not spontaneously or at random, of course, but in a highly organised and official way. Our bus drove us to an estate of tower apartment blocks, by no means pretty but certainly not worse than British municipal efforts of the sixties and seventies, and whose public areas, unlike their British equivalents, were not covered in graffiti and did not smell of urine.

The entire population of the estate was there to greet us. They applauded our arrival and the women, in long nylon dresses, waved – or in some cases shook, in a manner I found almost threatening – plastic flowers at us. When the flat-dwellers clapped there was no applause on their faces, only indifference. Their movements were mechanical and exhausted, like clockwork winding down.

We were split into small groups and led, like lambs to the slaughter, to our respective hosts.

It transpired that the apartment block in which my group's host lived was a little special: it was built solely for sportsmen. (There were also blocks for artists, writers, scientists etc). Our host was a world champion wrestler, and therefore more than a little privileged. For example, in a country where ownership of bicycles was not permitted, he owned a car. He had travelled to many parts of the world, and had photographs to prove it. He was a very short man, reaching only to my shoulders, but there was no mistaking the musculature that bulged under his clothes and made his suit look even more lumpen than it already was.

His wife greeted us demurely and we sat on the floor round a low table laden with food. This hospitality would have been more touching had a video camera for the television service and a tape recorder for the radio station not been present, and had our interpreter not been quite so hectoring in her insistence that we must enjoy ourselves and smile. I found the presence of portraits of Kim Il Sung and Kim Jong Il in every room somewhat inhibiting, too – the self same portraits, incidentally, that one sees in every room in the country (there is no freedom even to choose *which* protraits of the dynamic duo to hang). I also found that the martial music relayed through the open window by the public address system outside, from whose imperious broadcasts only stone deafness would have provided relief, failed to create an atmosphere of personal intimacy.

We were asked what we did for a living. I said I was a doctor, which was straightforward enough; but one young woman in our party with whom I had struck up a friendship said she was an ethnomusicologist.

'What is that?'

'I study music in different parts of the world.'

'And then?'

The question was a little difficult to answer. If she were lucky, she would teach ethnomusicology to others.

The conversation faltered. The cameraman moved around and pointed the camera at us, anxiously seeking out signs of life.

'Ask many things,' said the interpreter, with an edge of desperation in her voice, as though she would be held responsible for any *longueurs*. 'Please ask many things.'

I know of no finer cure for curiosity than appearing on North Korean television. Eventually, with the music entering the apartment despite the closing of the window, the wrestler asked me whether I liked sport.

Something inside me snapped. I was tired of lies: I felt as if an anodyne answer would make me an accomplice of a terrible crime.

'No,' I said, 'I hate it. I can't stand it.'

Probably the interpreter relayed my message as 'Yes, he loves to play volleyball.'

Immediately, I had one of those cries of conscience that so conspicuously mark out the western liberal. The poor wrestler was not to blame for the lies (the whole visit was a lie) manufactured by his government: he was only a pawn in a game in which individuals counted for nothing. Within the limits prescribed, he was probably trying to be hospitable; and if the visit was deemed a failure, he would also probably be blamed. Under normal circumstances, I shouldn't have dreamed of being so rude as to tell a world champion in his own home that I hated all sport. After all, a world champion is no less worthy of personal respect than anyone else. But I had felt very strongly, irresistibly, that to allow the visit to proceed smoothly along its prescribed, banal course was to play the regime's game for it, to dehumanise oneself, and that gestures of nonconformity, however tiny, were of vital importance, for they were signals to others that under an apparently robotic exterior there still existed a mind that turned towards truth.

It was time to leave the wrestler's apartment, but the final act of the charade was yet to come. This was the compulsory dancing in the concrete yard between the apartment blocks. The music blared from the loudspeakers; the women who previously had shaken plastic flowers at us came up to us and led us in the dance. There was no escape: almost cerebrally palsied when it comes to dancing, I shrank to the rear of the crowd, but a determined woman, mindful of the instruction that all foreigners should dance before the cameras to demonstrate the internationalist joy of the occasion, grabbed me by both wrists and led me to the front. It would have taken a considerable struggle to shake her off, quite possibly a punch on the jaw. She whirled me round: it was like dancing under arrest and in handcuffs. Her grip was unnatural, terrorised, and her face was fixed in a grimace of compulsory joy. She would not let me go, even between dances, for the Party had allocated a certain length of time for dancing with foreigners and to have let me go before that time was up would have been a dereliction of duty, if not a counterrevolutionary crime. And so on we danced, like the skeletons in a medieval woodcut of a *danse macabre*, she never once meeting my eye though we danced for fifteen minutes, her face resolutely turned away from mine thoughout.

Dancing on the same strange dancefloor was a liberated young woman from West Berlin, a supporter of good, or at least *bien pensant*, causes to judge by the way she dressed – an anti-war, anti-pollution kind of person. She too was being danced around in the vice-like grip of a Korean woman who would not look her in the eye. But our glances met, hers and mine; and I saw from a barely perceptible change in her expression that she understood for the first time what only the self-indulgence and self-importance of intellectuals could have hidden from her, namely that there was something more evil in the world even than the Berlin city council, or an Axel Springer newspaper.

Suddenly, I dissolved into a fit of the giggles. My legs went weak and I should have fallen to the ground like a puppet without its strings had not the redoubtable Korean lady, determined for the sake of her life that the show should go on, held me up. Of course she could not tell why this strange foreigner was laughing; but her face betrayed no interest in the matter. Her cheeks, her mouth, her eyes, were as granite as the heroic statuary found everywhere in Pyongyang. Truly the New Man: Kim Il Sung would have been proud of her.

No Aeroflot aircraft can have been boarded with such relief as mine. The airline has a poor reputation among travellers (Xan Smiley once told me in Moscow that he realised *glasnost* was something important and not just a cheap gimmick when an Aeroflot hostess smiled at him), but I had no complaints to make against it. On the contrary: now that the winds of change had swept through the Soviet Union, it seemed to me that the very air inside the aircraft was free by comparison with that of North Korea. When we were forced by weather conditions to land at Vladivostok instead of Khabarovsk, I looked at everything outside with benignity, and felt the romantic allure of the vast Siberian land stir within me.

We arrived home several hours later. There was a man just past the immigration desk at Heathrow Airport who stopped some of us and, without saying on what authority, demanded to see our passports and to know where we had been. His manner was abrupt and rude. Almost certainly he was from the Special Branch or M15. I cannot say that police interest in some of our party was illegitimate: there were several active supporters of the IRA among us, and those who did not think that the world would be a better place for a few strategically-placed bombs were distinctly a minority. But the clumsiness of the security service, its uncouthness, could not have fed more successfully the paranoia of those young people who believed, despite having just visited a land of forced labour, where everything was either forbidden or compulsory, and which out-Orwelled Orwell, that they suffered persecution without parallel in the history of the world.

ROMANIA

I was relieved when the Romanian customs official, preoccupied by a Romanian rugby team returning from London laden with semi-licit electronic treasures, waved me through without examining the contents of my suitcase, which included a memoir by a British intelligence officer of his days in Romania during and just after the war, and a biography of King Carol (both with their dust jackets removed, to avoid undue 'provocation'). These and other books eminently worthy of confiscation were destined for Romanian intellectuals whose names had been given me in London, and whose addresses I had committed to memory on the train to the airport. In the event of my memory failing I also had them, encoded on scraps of paper stuffed into odd pockets. I was uncertain whether I should remember my own code, though I had little doubt the *Securitate*, the Romanian secret police, would be able to crack it with ease. I was not cut out for clandestinity.

I was met by a *Comtourist* guide. She was holding up a placard saying *Welcome Mr. Daniels*, and though this was a pure formality – for which I had paid an agency specialising in travel to Romania quite liberally in advance – it nevertheless gave me a slight pang of conscience. For here I was, entering yet another country under false pretences, as a tourist rather than as a writer. The argument that I was helping to expose the evil that I supposed existed there did not altogether console me: for the evil I expected to expose was in large part the consequence of the doctrine that the end justifies the means.

Besides, the *Comtourist* guide belied the clumsy name of her organisation, and was young and charming. She had those soft, liquid brown eyes over which pre-war writers about Romania used sometimes to wax sickly. She was a medical student just entering her clinical training. I explained that I too was a doctor, who spent half his time practising and half travelling the world (I omitted my literary activities). My way of life I knew, of course, to be beyond her wildest dreams. After qualification she would most probably be sent to serve for several years in some unspeakably dreary concrete town with no meat or butter. But I assumed that, as a guide for foreigners, she was, despite her charm, a trusted employee of the *Securitate*, for whom some said a fifth of the Romanian people informed. I wanted to confront her ideology with a strong draught of freedom. This was before I realised that *no one* in Romania believed in the ideology, least of all its guardians, and that ideology was the last thing to motivate an agent of the *Securitate*. I had not yet readjusted once more to that strange looking-glass world where thought and speech, belief and action, were so radically divorced.

'I would very much like to travel,' she said quietly and humbly.

My flaunting of my own liberty in the face of her unfreedom seemed callous to me now, mere boasting.

We drove through the semi-darkness towards my hotel. The streets were ill-lit, the lights from the apartment blocks gloomy and yellowish, like the pages of old books. I wanted to ask the guide about Romanian hospitals, but she could scarcely have spoken frankly. Cars for foreigners are bugged, according to old Romania hands, and the driver might only have appeared to understand no English. But it mattered very little in any case, since I later found many people to describe medical services in Romania. They disagreed as to fine detail and I suspected that some of them exaggerated, but all were agreed that elderly people, especially from the country, were often denied treatment on the grounds of their uselessness to the economy.

Perhaps in this they were not entirely unfortunate, since sanitary conditions in hospitals for ordinary people were deplorable, there being insufficient nurses and no cleaners. Often there were two patients to a bed, drugs were unavailable and equipment ancient or broken down. Births were not registered until six months or later, an administrative method of keeping the infant mortality rate under control. Bribes were essential to obtain treatment, officially free. Doctors would not operate, nurses would not help patients, without the payment of *ciubuc*, Romanian baksheesh. Rags and scraps were often used for dressings in the absence of bandages and ambulances sometimes failed to attend cases for lack of fuel. Attached to gynaecological wards were policemen whose job it was to search out women who had illegally procured abortions. They checked the temperature charts of all miscarrying women, in whom fever was a crime. The dictator Ceausescu had decreed that there were not enough Romanians and it was every woman's patriotic duty to have at least five children (after which they might have an abortion legally if they chose). Childless men more than twenty-five years old were subject to a special tax.

We arrived at the hotel. It was in the outskirts of Bucharest, across the road from the *Scinteia* building, an enormous pile in the wedding-cake baroque style of the late Stalin era. Atop its tower was a red light, a beacon in the air-raid darkness of the city. A fraternal gift of the Soviet Union to Romania, the building contained the headquarters of the Party daily, *Scinteia*, which means Spark (as does the Russian *Iskra*, the name of the Party newspaper that played so important a part in pre-revolutionary Bolshevik history). The Spark was, of course, monu-mentally dull – unless one happened to be obsessively interested in the official activities of President Ceausescu and his wife. In the massive and clean forecourt of the building, constantly swept by a peasant woman in a scarf, stood a Pharaonic statue of the Spark's onlie begetter, Lenin. The rear of the edifice, which I later examined with some interest, was still like a building site, wasteland churned into mud and scattered with unused concrete blocks, the stone facing of the walls fast crumbling away. The front of the *Scinteia* building was all state power; the rear, neglect and decay.

When I arrived in Romania, it had been a communist state for over forty years. Before the takeover, engineered by the Russians, the Romanian communist party had 1000 members. The leadership soon began to quarrel and held show trials for one another. A 'hero project', the Danube-Black Sea Canal, which is said to have consumed the lives of 100,000 prisoners, was instituted, but never completed.

My guide and I parted at the hotel, her duty done. The hotel was of the socialist-Hiltonian type, a grey concrete tower with insufficient lifts so that one sometimes spent fifteen or twenty minutes debating whether to cut one's losses and climb the fire escape or wait just a little bit longer. How well I knew these hotels! I anticipated correctly the lack of plugs for either the basin or the bath, the mouldy jaundiced light, the mildewy odour of mummified dust emanating from the curtains, the inextinguishability of the bedside radio so that a faint lisp of rhythm without melody seeped from the headboard of the bed. Of course the telephone was tapped; and according to the chief of Romanian intelligence, Ion Pacepa, who defected to the United States in 1978 and wrote a scurrilous book (not without help, one suspects), there were microphones and infrared cameras installed in the walls of all hotel rooms used by foreigners. Welcome to Romania.

I can resist the allure of television everywhere except in hotel rooms. Hardly had the porter-cum-police-informer left with his 25 *lei* tip (whether it was generous or mean depended on whether one calculated it at the official or black market rate) than I switched on the clumsy monster in the corner. I discovered that it would not remain on unless I kept the button pressed hard down with my thumb, which soon became numb with the effort. That was not all: my mind was also soon rendered numb, deadened by the solemn recitation, lasting fifteen minutes, of the harvest results of farms around the country. The figures were as honest as the results of plebiscites awarding dictators further seven-year terms of office: Farm Number 3 of Ploesti had harvested 1427.36 kilos of tomatoes per hectare, while Farm Number 7 of Iasi, two hundred and fifty miles away, had harvested 1427.19 kilos.

This programme, I later discovered, was no abberration: the newsreader, who addressed his 'esteemed viewers' (of whom I must have constituted almost half, I should imagine), intoned the harvest results every night. When he finished, there was an equally enthralling programme about Romania's agricultural and industrial progress, thanks to the untiring and ceaseless efforts of the President of the Republic and General Secretary of the Party, Nicolae Ceausescu. Five minute sequences of tractors ploughing the land, with close-ups of the upturned soil, accompanied by a droning commentary, were followed by similar sequences (all in black and white) of slightly outmoded machinery whirring round producing something or other – there was never any indication of what, production being an end in itself, the ultimate triumph, regardless of whether anyone wanted or could use the thing produced. And then came sequences of factory workers lined up in rows at factory meetings, listening to – or hearing – speeches which they greeted with prolonged applause and chanting of Ceasescu's name. Later I was told that at both ends of each row there was a *Securitate* agent to ensure no one stopped clapping or chanting ahead of schedule.

Every twenty minutes or so, the programme would be interrupted by a burst of martial music, a picture of the Romanian flag fluttering in slow motion, and then by aerial shots of a vast complex of concrete apartment blocks. This was an advertisement for the 14th Party Congress, to be held in four weeks' time.

Later in my visit I discovered that people in Bucharest would queue for hours to copy down the list of Bulgarian television programmes displayed on the noticeboards of Bulgarian institutions in the city. That Bulgarian television should be considered a relief from boredom is surely a phenomenon entirely new in world history, something original and without precedent. The Bulgarians, long accustomed to Romanian assumptions of superior sophistication, delighted in the reversal wrought by the *Conducator* and his wife.

I went down to dinner, to the restaurant reserved for foreign guests. In the lobby of the hotel there milled half a dozen young men, watching for counter-revolution, dressed in suits that looked as though the linings were stuffed with pebbles.

'Are you group?' asked the waiter.

I confessed to being an individual and the waiter frowned. There were several clean and empty tables in the restaurant, but eventually he managed to find me a seat prickly with crumbs at a table that looked as though a 17th century Cossack feast had just finished there. It was a fine cure for appetite.

'What you like?' asked the waiter.

This turned out to be a superfluous question since – for individuals – there was only boiled beef and potatoes. The beef was as dry as the Atacama, the fried potatoes half-cooked, greasy, cold and infested with black bits.

'Vegetables?' I asked speculatively. 'Salad?'

'No,' said the waiter.

For dessert, there was chocolate cake in which lubricating oil had been substituted for butter.

Before the war, Romania was celebrated for the excellence of its cuisine. Nowadays artistry in the presentation of meals has been replaced by artistry in the concealment of microphones in ashtrays on restaurant tables.

I walked out into the darkness of a Bucharest night to digest Romania's equivalent of *nouvelle cuisine*. In the street I glanced behind me to see whether one of the men in lumpy suits who hung about on the steps outside the hotel was following me. No, I was alone. I quickened my pace just in case one of them changed his mind – I had been filled in London with suspicion and unease by stories of such men whose deliberately clumsy tailing was designed to frighten and intimidate.

It was October; there was an autumnal chill in the air and one could feel the fallen leaves underfoot. Such was the darkness away from the hotel that one could barely make out the ground beneath one's feet. Occasionally a car would go by, rattling over the cobbles, its lights piercing the blackness. Towards me came a small group of drunken revellers, each with a bottle grasped round the neck. In other countries I might have felt slight apprehension, but not here: one of the very few benefits of communism is the apparent rarity of street crime (though the

Soviet Union has recently, and for the first time, revealed its very high murder rate, crime mostly of the low-technology domestic variety). The revellers passed by, not noticing me. They were engaged in hilarity, which almost shocked me. How could anyone laugh in Romania? Desperation, hysteria? I was forgetting my own belief that life can never be encompassed by a few simple propositions. My journeys were turning me into an ideologist with rigid preconceptions, a case of travel narrowing the mind.

Bucharest was once known as the Paris of the Balkans, and next morning it was easy to see why. Many of the tree-lined streets and boulevards were built in imitation of Haussman's Paris. There is even an *Arc de Triomphe* in its own *Place de l'Étoile*, erected in 1922 in commemoration of the fleeting victories of the Romanian army during the First World War (before it was comprehensively defeated). Along the Soseaua Kiseleff are the homes, of the size and style of Normandy châteaux, of the former *haute bourgeoisie*. At the Piata Victoriei, where huge apartment blocks worthy of New Socialist Man were under construction, I caught my first glimpse of Ceasescu's plans to remodel the city, thus achieving immortality. Down the Bulevardul Ana Ipatescu, the architecture becomes cheerfully eclectic in style, a jumble of Second Empire, Bavarian Mad Ludovician, Bauhaus, and Viennese Classico-bombastic. Aesthetes tend to tut-tut over this admixture ('a savage hotch-potch', it was once called), displaying as it does the jackdaw or magpie tendency of the pre-war Romanians to appropriate the surface glitter of the occident: but I found it charming and, in its overall effect, original.

I walked long distances in the centre of the city. I was surprised to discover that many of the women were not only beautiful but elegant. There were also old ladies who, in their attention to their clothes and jewellery, would not have been out of place in the cafés of Vienna, eating Cellinian sculptures of cake and cream.

Being myself somewhat inattentive to personal appearance, in general I consider it of little importance in others, within wide though definite limits. Yet here in Bucharest elegance took on quite another quality, so that it was not merely pleasing to the eye but moving. For when one considered what was commonly available in the shops – cloth dyed the drab colours of hospital corridors, as in Abania – one began to appreciate the effort it cost women to dress well, the hours of frustrating search for material and then of needlework. Their elegance was not just vanity, therefore: it was a denial and rejection of the values imposed on them by the dictatorship, which everywhere preferred uniformity to individuality.

And so it was a strange thing to see an elegant young woman scramble for a place on a battered and overcrowded bus with large tanks of liquid methane on its roof (petrol and diesel being in such short supply), giving it the appearance of a huge mechanical scuba diver. And it was stranger still to experience the cafés of Bucharest, the last pathetic remnant of an otherwise vanished way of life. Here waiters in white jackets served customers who sat forlornly at outside tables drinking exactly the same drink, either acorn coffee or the nauseatingly sweet, brownish, sticky and chemical liquid with a bitter aftertaste known as orange, a mythical fruit mentioned in ancient texts: for it was beyond the organising powers of these cafés to offer a choice, even had choice not been a suspect concept from the ideological point of view. (Was it not Engels himself who said that freedom was the recognition of necessity?) The Plaza Athénée Hotel, which before the war was a louche hotbed of political rumour and intrigue, and where every employee was now said to be an agent of the *Securitate*, had a coffee shop that sold only one kind of chemical cake and no drinks at all, not even water. To have coffee and cake in Bucharest meant visiting more than one establishment and could well have been the work of an afternoon.

My first destination was the infamous Centru Civic, with its immense Boulevard of the Triumph of Socialism. Starting in 1984, more than 9000 homes were demolished to construct this insane monumental avenue, as were many churches, some of them ancient. An entire quarter of the old city was destroyed in a concerted assault not only on the monuments of the past, but on the past itself. And Ceausescu's idea of 'systemisation', whereby every Romanian was forced to live in near-identical apartment blocks, was meant to apply not only to peasants, whose ancestral villages were to be swept away, but to town-dwellers who lived in the unplanned and anarchic towns of the past.

Were these just the schemes of a mad dictator? Alas, no. There are plenty of mad dictators in the world, but only those steeped in the Marxist-Leninist philosophy, with its utter contempt for the 'unenlightened' past and for men as they are, combined with its boundless optimism about the perfectibility of Man and the gloriousness of his distant future, would engage in social engineering on so vast a scale, at once tragic and comically half-baked. According to the philosophy, the desired homogenisation of the world will have immense advantages (other than the convenience of the secret police):

The present poisoning of the air, water and land [wrote Engels] can be put to an end only by the fusion of town and country.

And Lenin had an even more poetic vision of the future. Socialism, he said, would bring:

> . . . a redistribution of the human population (thus putting an end both to rural backwardness, isolation and barbarism, and to the unnatural concentration of vast masses of people in the big cities).

Under communism, green is the tree of theory, but grey is life.

The Boulevard of the Triumph of Socialism is immensely long and wide, flanked on both sides by grandiose apartment blocks. Some of them were completed three years ago but have never been occupied. Recently, however, Ceausescu had opened the stores at ground level. They were supposed to be elegant, indeed Parisian, with brass fittings, polished plate glass, marble floors and gilded mirrors; but like the food, the elegance was *ersatz*, and missed the mark. It was elegance by decree; by decree, moreover, of a man without taste, of an apprentice shoemaker (as Ceausescu once was) who found himself in the position of Louis XIV.

Futhermore, the stores were not stores (a practical illustration of the truth of dialectical materialism which, it must be remembered, denies the Aristotelian law of non-contradiction). For they sold nothing: their stock of luxury items was for display, not sale. And these luxury items were themselves *ersatz*, if approached too closely. The packaging of cosmetics, for example, imitated that of cosmetics in the west; but the printing was shoddy, the ink ran, the gold lettering missed its allotted place, the cellophane went yellow. And this, presumably, was the best that could be produced in Romania, for nothing but the best was worthy of the great boulevard. A few 'customers', their voices hushed as in a museum, wandered desultorily through these strange Aladdin's caves of bad tennis racquets, unpurchasable sun-beds and Potemkin home appliances, no doubt recalling (how could they ever forget?) that not so much as two hundred yards away from the Triumph of Socialism a queue, hours long, had formed on the rumour of sausage or bacon.

No adequate word yet exists in the English language for these extraordinary establishments: pseudostores or parashops, perhaps.

The central reservation of the boulevard was given over to gardens and an immense system of fountains, constructed of concrete moulded into floral motifs of outstanding vulgarity. One could always tell when the *Conducator* (the Romanian word for *Führer*) was about to go by, or had just gone by: the fountains, otherwise dry, were switched on. Except for policemen, whose purpose was to bully pedestrians who, as a matter of principle, had to be told to walk along a path other than the one they had chosen, and peasant women in kerchiefs who swept the ground with witches' brooms, few people lingered. And at the top of a slight incline that overlooked the whole length of the boulevard was the building that, like Dracula's castle in a horror movie, made them look at their feet and hurry on.

This was the People's Palace which, though still imcomplete, had already become the subject of legend. Some said it had 4000 rooms, others 12,000; some said it contained Ceausescu's necropolis, others that there were as many rooms underground as above; some said it was for the dictator's personal use, others that all the ministries would have offices there, yet others that it would also house the central gaol and torture chambers for political prisoners. But everyone was agreed that Ceausescu visited the palace daily to supervise its construction, changing the plans constantly according to whim, thus delaying its completion.

The People's Palace was a vast edifice – larger in volume by three times than Versailles – in an architectural style best described, perhaps, as MGM-Babylonian. No doubt it was of the utmost solidity, designed to withstand both earthquake and nuclear war, but its white stone facade, eight storeys high, with every order of architectural decoration known to Hollywood, gave it the appearance of a film set. One half-expected thousands of extras, carrying spears and wearing breastplates, suddenly to swarm all over it. As you approached, however, you ceased to smile: for at the railings surrounding it were stationed every fifty yards or so brute-faced young men in lumpy suits who clutched walkie-talkies as closely as yuppies clutch mobile telephones. They eyed you with suspicion; a smile would have aroused their dumb hatred. Curiosity, like photography, was not permitted, especially with regard to the huge black subterranean entrance, wide enough to take tanks, that gaped beneath the entire structure.

The People's Palace was intended as an advertisement, not of a product, but of men's individual insignificance in comparison with the power of the state. Even the methods employed in its construction tended to this glorious conclusion. One might have expected, in a European country theoretically dedicated to technological advancement and modernisation, that a vast project like the People's Palace would have been undertaken with the latest methods available. On the contrary: I watched workers sifting powdered cement for stones by hand, like housewives sifting flour before baking a cake. The machines employed were few and by no means modern: an army of workers was used instead. This had the advantage of emphasising the Pharaonic nature of the whole enterprise, thousands of powerless helots having been dragooned into labour by the will of one man, their individual contributions an infinitesimal part of the worthless and whimsical whole.

At first I was amused by the palace, by its preposterous architectural rodomontade; then I was fascinated by it, for it seemed to me to raise in tangible form the very questions that my Romanian journey sought to answer. What was the nature of the authority that could direct the efforts of an entire nation not only to the construction of something utterly without merit, either utilitarian or aesthetic, but to the destruction of everything worthwhile from the past? Finally, I found that I could not look at the palace a moment longer: it made me too angry for my own good. I could no more stare at it than I could stare at the sun; I felt a strange tension building up within me that might lead at any moment to an irrational outburst. I walked away.

How did it affect Romanians, this Versailles without beauty, this tyrannous monstrosity? I watched as ordinary people went by, searching their faces for signs of anger or frustration. But there were none; they looked neither right nor left, but downwards or straight ahead as they hurried by. Tyranny had made them inscrutable (the Romanians were once known for their southern, or Latin volatility): they had adopted the only defence possible in the circumstances, what the Germans of the Nazi era called 'inner emigration'.

It was time to visit the people whose names I had been given in London. I felt at first a certain reluctance: fear. This was irrational, for the worst that could have happened to me as a foreigner was arrest, interrogation and expulsion, all grist to my mill, and certainly not without interest. But fear in Romania is like a miasma, the ethereal, gaseous product of the earth that in the middle ages was thought to originate and communicate disease. The means by which this terrible contagion spread was one of the things that interested me.

Do not take risks, I was told in London; if, on your way to see someone you suspect you are followed, abort the visit. Err on the side of caution: the consequences for the person you are visiting can be drastic.

Sometimes (I was told) the *Securitate* wish to intimidate you by making it clumsily obvious they are following you; at other times, they follow with the greatest of skill, so that it is difficult to detect them.

I hired a car during my two weeks in Romania. About nine tenths of the cars there are Dacias, Renaults of old-fashioned design built in Romania. In this classless society, the colour of one's car indicated one's occupation or rank – black cars for very senior apparatchiks, white for directors of institutions, pastel colours for people of intermediate importance. My first car was red (until I had to change it for a light blue one when I ran out of petrol because the contents of the tank had been siphoned off and the fuel gauge interfered with in the hotel car park). The car had a special number plate to make me conspicuous to all authority. As I drove around Bucharest, I glanced nervously at my rear view mirror every few seconds. Any car that remained behind me for more than a hundred yards was following me; every policeman who spoke into his walkie-talkie was relaying information about my movements. It was only after I had driven circuitously round back streets that I was able to convince myself I was alone. Naturally, I parked at some distance from my destination; and even then I thought that anyone standing casually in a doorway was observing me.

Having abandoned the car, I walked swiftly and purposefully to the address. It was important, I was told, that I should look confident rather than furtive. But my frequent glances over my shoulder might have given me away, had anyone been observing. I was mildly put out that, after all my elaborate precautions, no one was.

I cannot, of course, describe my visits in too great detail: to do so might endanger those I visited. Romanians were supposed to report, verbatim, any conversations they had with foreigners to the police within twenty-four hours, and failure to comply with this regulation was taken as evidence of disloyalty and even dissidence. It was not actually forbidden to speak; only to say anything.

The people I met were literary intellectuals who knew either English or French. They were not a representative sample of the population, but they told me nothing about daily life in Romania that was not confirmed by people I subsequently met by chance as I drove around the country. Their privations were both physical and spiritual; the former would have been supportable, they said, had it not been for the latter. They saw no light at the end of their tunnel; they were gloomy and dispirited.

The first man whom I contacted, an economist, had just spent four hours queuing for eggs (and failed to obtain them). Did the fact that such experiences had been commonplace for a generation render them more acceptable, less aggravating? A Swiss friend of mine once saw people in Bucharest *fighting* over potatoes. One effect of the unceasing and time-consuming search for everyday commodities was a general slowing of the pace of life. In all probability, the Romanians were never celebrated for their expeditiousness; but with the coming of the new dispensation, a task which in western Europe would have been the work of a few minutes (such as buying butter or lightbulbs), to be fitted into the day's myriad other activities, had become the legitimate work of a whole afternoon or even of a day. Calculated by the length of time expended upon it, queuing was probably every Romanian's most important waking activity.

In the Era of Light, as Ceausescu sometimes called his 'epoch' when he grew tired of calling it Romania's Golden Age, there was such a shortage of domestic gas that, during winter, people had to cook after midnight, when the pressure was a little higher. Even so, it took half an hour to heat sufficient water for a cup of tea. The light of the Era of Light was, of course, strictly metaphorical: during winter, when there was not an outright power cut, rooms were allowed not more than one 40 watt bulb each.

Some might consider this ecologically sound, the epitome of the 'sustainable lifestyle'. Let them, therefore, inspect Romanian factories, which used up the country's power and whose principle product was pollution.

There were shortages of almost everything (even in my privileged capacity as tourist I was not to eat fresh vegetables once in Romania). There was a black market in books – not in forbidden ones alone, but in all kinds. A novel might cost half a month's salary (I hope I cannot hear embittered authors murmuring that at least they appreciated literature at its true worth there). As for coffee and Kent cigarettes, those – not crumpled, dirty *lei* – were the true currency of Romania.

But it was the stifling spiritual atmosphere of Romania that most preoccupied the people I met. Everyone lived in fear; fear was the universal, all-embracing condition, the daily experience of everyone in the country. I had sensed it in North Korea; but my inability to communicate with the Koreans, as well as the enormous cultural differences between us, kept alive in my mind the possibility that I was misinterpreting what I saw. Here in Romania there was no such possibility: whenever I entered a house, conversation was postponed

until the telephone was removed from the room, it being assumed not
only that telephones were routinely tapped, but that there was a
microphone within each apparatus to monitor private opinions
expressed in the home. One of the people I visited, who thought himself
under constant surveillance, drew all the curtains and turned on the
radio before he indicated it was safe to speak.

Was he paranoid? These precautions, it seemed to me, were more likely
to draw the attention of the police to him than the reverse; but he told me
they were necessary because he had been called to the police station for
interrogation after the last foreigner (who, like me, thought he was not
being followed) had visited him, and though he had been offered no
physical violence there, he had endured prolonged verbal abuse. Next
time it might be worse. Was he dramatising his situation to impress me, a
person of limited experience? He had a strange intensity about him, a
burning quality, that reminded me forcibly of Solzhenitsyn. Was it real,
this similarity, or assumed? Everything he did was on a grand scale: giving
me food, bread and cheese, he cut hunks with the passion of Goya's Saturn
devouring his own children. He was writing a novel in the style of Gogol
(realism was insufficient to capture the madness of Romania, he said) and
he wanted me to find a way of smuggling his manuscript out to a publisher
in London. Once it was published, he added, he would have become a
full-blown dissident rather than an unknown man living, as he now was,
on the margins of clandestinity. Therefore it was essential that I and others
provide him with the maximum of protective publicity, for it was only
limelight from the west that prevented the regime from 'disappearing' its
opponents.

Various people suggested to me that he was an *agent provocateur* and
warned me to be wary of him.* I felt out of my depth, or as though I
had, like Alice, stepped through the looking glass and entered a world
where everything was familiar yet changed, where nothing was what it
appeared to be, where ignorance was guilt and trust foolishness.

> Logic [wrote Elie Wiesel on visiting the Soviet Union] will not help you
> here. You have your logic, they have theirs, and the distance between you
> two cannot be bridged by words. The more you see of them the surer you
> become that everything you have thought or known till now is worthless;
> here you must begin anew.

I did not take the Gogolian manuscript, of course; but I did take a

*This was nonsense, but in the Romanian atmosphere of the time, appeared
plausible.

message of love to an English woman whom he had met briefly in Bucharest a few weeks before. It was not a very satisfactory way to carry on a love affair, but the only way open to him in the circumstances.

I discussed the prevailing state of fear with everyone I met. Each had his own interpretation, but all were agreed that it resulted not only from physical threat but was something deeper. Of course, the regime was prepared to be brutal if need be: it had no 'bourgeois sentimentality' about the worth of individuals, or about their rights. It had tortured and killed many, many people. Yet the fear was not merely that of brutality. It was something subtler, deeper, less tangible, almost puzzling and enigmatic. One might almost call it ontological. Certain intellectuals even blamed themselves or the Romanian people, implying that the traditional Romanian craftiness, passivity and patience exhibited in the face of overwhelmingly powerful enemies during the past millennium was really nothing more glorious than cowardice or pusillanimity. One of them mentioned a student in the city of Brasov who had immolated himself publicly the year before like Jan Palach, the Czech student who set fire to himself in protest against the Soviet invasion of Czechoslovakia in 1968. But unlike Jan Palach, the Romanian student's sacrificial protest found no answering echo in the country: shamefully, even his name was unknown, and almost everyone had forgotten his very existence. This was not because Ceausescu's regime enjoyed support, far from it: it was simply that Romanians were unable to organise opposition, both because of their fierce individualism and because the *Securitate* would soon infiltrate an organisation of more than two or three. They lacked the requisite determination to free themselves: theirs was a thousand year Reich.

A lack of determination is not necessarily an unattractive quality. Alone of the people I met, the Great Writer of the Romanian Land (or *agent provocateur*) possessed the hard edge of ruthlessness; but I preferred the others, though their achievements might in the end be less than his, for they spoke as much in sorrow as in anger and were therefore less likely – if their day ever came – to commit injustices of their own. Furthermore, there was something bittersweet about the physical surroundings in which we met. Many of them retained flats in pre-communist blocks. These flats were innocent of modern appurtenances and their floors were strewn with eastern rugs; their furniture was heavy, antique and dark. Nothing had been thrown away, for nothing was replaceable. The whole atmosphere was that of a vanished civilisation: cultivated, ployglot *Mitteleuropa*. A historian told me he felt like a member of a dying race; once his flat had been systematised and all traces of the past obliterated (Ceausescu's great dream), then truly his life would serve no purpose.

I heard mild criticisms of Romanian intellectuals when I returned to England: they did not protest enough, they did not unite, they had no programme in common. These were criticisms I felt I could not make . . .

By an extraordinary irony, these were the last words of this chapter I wrote before the Romanian revolution broke out six weeks after I left Romania, during which millions of unarmed Romanians faced rifles and machine guns rather than endure another day of the *Conducator*'s rule. At the time, I was also engaged on chapters about Albania, North Korea and Vietnam, but I had planned – more or less – what I was going to write about Romania.

I followed the course of the revolution with more than mere interest: passion would be a better word. I listened to every news bulletin without fail, and when I heard that Ceausescu and his wife had been winched aboard a helicopter from the roof of the Party Headquarters, that they had fled, I felt a depth of satisfaction, happiness, that no other piece of news has ever given me. My heart raced, I hugged myself, I wanted to jump and dance: I felt I had to share the joyful tidings with as many people as I could. I went to buy a newspaper in the small town where I was writing (and where the postmaster, confronted with a letter to Romania, was likely to ask whether Romania was in Asia or Africa).

'Ceausescu has been overthrown,' I said to the lady at the till.

'Oh dear,' she replied.

'What do you mean, oh dear? He was a monster.'

'Perhaps it's just as well, then,' she said, unconvinced.

But there was no doubt that the revolution presented me with a few small problems. Should I scrap my chapter or continue it as though nothing had happened, should I write with the not inconsiderable benefit of hindsight, should I lay claim to more political perspicacity than in fact I had at the time? Should I write of Ceausescu as if he were still alive, or as if he were consigned to that infinitely capacious vessel of Marxism, the dustbin of history?

There were problems that went beyond those of mere style. Could I now safely reveal the identities of the people to whom I talked? When I resumed this chapter, there were doubts about the character of the revolution: too many of the old guard were still in place. And was it safe yet to reveal that when I 'talked' to officials at our embassy in

Bucharest, we went into a 'safe' room, believed not to be bugged, and even there communicated by passing notes to each other?

I decided to continue as I should have done had there been no revolution, as far as possible not allowing subsequent events to colour my descriptions of what I saw, though hindsight would inevitably affect my interpretation of what I saw. To prove my good faith in this regard, I shall mention an article I wrote that caused me grave embarrassment when it was published in a magazine in the United States, six weeks after I wrote it, on the very day of Ceausescu's overthrow, and several days after the *Securitate* had shown their true ferocity, which I – no friend of the regime – grossly underestimated. In the article I stated that the terror in Romania was Kafkaesque, having almost as much to do with metaphysics as with torture. I had come rather hastily to this conclusion because I had met people who had been asked several times to inform for the *Securitate*, had refused, and yet had suffered no obvious reprisals. There could hardly have been a less opportune moment at which to publish such an opinion. I did not then know that every police station in Romania had its torture chamber. On the other hand, I did predict that Ceausescu would not last as long as the pessimists in Romania had suggested to me.

I have one further confession to make. When I saw film of Ceausescu speaking from the balcony of the Party Headquarters on the day before his downfall, and suddenly become frightened and bewildered when the crowd turned against him, I felt almost sorry for him, forgetting for a moment who he was and what he had done. I saw only a lonely old man facing the abyss. Surrounded for years by time-servers and flatterers, perhaps he really had imagined he was the nation's favourite son. All the telephone tapping, the espionage, the denunciation, the blackmail, the torture, had not helped him discover the most elementary and obvious truth: that he was a man who inspired the uttermost loathing and contempt, loathing of a depth quite unlike that inspired by any other political figure I have ever encountered, a loathing that reached into every fibre of every Romanian's being and that was reinforced by each day of his dictatorship.

During the revolution I recalled a painting in the Bucharest Museum of Fine Art that was of quite a different quality from all the other paintings exhibited there. It was by Breughel, and it was called *The Massacre of the Innocents*. I went three times to see it, arousing the suspicion of the staff (for the museum was otherwise empty). The painting shows a party of cavalry arriving in a village in winter. At first one admires the beauty of the composition, the blue of the sky, the landscape, the perfect arrangement of the figures. Then, as one approaches closer to the canvas, admiration gives way to horror, as one sees dismounted soldiers piercing babies with their swords or dragging children from their frantic parents. They do this with the calmness of those simply going about their duty (I am only obeying orders, one can almost hear them say). The mounted soldiers look on indifferently. Worse still, some of the villagers appear to be helping the soldiers in their 'work', and in the foreground two dogs frolic, as if to underscore the truly bestial unawareness of one of the soldiers who urinates happily against the wall of an inn while the innocents are massacred.

I do not know whether this wonderful and terrible picture survived the revolution. The Museum, just around the corner from the Royal Palace and the Party Headquarters in the Piata Republici (a square, it was once said, that awaits the *coup d'état* for which it was designed), was badly damaged. If the picture survived, and if it is exhibited again, I wonder what message it will convey to the Romanian people, so many of whom co-operated in their own enserfment?

Meetings with people in Romania had a special and quite extraordinary intensity. All frivolous chatter was excluded; within the hour, one felt united by indissoluble bonds of friendship (and more than friendship). On three occasions I spoke for several hours to a historian in Bucharest, a man whose father and grandfather were historians, not noticing or caring about the passage of mealtimes. He was not a dissident and would have laid no claims to exceptional bravery. But he had refused to join the Party, and thus remained on the lowest rung of the academic ladder, earning the equivalent, at the age of forty, of $25 a month. Moreover, he wrote only the truth – as he saw it – though this confined him to historical subjects so arcane that even the ideologues ignored them. He hoped that by patiently publishing the results of his investigations on small and seemingly unimportant matters, he would eventually, like a pointilliste, achieve a large picture: a picture totally opposed to the preposterous official caricature of Romanian history that was propagated everywhere.

Was his a worthwhile project? In Romanian circumstances, did not research into the church in 17th century Wallachia bring to mind the old Romanian proverb: the whole village is on fire, but grandmother wants to finish combing her hair? Should his project be construed as cowardice or essential groundwork for the eventual recovery of the Romanian nation from the damage inflicted on it by communism and

Ceausescu? If he had compromised a little with evil, who was I, who had done the same in far less dire circumstances, to blame him? Exceptional courage is a virtue, but it can never be a duty. Still, there are those who might say he should have chosen exile rather than prevaricate over truth: but it is a terrible thing for a historian to be separated from his language, his culture, his subject matter. It is a kind of death. And would it really have been better for Romania had the field been left entirely to hacks of the most abject stamp?

The historian and I explored together the workings of totalitarianism. He spoke from experience and intimate knowledge, I from superficial observation and a certain amount of reading. I was rather proud of my deduction – which admittedly it took me an unconscionable time to make – that within an established totalitarian regime the purpose of propaganda is not to persuade, much less to inform, but rather to humiliate. From this point of view, propaganda should not approximate to the truth as closely as possible: on the contrary, it should do as much violence to it as possible. For by endlessly asserting what is patently untrue, by making such untruth ubiquitous and unavoidable, and finally by insisting that everyone publicly acquiesce in it, the regime displays its power and reduces individuals to nullities. Who can retain his self-respect when, far from defending what he knows to be true, he has to applaud what he knows to be false – not occasionally, as we all do, but for the whole of his adult life? How else could one explain the insistence of the Ceausescu regime that it had brought the Era of Light, at the very time when light itself was rationed?

The historian was passionate about the preservation of the past precisely because so concerted an attack had been made on it. His admiration for Orwell knew no bounds (I have found the same admiration all across eastern Europe). Never to have lived in a totalitarian state and yet to have understood so well – that was genius! For to understand eastern Europe one needed not just information but imagination. Orwell grasped intuitively but with astonishing precision the importance to a totalitarian regime of control over the past. But I said that his conclusion in *Nineteen Eighty-Four* was nonetheless mistaken: Winston Smith could not be made to love Big Brother, only to pretend that he did. I said that in 1988 I had witnessed a hundred thousand people singing the Latvian national anthem for the first time in nearly half a century, despite its previous total proscription, despite the years of terror, deportation, murder, collectivisation, indoctrination, untruth and destruction. This had convinced me that the annihilation of the human spirit was not possible.

But here in Romania, said the historian, the evil was etched into people's souls, and it would take two, three, even four generations to erase it (an observation not entirely contradicted by events subsequent to the revolution). From time to time as he spoke, he would glance out of the window to see if there was anyone below in the street: his apartment block was next door to an embassy which was guarded day and night.

Then I spoke of the other deduction of which I was rather proud: that in a tyranny such as Ceausescu's, shortages of material goods, even of necessities, were not a drawback but a great advantage for the rulers. These shortages were not accidental to the terror, but one of its most powerful instruments. Not only did shortages (which were known to be permanent, not temporary) keep people's minds strictly on bread and sausage, and divert their energies to procuring them so that there was no time or inclination left over for subversion, but they – the shortages – meant that people could be brought to inform, spy and betray each other very cheaply, for the sake of trivial material benefits that obviated the need to queue. (Let him who has not queued for hours a day cast the first stone.) And since everyone in Romania had to resort to the black market to live, everyone laid himself open to blackmail by the authorities, who could threaten him with 'justice' unless he co-operated.

This was all very true as far as it went, said the historian, but I had not plumbed the depths of the Romanian degradation even yet. Totalitarian regimes created a debilitating psychology of complicity. Because they owned and controlled everything, and recognised no limits to their own power, every mouthful of food, every moment of rest, every item of consumption, was enjoyed solely by their grace and favour, which could be withdrawn at a whim. Therefore even the most everyday of activities served to remind everyone that they lived on dictated terms, that they had compromised their principles for a potato or a piece of paper. Even freedom – that is to say, non-incarceration in a penal institution, the highest form of freedom known at that time in Romania – was a privilege, not a right, and a fragile one at that. To walk the streets at liberty was conditional on not raising one's voice against injustice as one ought. Thus even this limited liberty was bought at the cost of moral emasculation. Everyone – except out and out dissidents – was an accomplice of the regime; to live in Romania was to be stained by its indelible corruption. Everyone was both victim and culprit at the same time: that is why it would take generations to repair the damage that had been done, to unmake the New Man, now entering his fifth decade and third generation as a toady, a sycophant, a hypocrite, a coward, a blackmailer, a gutless doublethinker . . .

There was an irony in all this, of course: which was that everything he said confirmed the Marxist idea, adumbrated in the *Theses on Feuerbach*, that man's social being was not determined by his consciousness but that his consciousness was determined by his social being (*au fond* by the relations of production). The historian believed that communism had really wrought a change in people's souls, in their innermost being. I was not so sure (though I could hardly say so to a man who had lived forty years in a cesspit which I was visiting for only a few days): repeatedly in Romania I met fine people, many born well into the communist era, who made compromises, it is true, but who never lost sight of what they were doing. Indeed, I never met a Romanian who did not passionately abhor what had been done to his country. And it seemed to me that as long as this was the case, the New Man had only a shadow existence. Hypocrisy is no doubt a vice in itself, being the compliment that vice pays to virtue: but a hypocrite still knows what is virtue and what is vice, and there is therefore still hope for him. The New Man, by contrast, has lost the capacity to tell the two apart.

In the Moldavian city of Iasi, 250 miles to the north east of Bucharest, I met a historian who lived among books stacked three deep against the walls and up to the ceiling of his room. He was a gentle man, as bookish people often are, reserving his venom, insofar as he had any, for scholars with whom he disagreed. He spoke in a lowered voice, as if afraid of discovery with a foreigner. I took him Bulgakov's *The Heart of a Dog*, which he received with delight. I rather assumed by his manner that he was a timid man, more Hamlet than Don Quixote.

I was mistaken. On the 400th anniversary of the birth of Michael the Brave, the prince who briefly united the provinces of Romania for the first time, he arranged not a demonstration but an unofficial celebration. This was before 1965, the beginning of Ceausescu's Era of Light, when Michael the Brave was still considered a bourgeois nationalist and not a national hero. To celebrate the anniversary of his birth, even with a cake, was then regarded as a sign of deviation from the True Path of Socialist Internationalism. The young historian was sentenced to ten years' hard labour in a prison camp. He passed over his sufferings there (he served six years) with a lightness that was as eloquent as any harrowing description. He was released in the first flush of Ceausescu's 'liberalism'. That he had asserted something that subsequently became orthodoxy had nothing to do with his release. 'Objectively' – in the Stalinist sense – he had been mistaken. For truth in totalitarian countries does not depend on correspondence to reality; it depends merely on *who* propounds it, and when.

On his release, the historian returned to his books. He was a specialist on Romanian historiography and had at various times been offered scholarships abroad, in Germany and France. Why had he not gone, I asked, and stayed where he could have worked in peace?

'I wanted to show my students that it was possible to live in Romania and still be a human being,' he said.

And was this not a dangerous project?

'I am not afraid. I already know what hard labour is like.'

One man against the state: Don Quixote against not just windmills but armoured cars, tanks, tear gas, informers, torture, prison camps, blackmail and murder. My habitual pessimism now seemed to me rather a cheap stance towards the world.

All the same, a cynical thought recurred to me every time I met Romanian intellectuals: if totalitarianism were ever defeated in Romania, would they not soon come to miss it? In a strange way, its very denial of the value of life gave value to life. The evil of the regime was so overwhelmingly omnipresent that one didn't have to worry about complex and boring questions such as the level of income tax that maximised both justice and economic efficiency, or the best way to organise old age pensions or scientific research. One went straight to the large issues of human existence, bypassing mere administrative details.

And secretly I fell prey to the one of the besetting sins of western intellectuals, which normally I abhor: I began to experience envy of suffering, that profoundly dishonest emotion which derives from the foolish notion that only the oppressed can achieve righteousness or – more importantly – write anything profound. I thought that if only I had lived through even a little of the Romanian experience, my literary problems would solve themselves: there would be no casting around for subject matter, I should write under feverish compulsion and profundity would come of itself. As for the suffering entailed, I accepted it in advance with a light heart: for even if I were wrong, and suffering does not necessarily give meaning to artistic endeavour, artistic endeavour certainly gives meaning to suffering.

My historian in Bucharest had an almost unmentionable professional interest: the history of the Jews in Romania. This was a subject on which no work was done or published in Romania; an impenetrable veil of silence had descended on the fate of nearly a million people, of whom only a mere 20,000 remained, and anyone who sought to lift this veil was regarded as an enemy of the state. Though he was gentile, the historian well understood the importance of preserving the memory of this once large community from all the official efforts to forget it had ever existed, for no country can regain its own health while so terrible a crime remains unexpiated, or worse still, unacknowledged.

The official silence about the extermination during the War of so considerable a part of Romania's population was the result of several mutually reinforcing factors, the first and not least of which was the anti-Semitism of the Danube of Thought, the *Conducator* himself, who in this respect shared the prejudices of a large percentage of his people. According to Ion Pacepa, Ceausescu constantly reiterated that two of Romania's greatest assets were Germans and Jews, since both could be held to ransom for hard currency. Outright public anti-Semitism was impermissible, of course, ever since the Holocaust; what greater revenge on the Jews, then, than simply to forget they had ever lived in Romania in large numbers? This inhuman amnesia was made all the more diabolical by the presence of a pathetic Jewish remnant, too terrified to protest against present persecution, too aware that everything could be worse to demand that anything should be better.

Irony of ironies, therefore, that – as the historian told me – there was a notice on the door of the Chief Rabbi of Romania's office stating 'We do not accept conversions'. Why was such a notice necessary? Because every day before it was posted, the office was beseiged by Romanians offering to convert to Judaism in the hope that they could thereby escape from the Romania of the Era of Light to evil, Zionist Israel and thence to the west. More poignant still, I found myself in my hotel dining opposite two elderly Jewish ladies who lived in Israel but had been born in Romania, and who spoke to each other in Romanian, their mother tongue. Ostensibly they had come for treatment for their rheumatism, as they did every year, there being some bogus Romanian remedy involving mud and injections (available only for hard currency) for this condition. But really they came so that they could joke with a waiter – even for a short while – in their own language, in a language that was not forever foreign, and to enjoy for once the pleasures of speech without translation.

At first I wondered how anyone who had lived through suffering such as they must have witnessed could bear to return to the scene of it; but I was forgetting the importance to human beings of language, greater perhaps than that of any subsequent experience. How should I survive separation from the English tongue? English, of course, has many lands of exile; but if you are Romanian, where can you go to hear your language except Romania itself (or Soviet Moldavia where, incidentally, I was told they speak the purest Romanian because Russian was until very recently the official language, and thus Romanian had been preserved from the distortions of communist *langue de bois*, and was used only for the transactions of daily life)? The Israeli Romanians were so delighted by the sound of the waiter's speech that they minded neither their memories nor the disgusting food they were served.

When I returned to Bucharest after two weeks travelling round the country I visited the historian again: by now he was my guru on all matters Romanian. Knowing his interest in Jewish history, I mentioned that in the far northern town of Sighetu Marmatiei I had unexpectedly come across a monument in Hebrew and Romanian, commemorating the deportation of Jews in 1944 from the town to death camps elsewhere. But in Iasi, a third of whose population before the war had been Jewish, I found no such memorial, not the faintest indication indeed that Iasi had ever been other than it was now, *Judenfrei*. Watching people go about their business in Iasi – not very cheerfully, it is true, but for reasons other than their city's cataclysmic history – I wanted to stop them and ask where all the Jews had gone. Did they know, did they care? People cannot live by recollection alone, of course; but can they live entirely without it?

I speculated on the difference between Sighetu Marmatiei and Iasi. I guessed that the memorial to Transylvanian atrocities was permissible because Transylvania was then under Hungarian jurisdiction, and it was the Hungarian gendarmerie who had rounded up the Jews of Sighetu for extermination; whereas in Iasi, the same task was performed (all too willingly) by the Romanians themselves. This unfortunate fact was indigestible from the point of view of official Romanian historiography, according to which the history of Romania has been a continuous triumphal progress to the glorious present, any negative phenomena being solely attributable to foreigners or a handful of anti-national members of the ruling class. The monument in Sighetu was not in mourning for the Jews; it was anti-Hungarian propaganda.

My surmise was essentially correct, said the historian. The rabid nationalism by means of which Ceausescu sought to give legitimacy to his dictatorship was a straightjacket in which all serious thought about historical or political matters was impossible. It was at this point in our conversation that I mentioned a curious volume, half in English, half in French, that I had found in a Bucharest bookshop: *The Priority of Paulescu in the Discovery of Insulin*. The purpose of this book, first published in 1977, was to establish that insulin had not been discovered in Toronto by Banting, Best and Macleod, as described in almost all textbooks, but by Paulescu in Bucharest, and that the Canadians had nefariously deprived Paulescu of the credit (and hence of the Nobel Prize).

The historian asked whether I had ever heard of Popov and he was surprised to discover that I had. Popov was the man the Russians claimed had invented radio before Marconi. I knew of him because my father had possessed a huge book about the Soviet Union, published in Russia in 1947, which claimed every conceivable achievement for both the Soviet Union and pre-revolutionary Russia. The book was cream coloured and the arms of the Soviet Union were embossed in gold on its front cover. Inside were sepia photographs of buxom peasant girls in national costumes holding baskets of fruit in fields of waving corn, a row of combine harvesters reaping plenty on the distant horizon. The book was arranged like a religious calendar, every day of the year commemorating a political event or the birthday of a Russian genius. As a child, I spent many hours with the book, looking at its pictures and committing the exotic names – Mendeleyev, Mussourgsky, Lunacharsky, Dzherzhinsky, Zhdanov – to memory. And it was from this book that I learnt of Popov.

'Paulescu is the Romanian Popov,' said the historian, laughing.

Actually, the book was very convincing. Paulescu was a physiologist of considerable renown who published the results of his work on an extract of pancreatic gland several months before the Toronto group. For some reason, it was not taken up by the scientific community (Paulescu published in French, but in those days English had not yet reached its complete preeminence in the scientific world). The Toronto group knew of Paulescu's work, but persistently misrepresented it in their own papers. According to the author, they realised at once that Paulescu had already discovered what they had also set out to discover. They therefore deliberately misunderstood his work so that they might claim priority in the discovery.

I started to read *The Priority of Paulescu in the Discovery of Insulin* with something of a superior sneer on my face. I assumed I already knew the story of that discovery (I have a degree in physiology), and no doubt there was more than an element of cultural arrogance in my reluctance to concede that so important a scientific contribution could have been made in a Balkan backwater. But the documentation in the book was decisive; and the subsequent evasions of the Toronto scientists were not pleasant to read. I understood the feeling of outraged national pride that such devious and discreditable behaviour were likely to inflame.

Nevertheless, one thing puzzled me about this book, and that was its date of publication. A retired British physician had drawn attention to Paulescu's claim to priority several years earlier in the *British Medical Journal*; and according to the historian, the book's author had struggled for many years in vain to bring posthumous lustre to Paulescu's name. The author was himself a physiologist who had been taught by Paulescu, succeeding him to the chair of physiology at Bucharest University; the book was written in a spirit of filial piety rather than nationalist vehemence.

But why, I asked, had it taken so long for Paulescu to be recognised even in the country of his birth? Because Paulescu later became an intolerant Roman Catholic, a fascistic anti-communist who in addition to his scientific papers wrote vile anti-Semitic pamphlets. It was decided only latterly that the glory to Romania of his scientific discovery was greater than the risk of having to admit that a man could be both a brilliant scientist *and* a fanatical anti-communist (for in the official world-view, which declared itself scientific above all else, anybody who achieved anything worthwhile prior to the revolution must have been at the very least a communist *avant la lettre*).

Before Paulescu's rehabilitation, therefore, you could not mention him because he was a fascist; after his rehabilitation you could not mention he was a fascist because he had been rehabilitated.

In these circumstances, the historian asked, was it any wonder that intellectuals were leaving Romania as fast as possible? He felt he would soon be the only one left. He asked a favour of me: as I had been so successful in smuggling books into Romania, perhaps I wouldn't mind smuggling a few out? An archaeologist friend of his was leaving for France, but couldn't bear to leave his painstakingly acquired library behind. It was illegal to export secondhand books from Romania, which were regarded as national treasures even when it was not permitted to read them. When he left he would be allowed to take none of his library with him, which would be forfeit to the state. If every sympathetic visitor took one or two of the most important volumes to the west, the library could perhaps be salvaged, at least in part. I agreed, though I was alarmed to discover that the books allotted me were in Greek and Russian, neither of which I read. But at the last minute, the risk both to the books and to me was considered too great and my mission of bibliographic mercy was aborted, not without a certain relief on my part.

The first time I visited him, the historian gave me a very valuable piece of advice: I should go to the National Historical Museum which, like Gaul, was divided into three parts. The most important part, admittedly from my slightly peculiar point of view, was that devoted to 'Proofs of the love, high esteem and appreciation that Preident N. Ceausescu and Comrade E. Ceausescu enjoy'. The museum was in the Calea Victoriei, the once fashionable central street of Bucharest which was now permanently closed to all traffic except the *Conducator*'s motorcade *en route* twice a day to or from the grim and sinister Party Headquarters, and along whose pavements people queued at midday to buy little balls of glutinous starch fried in rancid oil for their lunch. I bought my tickets for the museum and made straight for the Proofs of Love section.

This was housed in three or four large rooms, the first of which contained in glass cases all the decorations and academic awards bestowed on the happy couple during their voyages abroad. Here were sashes and medals from every country in the world, including – I am ashamed to say – my own, which awarded the *Conducator* an honorary knighthood, withdrawn shortly before he was shot. The Royal Institute of Chemistry elected Elena to its fellowship, apparently under the misapprehension that she was some kind of chemist (she had chosen to be known in Romania as a 'world-ranking scientist', though she was as much a chemist as Marie Antoinette was a shepherdess). There were gaudy sashes from Africa, complete with large bronze stars embossed with elephants and zebras, medals from Italy and West Germany, and honorary doctorates from Peru and the Philippines. The last came with a citation, which was at the bottom of a glass case near floor level. It was so odiously sycophantic that I had to copy it down, and I went on to my knees to do so:

For your lifelong commitment to national and social liberation from the forces of fascist and lawless regimes, a commitment which earned for you the honor of having been incarcerated for your political beliefs, thus joining

that distinguished company of true leaders of men who, even while political
prisoners, affirmed the integrity of the mind through the resoluteness of
their will and the strength of their ideas . . .

It was at this point in my copying that I noticed I was joined by a
policeman's boot on my left side. I looked up and there, as they would
say in Nigeria, was a whole policeman. The frumpish museum
attendant, who had in any case found my entry into the Proofs of Love
section highly suspicious, had fetched him as soon as I started my very
odd behaviour. I tried to explain to the policeman that I was only
copying down this Philippine eulogy to his employer, but it was clear
that voluntary devotion to the cult was unwelcome, first because it was
voluntary and any voluntary action was suspect, implying as it did the
ability to choose and therefore to think, and second because it was
obviously mad. My efforts to persuade him of my harmlessness were to
no avail: he insisted that I discontinue. Rather than risk confiscation of
what I had already written – the only notes I took in Romania – I
complied. In any case, the rest of the citation was worded in the same
rolling thunder eloquence and was without interest, except as evidence
of how completely wrong or cynical in their judgments it is possible for
humans to be.

I went from the awards and decorations to the gifts given to the
Ceausescus on their journeys round the world. The gifts were divided
geographically by continent, and I was particularly anxious to see the
certificate of Nicolae's honorary citizenship of Disneyland, conferred
on him by Mickey Mouse. Alas, the room was very ill-lit, and I could
scarcely make out the words. In the American section I was surprised to
discover that American astronauts had carried a small Romanian flag to
the moon, at a time when Ceausescu was considered the 'good'
communist and it was hoped he might prove a Trojan horse in Eastern
Europe.

The gifts displayed were worthless, cheap junk such as tourists bring
home from two weeks on a foreign beach. There were coconuts with
carved husks, tropical landscapes made out of seashells, cups and
saucers with municipal coats of arms, small dolls in national costume,
mass-produced tribal masks and shields, and little bronze cathedrals.
By all accounts the Ceausescus, crudely avaricious, kept for themselves
anything of value that they acquired. But it was in the final room of the
Proofs of Love, whose lights had to be switched on specially for me by
the incredulous attendant because no one had visited it for days or

possibly weeks beforehand, that kitsch really came into its own. Bad taste was here elevated into a government policy. The final room of the Proofs of Love contained gifts given to the Ceausescus by people and organisations from all over Romania.

Hung on the walls were portraits of the presidential couple in oils, mosaic, tapestries, batik and carpets, all in primary proletarian colours. Madame Ceausescu, with her beehive hairdo, generally clutched a bouquet of flowers while her husband waved to a crowd of adoring children; in several portraits Ceausescu appeared in immanent proportions against the sky (in fact, he was a small man who used to receive visitors in his office sitting on a raised platform to ensure that he had to look down rather than up at them), the crowds of tiny people below reaching up to him as though he were distributing celestial chocolates. Naturally, there were white doves everywhere. In one portrait with faintly biblical overtones the couple were framed by a brilliant rainbow, their convenant no doubt to the people of Romania. But best – or worst – of all were the huge porcelain vases with painted portraits of the *Conducator*, produced 'in their spare time' by workers at porcelain factories. These were the purest throwbacks possible of the Stalin era: once again I recalled the hours of my childhood spent with that Soviet volume, with its colour plates of Stalin vases, 'the largest in the world', gifts to the *Vozhd* from workers grateful to him for their fruitful, happy lives etc.

Before I left the Proofs of Love, I bought the nearest thing to a catalogue, which contained badly printed pictures of the happy couple inspecting the proofs of the love and high esteem in which the whole world held them. I bought it in the hope and expectation that it would soon become a collectors's item.

Out of the frying pan into the fire. Next to the museum was an exhibition hall into which I watched a large party of schoolchildren, all with red neckerchiefs, file under the direction of their teacher. I followed them in: it was an exhibition of Romanian economic achievements, under the guidance of Nicolae and Elena Ceausescu. At the end of the hall was an enormous Romanian flag, red, yellow and blue, with the communist coat of arms on the central yellow stripe. On another wall was a huge photograph of Ceausescu standing in a field of corn, a group of peasants gathered round him (at a respectful distance) hanging on his every word as he, the former shoemaker, explains to them how to grow cereals. So that his words should not be lost to posterity, so that they could be entered into Volume Sixty-Three of his

Collected Works, there stood next to him a man with a notebook, leaning forward with just the right degree of eagerness and obsequiousness to catch the falling pearls. The *Conducator* himself was wearing silver mohair trousers and jacket, halfway in design between a safari suit and a Mao costume. He also wore a flat cap of the same material, which was a neat iconographic resolution of what dialectical materialists would no doubt call a contradiction: on the one hand the need to appear unique (everyone else in the picture was bareheaded, and no one else wore silver mohair) and on the other to appear proletarian – hence the flat worker's cap.

As for the exhibits, they were material evidence of the enormous economic strides that Romania had made – precisely the same strides as Albania had made. Displayed in glass cases were telephones, bottles of apple juice, electrocardiographs, cups and saucers, vials of antibiotics, tomato ketchup, radios, plastic cucumbers, chocolate, wheelchairs, indeed a gallimaufry of the products of Romanian industry, which brought to mind the exclamation of an exasperated Soviet author, 'When will we stop regarding a sausage as an economic achievement and simply as something to eat?'

The children were given a turgid lecture by an attendant as they went round the exhibition (I could tell the lecture was turgid even though I understood only a few phrases, and I could tell also that the attendant didn't believe a word of it, for she spoke with the passion of a tape recorder). I am glad to say that the children spent far more time looking at me than at the exhibits, and I likewise looked at them. How beautiful and lively were the girls, with chestnut hair and dark brown eyes, slim and too young yet to have succumbed to the southern tendency to fat. Before long the teacher, noticing their distraction, tut-tutted and shepherded them away from me, so that they should concentrate on the glories of socialist ketchup, unprecedented in the world.

I visited two more people in Bucharest: a former diplomat who was writing his memoirs and a poet, both under surveillance, the latter for writing love poetry of no political content, which automatically made him suspect in the eyes of the authorities. Both had signed a letter protesting at the expulsion of a writer from the Writers' Union, which had caused displeasure in official circles but so far no harsher penalties than prohibition from publication – a mildness of response for which it was possible that visits from westerners were responsible.

I left Bucharest after a few days without any clear itinerary. By now I had such an aversion to planning that I refused to think ahead, even in simple personal matters.

I made for Brasov, on the borders of Transylvania, by way of Ploiesti. The latter is an oil town, thirty miles from Bucharest, with an interesting history and a foul smell. One of the first oil refineries in the world was set up there in 1856. In 1916, the British-owned oil installations were destroyed by British agents to prevent them from falling into the hands of the Germans. Subsequently, the British demanded compensation which the Romanians reluctantly paid. Then the British sold out to the Germans before the war and bombed the installations once more in 1944, in the process destroying the town altogether.

Ploiesti had been rebuilt in a style typical of communist modernity, rectangular concrete block after rectangular concrete block, like a blueprint for paradise drawn up by Le Corbusier, except that standards of actual construction were so abysmally low. Of all building materials concrete is the least attractive, the most impossible to humanise, and therefore beloved of communists (and British architects). At best, its widespread use creates a bleak wasteland; but where, as in Romania, its use is accompanied by wide, grey, treeless boulevards which act as wind tunnels and are without traffic, and empty shops called simply 'Shoes' or 'Groceries' or 'Books' or 'Clothes', the effect is to call into question the very meaning or purpose of life, to induce a state of apathy and hopelessness. Ploiesti is such a town, with a sulphurous pall of various shades of grey and blackish mauve hanging over it.

I ran out of petrol just outside Ploiesti, my petrol gauge still showing half-full. I stood by the side of the road and waited for someone to take me back to the town, from where I hoped to telephone the car hire company in Bucharest (at this stage I did not know the problem was lack of fuel). A passing bureaucrat gave me a lift, and deposited me in the largest, most important hotel in the town, from which I was able to telephone for help. I waited an hour and a half in the lobby, a fine example of Romanian modernity, dispiriting in its deadness. There was nowhere to have tea or coffee, there were few people around, and the concrete walls absorbed all sound, muffling it in an almost sinister way. At least there was no muzak. I read and was entertained for a time by two workmen who came to remove a large plastic pot plant from the lobby, which proved difficult to manoeuvre through the door. Where were they going with the plant, I wondered? Was an important visitor arriving at Ploiesti party headquarters, which had to be made attractive for him? Perhaps the whole town possessed only this one plant (plastic at that) which was moved from office to office as need be. Here indeed was a theme for a Gogolian novelist . . .

The men from Bucharest arrived while I was having lunch in the hotel restuarant, a vast expanse of tables with not many customers and a dearth of waiters. I had excellent red cabbage soup with sausage and general leftovers, followed by meat of uncertain provenance cooked some time in the nineteenth century, served with vegetables of postively British mushiness. The men from Bucharest decided to have lunch too, but did not sit at my table.

We drove to my stranded car afterwards, where they proved beyond all doubt that I had run out of petrol. The fuel gauge, they said, had been interfered with by the siphoners of my petrol. I must be very careful in future, because petrol was scarce in Romania and people were always stealing it from each other. (At the beginning of the month, when car owners received their petrol ration coupons, the queues outside petrol stations were not hours but days long.) Unfortunately, my petrol tank had no lock, so their warning was of little value: I could hardly spend the nights standing guard over the tank. They brought me a new car in exchange for the old, even though, with fuel, the old was perfectly all right. Regulations, they said. As payment they demanded only petrol coupons: considerably more than the fuel they could have expended to reach me and return to Bucharest. I suspected they were trading on their own account, and that I was being robbed of yet more petrol. Still, they had helped me not a little, and I gave them some Kent cigarettes as well. In other communist countries they prefer Marlboro.

I decided against visiting one of the only tourist attractions in the vicinity of Ploiesti, the prison of Doftana. It was here that participants in the great peasant uprising of 1907 were imprisoned and tortured. Later the prison was used for communist leaders, including Gheorghiu-Dej, the Romanian leader, until his death from throat cancer in 1965, after whom a boulevard in every town in the country has – or had, before the recent revolution – been named. (Ceausescu believed that the Russians gave Gheorghiu-Dej cancer by irradiating him while he was in Moscow, and was terrified of meeting the same fate.) There was, apparently, an exhibition in Doftana of the instruments of torture used on communists, of the old police files about them and of the little devotional Marxist tracts they kept hidden in their cells to restore their spirits. If ever there were a refutation of the popular fallacy that the persecuted are in some manner more devoted to justice and freedom than others, the prison of Doftana was that refutation. Here was evidence, if any were needed, that it is perfectly possible to be staunch and brave, heroic even, in pursuit of undesirable ends. I sometimes wonder whether intellectuals will ever realise that the worth of a cause is not necessarily proportional to the lengths to which people will go to promote it.

On the way to Brasov I passed through Sinaia in the Bucegi mountains. It was cool and the countryside was magnificent, clouds slipping silently over the edges of awe-inspiring escarpments, the slopes of the mountains dark green with fir trees. As for Sinaia itself, it was a somewhat Germanic alpine settlement with timber-framed chalets and a mad Teutonic *schloss*, the whole town being in a state of decay caused by the absence of any commercial incentive to keep it attractive. Its tourism was now internal, and opportunities for Romanians either to earn or to spend their virtually worthless currency were almost non-existent. Romanian holidaymakers milled around aimlessly, as though simply waiting for time to pass. Released for a time from their daily drudgery, what purpose did these people have? Unanswerable questions that transcended politics, concerning the meaning of life, rose unbidden to my mind.

The countryside restored me somewhat: sufficient unto the day are the pleasures thereof. But the approach to Brasov itself brought radical pessimism flooding back. For what seemed like several miles, there was a grey boulevard running like a cavern through cliffs of concrete, proletarian apartment blocks from whose windows hung washing like trophies from some inglorious war. There was no life on the street, no vulgar commerce (how one misses it when it is not there, how one criticises it when it is), only Lowry-like figures endlessly trudging, probably in search of potatoes, in that inhuman landscape created by humans.

The centre of the city belonged to a different age. Such was one's relief to see architecture of a humane type, buildings constructed for various proper purposes and not for some overarching plan to reduce human consciousness to absolute uniformity and unthinking obedience, that one began at once to romanticise the past, always a dangerous thing to do, especially in the case of Romania. Could a civilisation that produced such a city really have been so terrible? At least it had *something* in its favour; I should be hard put to it to find anything to say in favour of Romanian civilisation today.

Brasov was what in communist parlance would be called a 'Hero

City': anti-government riots broke out there in November 1987 at a time when everything seemed under control, at least from the executioner's point of view. It was said that thanks to this manifestation of discontent, the city was under particularly strict surveillance by the *Securitate*, and that foreign visitors would be even more closely watched here than elsewhere. I don't know whether this was so in my case; all I can say is that the lady in the lift of my hotel, whom I naturally supposed to be an agent, or at the least an informer, of the *Securitate*, made about the clumsiest attempts at seduction I have ever witnessed, hitting me several times between the ground and second floors with her vast peasant bust (which came up to just above my waist) and fluttering her artifical eyelashes, all gluey with mascara, at me in a manner one might have expected to see in an early silent movie of the life of Mata Hari. Did she want to compromise me, as in a spy novel, or were the Kent cigarettes I gave her the real object of her behaviour? Having experienced a few torrid moments cornered in the lift (she was built like a wrestler), I subsequently chose the fire escape.

In Brasov I met another historian, a young man struggling to survive on the lowest salary level. He was approaching the age at which he would be fined for not having children, but he preferred a fine to bringing a child into the world in impossible conditions. His young wife was still a student. Originally she had wanted to study philosophy, but her brother had escaped to Yugoslavia and thence to America, thus bringing suspicion on the whole family. Only students with an irreproachable family record of loyalty to the regime were permitted to enter the philosophy faculty: she had to content herself with Romanian instead.

The historian told me of the conditions in his small institute. He knew well enough who was the head of the *Securitate* in the institute – everyone knew, for he made it perfectly clear – but as for the rest of his colleagues, it was impossible to tell. What a charming atmosphere in which to conduct research! The *Securitate* had approached him twice to ask him to inform on his colleagues, in return for coffee, money etc, but he refused and had not even been threatened as a result. It was quite possible, though, that everyone else in the institute had succumbed, so that informers informed on other informers, and vice versa. At some point, I thought, this mania for espionage must be counterproductive, with nobody being able any longer to distinguish real information from vague suspicion, thanks to an infinite regress of paranoia. It was almost as though the model for the *Securitate* were not the Cheka or the Gestapo, but Feydeau and the French *farceurs*.

A Zimbabwean rugby team was staying in my hotel, and I overheard their bewilderment at the lack of anything to do in the town at night. Down the Strada Republicii, it was true, one could hear a rather desperate band playing in a café, but one's ears soon tingled with the sheer volume of sound it produced and spurred one to leave before catastrophe, in the form of burst eardrums, struck. So the rugby team stayed at its table in the restaurant (another joyless canteen, where foreigners were seated separately from Romanians) and drank the kind of beer that produces a hangover well this side of drunkenness. The waitress, though, made up for it with her charm. She told me that, with a little bit of negotiation on her part, she could find some 'big chicken' in the kitchen, a real delicacy. I waited for it in suspense, drinking beer from a brown bottle with no label. 'Big chicken' turned out to be duck, cooked in that extraordinary manner that I thought only the British had fully mastered, namely par-boiled and half-roasted without seasoning, with limp skin and served lukewarm. Still, it made a change, worth every one of the Kent cigarettes I gave the waitress. After dinner I walked the crimeless streets of Brasov composing anti-Ceausescu tirades in my mind.

I moved on, further into Transylvania, travelling 50 or 100 miles a day. I passed through the Burzen Land, taking the smaller side roads. The landscape here was of rolling hills and villages with fortified Saxon churches of the fourteenth and fifteenth Centuries. The Saxons were invited into Transylvania by the Hungarian king, fearful for Hungarian control of territory inhabited mainly by Romanians. The Saxons, hard-working and thrifty, soon become rich; they controlled all trade and ruled the towns, eventually becoming a caste apart, so that mere Romanians (then called Vlachs) were not permitted to reside within the walls of Transylvanian towns. The Saxons later lost their privileges, of course, though they retained their culture; and during the fascist years, many of them volunteered for service in the SS, which is why, perhaps, the world was less than indignant at Ceausescu's policy of selling them into freedom on payment by the West German government of a ransom of DM8000 each.

On one of the smaller roads pointing eastward, I picked up a hiker, obviously a manual worker to judge from the roughness and deeply ingrained greyness of his hands. He was dressed in everyday clothes of coarse twill, and he wore a real workman's cap of overalls-blue. He was fascinated by my excellent road map of Romania, staring at it with great intensity. Then he pointed to Yugoslavia. Romania was no good, he

said; there was nothing to eat. He indicated that Yugoslavia was where
he was headed, and he mimed his swim across the Danube. I set him
down at a crossroad and wished him luck. By nightfall, he would either
be free or dead. But what about his family, I wondered as I watched him
disappear from my rear view mirror.

I reached Sighisoara, perhaps the most perfect of the Transylvanian
towns. It is Germanic in architecture, if no longer in atmosphere. One's
eye is drawn to the ramparts of the citadel on the hill where the old town
was built, and in particular to the magnificent clock tower, with its roof
of patterned tiles and a clock that sends out a different medieval figure
each day of the week to mark out the passage of the hours. In the
shadow of the tower stood the small house where, in 1431, Dracula was
born. It was now a small bar and restaurant. Surprisingly, fish was on
the menu (though nothing else was), and as I ate a sentence that I
thought I should one day use at dinner parties at home ran through my
mind like a record with a stuck needle: I have eaten fried fish in
Dracula's birthplace.

The cobbled lanes of the old town with their neat, pastel-coloured
houses reminded me of Tallinn in Estonia, another transplanted
German settlement. There, of course, Hitler destroyed the centuries-
old German community once and for all; surely the Romanian Saxon
settlements would not long survive the miseries of Ceausescu combined
with the attractions of the Federal Republic.

At the very summit of the hill stood the *Bergkirche*, approached by a
covered wooden staircase. All around the simple white-walled
Lutheran church, which was closed, was the wooded German
cemetery, overgrown with weeds and ivy, the grandiose tombstones
everlasting to the memory of people now entirely forgotten. These
tombstones were made of marble and granite and carved with Germanic
precision, and I was surprised to see that even the graves of the last few
years maintained this tradition. The tombstones in the German
cemetery were the only modern objects I saw in Romania manufactured
to the highest standards.

On the way from Sighisoara to Tirgu Mures I gave a lift to a young
factory worker. He spoke a fair amount of English, and lost little time in
describing the hardships of life under Ceausescu. When we arrived in
Tirgu Mures we had a drink of rasping Romanian cognac in the bar of
my hotel, and then set out to explore the town. My companion took me
first to the supermarket, so that I should experience for myself the
pleasures of shopping during Romania's Golden Age. Whatever was for

sale was not wanted; whatever was wanted was not for sale. All the goods were of the quality one associates with prizes won at the fairground, crude in design and rough in manufacture. Although my companion was young enough to have lived his entire life in this atmosphere of ugliness, and had never experienced through travel abroad anything different, he was not reconciled to it. He picked up objects for me to examine, the better that I should appreciate their shabbiness. He did not doubt that beauty in small things improved the quality of life: when he had looked at my road map of Romania (produced in West Germany), how much pleasure had he derived from its beautiful printing, and with what deep respect had he handled it!

The supermarket was large and drab, on three extensive floors in a construction of unadorned concrete. The goods on display, if gathered together, would comfortably have fitted into half a floor or less. Rack after rack was empty, shelf after shelf. The whole store was like a vague and unspecified promise that one day in the not-too-distant future all this space would be needed for an abundance of goods hitherto undreamed of. No one took this promise seriously, of course, as they shuffled round the store looking for something that had not remained unsold for three years.

From the supermarket we went to a bookshop nearby. Displayed in the window to the exclusion of everything else were the works of Nicolae Ceausescu and his wife, World-Ranking Scientist and Academician Dr Elena Ceausescu. Given prominence was a large volume devoted to the spectroscopy of beta-blocking antihypertensive drugs (a subject dear to the hearts of the population of Tirgu Mures), allegedly edited by *la* Ceausescu. Why she chose to pretend to be a chemist rather than, say, a microbiologist or a mathematical physicist is shrouded in mystery; but the pretence gained for her the direction of all of Romania's scientific research.

Inside the shop, the works of the presidential couple took up the space occupied in our bookshops by alternative health, radical politics, self-development, the Third World and the occult combined. I bought a book in English by Ceausescu's brother, General Ilie Ceausescu PhD, concerning the dispute with Hungary over which population, the Hungarian or Romanian, arrived in Transylvania first. By coincidence, most Hungarian historians have found that Magyars arrived first, while most Romanian historians have found the opposite, claiming that the present-day Romanian inhabitants of Transylvania (the majority) can trace their occupation back to pre-Roman times. The latter assertion had become unquestionable historical dogma in Romania (where there were museums of 'Two Millennia of Continuous Occupation'), and all writing on the subject had become apologetic, grist to the mill of ancient enmity, and supposedly useful for lending spurious nationalist legitimacy to the *Conducator*'s regime.

I took a last look at the bookshop window and laughed.

'You laugh,' said my companion, 'but we did not laugh.'

He showed me Tirgu Mures' Palace of Culture, an astonishing and elaborate edifice built just before the First World War, when the Hungarians ruled the Transylvanian roost. Dark and gothic, one felt its style was not governed by aesthetic preference alone, but by an imperative to establish a distinctive national architecture that would somehow justify political domination of the numerical majority. Nevertheless, it was not aesthetically a failure.

We had dinner in a *fin de siècle* restaurant, with mirrors and plaster cherubs, whose atmosphere had been completely altered by the reversal in the social status of the waiters and customers, and by the presence of dusty plastic flowers in the moulded vases. The waiters were the bosses here, the customers the ones who had to obey and grovel for tips – for in a country where food is rationed, the waiter is as powerful as a mayor (and better fed). It is the waiter who determines who shall enter his establishment, how long the customers need wait for a table and whether they shall have a slice of cucumber; it is the all-powerful waiter who decides whether or not wine is available. Woe betide anyone who offends him, or answers back.

We secured a table by the usual argument: that I was a distinguished foreigner whom it would be inhospitable to refuse. And so we ate in such luxury as Tirgu Mures could afford, all the town's officials and some of the policemen eating precisely the same meal. A band began to play, very loudly and not at all well, and couples, lumpish from a lifetime's consumption of starch, began to dance. It was like a scene out of a film by an acclaimed East European film director; and though the scene appeared superficially to be in colour, really it was in black and white. At half past nine precisely, the band stopped playing and everyone left. My companion insisted on paying the bill, though it was nothing to me and a fortune to him. I could not very well refuse him his gesture of friendship, however. By this time I had drunk rather too much wine and, slightly inebriated, tottered back to my concrete hotel. The streets were as deserted as during a curfew.

In the next restaurant in which I ate, in the city of Cluj, renamed

Cluj-Napoca by Ceausescu in 1978, and known in the days when it was the regional capital of Hungarian Transylvania as Kolozsvar, I sat at the same table as three young Romanians who at first were very wary of me. It was Sunday lunchtime, and I had the impression that all the city's *beau monde* was present. At any rate, the restaurant was full, many of the women were dressed with elegance and everyone who smoked made sure their packet of Kent cigarettes was prominently displayed on their table. The waiter was charming, and appeared to be doing his best to accommodate everyone: conduct, in Romanian circumstances, not merely pleasing but positively heroic.

The three Romanians at my table were a young couple and a slightly older friend. We started to speak when the young woman, who was very pretty, drew out of her bag an old copy of *Art and Artists*, an English magazine for painters and sculptors. They began to discuss with obvious intensity the advertisements for artists' materials, and I interrupted them by enquiring whether they spoke English. The ice was broken: they gave me a glass of wine, and soon we were friends.

The young woman was an art student and her husband was an engineer. Their friend was a teacher of mathematics. It was not possible to talk in such surroundings, and so, taking their courage in their hands, they invited me back to their flat.

It was in a once grand *fin de siècle* building, whose entrance hall was dark and damp and smelt of rotting garbage. The walls were grey with mould and other stains. We had to move quickly, for fear of being seen by the neighbours. In Ceausescu's Romania, to spy and inform on others was not the work of a few, it was the duty of all. *Not* to have reported the arrival of a suspicious stranger to the authorities would have been a crime. Therefore we slipped into their flat as quietly and quickly as possible.

The flat itself was pleasant, their small kitchen comfortable and surprisingly well-equipped. The other two rooms, their bedroom and living room, were rather bare, but they were of a good size (the building had obviously once been home to the bourgeoisie) and had magnificent old-fashioned ceramic stoves to warm them, now converted to gas, whose pressure of course was quite insufficient to warm the rooms in the winter. But as a whole the flat was very much better than many I had seen in England, where millions live dingily enough.

In lieu of children, my Romanian friends had a small and sweet fluffy dog called Charlie who, in the course of my visit, ate his master and mistress's only tomato. When Charlie had to be taken for a walk, I could not go with them, for it would have been dangerous for my hosts to be seen in public in my company. During my visit a neighbour called, and I felt the tension rise. Had she seen my arrival? Was she asking who I was? No, she wanted only to borrow some sugar, which was in very short supply these days. The relief when the front door closed behind her was great, and we were able to resume our conversation.

In these conditions of fear and circumspection, how quickly the bonds of friendship formed! As a foreigner they knew I was free of all possible association with the *Securitate*, and therefore they were able to speak to me unreservedly. They longed for culture, the kind of geniune culture that was not decreed by the state for the purposes of the state, but was the product of free people trying to give meaning to their lives. Rather touchingly they associated this kind of culture with western Europe, and I grew ashamed of the use (or lack of it) to which so many of our citizens put their freedom, and of their not infrequent disparagement of that very freedom itself. It seems one appreciates only what one does not have.

A discussion broke out between the engineer and the teacher of mathematics about the Hungarian question. The latter maintained that the Hungarians had not been badly treated by the regime, that they had outlets for their culture etc. (As a friend of mine once pointed out, under communism all minorities dance.) The engineer calmly disagreed; he pointed out that the Hungarian language university of Cluj had been closed in 1959, that people with Hungarian names laboured under several disadvantages, that there was less and less teaching in Magyar, and that Hungarians were continuing to leave the country in large numbers for Hungary. The teacher responded with the historical injustices inflicted on the Romanians by the Hungarians, which were, of course, not relevant to the argument, except psychologically. In what he said, in his increasing agitation as his friend countered with what sounded to me like reason, I thought I detected the terrible resurrection of Balkan chauvinism. I was pleased when the subject was changed.

We talked of their humiliation by the communist system. Even the engineer's work was humiliating. This was not because he was forced to work so hard, but because he had so little work to do. Whether he did it or not made no difference to anybody or anything. Using obsolete methods superseded elsewhere, he made a few mathematical calculations each day, but most of his time at work was, if not free, at least vacant. Thus, young and capable as he was, he was already a kind of pensioner of the state, deep in the slough of mediocrity; the self-respect that comes from doing a worthwhile job properly would never be his, and if he were to demand it he would be highly suspect in the eyes of authority.

Worse still, of course, was the fault line in everyone's personality that ran between their public and their private persona. To be an honest man in Romania, one had to be a hero; otherwise, one asserted in public what one did not believe and believed what one did not assert. Everyone knew himself to be a hypocrite, and knew that everone else was a hypocrite too. One lived in inner squalor.

After dinner – grilled meat, fried potatoes and Cuban rum – the engineer had to catch the night train to Bucharest. I took him to the station and on the way he asked me to send them postcards from around the world, wherever I might be, just to remind them that another life existed, and to make them feel a little less isolated. When we parted at the station, he said something of which I felt unworthy:

'You have made us feel free for a day.'

His words have often run through my mind since then, together with those of my companion in Tirgu Mures:

'You laugh, but we did not laugh.'

Behind the simplicity of these words lies a depth of suffering which must never be forgotten, which must always be remembered, to which end I hope this book is a small contribution.

After nearly two weeks, I was coming now towards the end of my time in Romania, and I drove north from Cluj into the remote land called Maramures. The rolling green hills had grassy meadows and pleasant copses of deciduous trees. The farms were not as comprehensively collectivised in Maramures as elsewhere in Romania, and it showed. Elsewhere in the countryside, one saw huge fields, poorly demarcated from their neighbours, either ploughed without care or overgrown with weeds. In some of them one saw large contingents of people who used to be peasants but were now agricultural servants of the state picking potatoes from the field by hand, as if posing for a pre-revolutionary figurative painter with a social conscience.

Everywhere one saw the harvest stacked in the fields, but storage and transport were inadequate, and half of what was produced would surely have rotted there. (This is one of the reasons why figures for production can rise relentlessly in countries like Romania, yet nothing ever appear in the shops.) There were horse-drawn carts as soon as one left the cities, ecologically sound no doubt but insufficient in numbers to compensate for the lack of mechanisation. Not many of the villages had yet been systematised, but not a few contained a little quarter where uniform blocks of apartments – of the same design throughout the country – had been built, in earnest of the Ceausescu dream of a nation living in bugged, ill-lit, cold, waterless yet damp cells, in total dependence on the state for everything they consumed.

Maramures was different. The fields were cared for, they had proper hedges and fences, and the villages were beautifully preserved, each wooden house with a splendidly carved gate and bright painted decorations of stars and flowers that somehow communicated the villagers' deep love of their world and what it contained. (I was surprised that such a completely subversive outlook, from the regime's point of view, had been permitted to survive; perhaps Maramures was too remote and insignificant to worry about, at least for the present.) Off the main road, some of the villages had the most beautiful wooden churches, two and a half centuries old and with steeples over a hundred and fifty feet high. The most exquisite of all was in the village of Surdesti, covered in oak shingles, whose dark interior was opened to me by a man who lived in the nearby painted house. How difficult it was in the churchyard, nestling in a little valley between gentle hills, with a nearby stream and ancient trees all around, not to fall prey to the illusion that here was an arcadia, an illusion all the more powerful because of the sordidness of life elsewhere in the country. To be left alone is the whole secret of happiness in a dictatorship.

In the village of Sapinta is the famous *Cimitrul vesel*, or Merry Cemetery, where a peasant carver, Stan Ion Patras, began his work before the war, carving wooden headstones with a painted scene from the life of the deceased and accompanied by a limerick, not necessarily flattering to the memory of him or her: Avarice – 'He who sought money to amass could not escape death, alas!' – and violence – 'Griga, may you pardoned be, even though you did stab me' – were not passed over in silence, but peasants who had escaped the village to the world beyond, and become bureaucrats or agronomists, were celebrated too, portrayed in the uniforms of their success, a suit and pork pie hat in the former case, a clinical white coat (with cows in the background) in the latter. Although the cemetery was permitted to exist and its tradition even fostered – Stan Ion Patras had died, but his followers worked on – it would be difficult to conceive of anything more antithetical to the world outlook of Nicolae Dracul (dracul is the word for devil in Romanian) than this cemetery that commemorates the irreducible individuality of men.

I drove across the north eastern corner of Romania, through the Prislop Pass, into Moldavia, *en route* giving a lift to a geology student who had just been on a field course in the mountains. His mother was second in command of the party in a *judentul*, the administrative equivalent of a county, but this did not mean the student was an apologist of the regime, very much the reverse. He spoke with withering contempt – in fractured English – of the bureaucracy, the Party, the ideology, the leadership and its privileges. Yet he talked with tenderness of his mother, who he said was a wonderful person, despite her service (above the call of necessity, surely) to the very evils he had just denounced. What peculiar states of mind this tyranny gave rise to, what dissociative feats of filing in separate compartments of the mind it required!

We stopped for a late lunch at a roadside restaurant famous for its sausage, not available to everyone, but my companion knew how to wheedle it out of the management (mention of his mother helped). I found the sausage distinctly mundane, but the geology student, who was broad and muscular, consumed it with gusto, washing it down with a whole bottle of red wine in about ten minutes without apparent effect.

We continued on our way, and he asked me whether I should like to meet a friend of his, the gynaecologist in a small town on the way to Iasi. Certainly, I said; gynaecologists were in the front line of Ceausescu's assault on the people.

We reached the town in the dark. The gynaecologist lived in an ordinary flat, crowded with cheap furniture and ornaments. His wife was ill in the bedroom, but he welcomed us all the same, after removing the telephone from the living room. With some ceremony, he placed a full bottle of Scotch (payment for an operation) on the table and we began to drink it. I hoped that he might grow indiscreet about his work, but he was conspicuously silent on the subject – especially considering I was a fellow doctor – except to say that he did his best for his patients in the circumstances. More than this he would not say. If it were true that gynaecologists examined women monthly at the behest of the state to ensure they were using no artificial means to prevent conception, so that there should be twenty-five million Romanians by Ceausescu's 75th birthday and thirty million by the year 2000, it was not something they would readily wish to confess to a foreigner at a first meeting. When my inquiries were turned aside, I inquired no further.

We finished the bottle of Scotch and then the hard stuff was produced: absolute alcohol with a few wild raspberries thrown in to give it colour and, if drunk with the tongue of faith, a little flavour. By now conversation had degenerated into slurred protestations of eternal friendship, and I thought it wisest to pour my share of the raspberry alcohol into the pot plants, which I hope did not suffer unduly as a consequence. The student of geology was soon very drunk indeed, and when he tried to stand up it was as though there were a large but invisible hand pushing him back down into the chair.

The gynaecologist rang the local hotel to ask for two beds for us, since we were in no condition to continue our journey. This was not a town where tourists stayed, and he tried to sound casual when he mentioned that one of the beds was for an English doctor.

About an hour later the hotel called back to ask where we were. They were tired of waiting and said they would lock the front door soon.

The student was stood up with difficulty, the gynaecologist and I acting as scaffolding. We staggered down the stairs, into the street, and several hundred yards to the hotel. The gynaecologist wished us goodnight and said he would meet us for breakfast. It transpired that it was not just the hotel staff who had been waiting for us. Two men with rodent-like faces were seated in the office: *Securitate* agents. I handed them my passport in my best amiable idiot manner, as though I hadn't the faintest idea who they were or why they were interested in me. They looked through my passport as though they expected to find pornographic pictures in it. They noted its number and then turned to the student, asking for his identity documents. They asked him a few questions but he was so drunk that he threw caution to the winds and told them what he thought of them in no uncertain manner, and almost spat at them as he swayed before them. (Perhaps the importance of his mother in the Party fortified him as much as the alcohol.) For the moment, at any rate, there were no consquences of this defiance.

The receptionist asked for our money. The student was charged 18 *lei*; I was charged 512 *lei*.

Once in his room my companion punched the walls, not lightly but with his full and considerable strength, so that the plaster flaked off and his knuckles bled. By this time, he was too drunk for speech, and I was unable to guess whether his punches represented a show of bravado or a realisation of what he had done in offending the *Securitate*.

Next morning, he looked considerably fresher than I felt. The bottle of wine and the bottle of spirits he had drunk left him with no ill-effects.

We continued our journey. In the next town, I tried to buy some petrol, but the woman at the garage said there was none. By chance, the student saw his mother's car parked outside the town's Party headquarters and he said he would ask for her help. He ran into the headquarters and after a few minutes emerged with his mother, dressed smartly in the communist fashion, in a green and cream check suit of greater durability than elegance, and a beehive hairdo. We shook hands and her son explained that she had ordered the garage by telephone to release thirty litres of petrol to me. We returned to the garage where, looking sullen and defeated, the attendant delivered thirty litres as ordered, for which I paid in *lei*, thus reducing the cost to me by 80 per cent.

So this was how the dialectic worked in Romania. Thesis: there is no petrol. Antithesis: an order from the Party to deliver it. Synthesis: thirty litres.

I had qualms about accepting the Party's bounty, of course, as though in doing so I were demeaning myself. This was the way the Party produced a psychology of complicity: by extending favours to evade the multitude of frustrations it created itself. At the first hint of an inconvenience, I had caved in and accepted such a favour. How, then, could I blame people who had experienced a lifetime of such inconveniences (and incomparably worse than inconveniences) for their failure to protest, for their seeming acquiescence in the monstrous system of privilege whose pillars were monopoly, incompetence inefficiency and corruption?

At Bucharest airport my name was entered into a computer and I was asked to step aside. The police took my passport and my baggage was searched for a second time. Though I was treated politely, they looked at me with feral eyes.

It was half an hour before they returned my passport. Far from being nervous, I was elated, though I remained calm. To have been suspected of anti-state crime by the *Securitate* was the highest, the only compliment they could have paid me.

VIETNAM

Entering Thailand, one is asked to declare 'monetary instruments' in excess of $10,000; entering Vietnam one must declare one's T-shirts. Persons 'having the action of tricking' in the latter regard will, according to the customs declaration form headed with the national motto, *Freedom, Independence and Happiness*, be punished as prescribed by the laws of the Socialist Republic of Vietnam, which are no doubt of exemplary severity.

What kind of economy could be seriously imperilled by undeclared T-shirts? I arrived in Vietnam in December 1989, 13 years after the communists entered Saigon, with a friend, Ingo, who was once a refugee from East Germany when Ulbricht was in Berlin and all was right with the world. He recognised the mentality at once.

Actually, everything was changing fast in Vietnam, according to an Australian businessman we met as we waited for our luggage (the less busy the airport the longer it takes to unload). The nonsense about T-shirts was a hangover from the *ancien régime*, he said. Every month, no, every week there were reforms and improvements. For example, when he – the Australian businessman – left Saigon only a fortnight ago, there was no conveyor belt for luggage at the airport, a deficiency that had been rectified in his absence. It now took only an hour to retrieve luggage instead of three. There had also been no public address system when he left; now it was very much in evidence. Let there be muzak, said a commissar; and there was muzak.

It seems that progress, like freedom, is indivisible.

From the purely selfish point of view, I found the optimism of the Australian less than pleasing. It wasn't that the commercial project upon which he was engaged struck me as strange, even bizarre (he was planning to bring a floating luxury hotel, with rooms at $200 a night, to a mooring in the Saigon River); rather, it was that I was writing a book about countries in despair, and amelioration made my task more difficult.

We drove to the centre of Saigon (no one calls it by its new name, Ho Chi Minh City). I was struck at once by the complete difference in atmosphere between Saigon on the one hand and Tirana, Pyongyang and Bucharest, which were still fresh in my memory, on the other. Not only was there little in the way of political iconography to be seen in Saigon, and that little so faded by time and climate that it had achieved the status of relic, but there was life on the streets, there were shops, little cafés, stalls, discussion groups, mechanics and – it must be said – beggars. Bicycles, motorbikes and a few cars wove their way anarchically through the tree-lined avenues (more than one Vietnamese remarked on the French legacy of trees in the cities of Vietnam), tinkling bells and honking horns. Everything was shabby and run down, one could almost smell the mould everywhere; but the people were alive, not undead.

As soon as you take your first walk in Vietnam, you become aware of a certain crudity, not in the people around you but in yourself. I am neither fat nor unusually tall, and yet I felt my movements were awkward and lumpen compared with those of the Vietnamese, who seem to perform even the most ordinary tasks with physical grace and suppleness. This impression was powerfully reinforced on our first night in Saigon when we were directed, somewhat against my will, to a performance of 'folk' singing and dancing. Such performances in communist countries, which take place in the caverns of international hotels where ordinary citizens may not penetrate, are as authentically traditional as John Wayne's films are authentically historical. So it was on this occasion, with young Vietnamese men in traditional costume playing their traditional electronic instruments, to whose sound heavily made-up peasant women danced peasant dances under coloured spotlights. With the exception of Ingo and myself, the audience was Russian, to whom such entertainments were no doubt thoroughly familiar.

When the singing and dancing were over, one of the Russians got up on stage to make a speech. No one forced him to do so; heir to seventy years of official evasions and falsehoods, he spoke fluent *langue de bois*, managing to disregard entirely the absence of Vietnamese in the audience as he extolled the virtues of international solidarity and friendship. His appearance among the slender Vietnamese performers, however, was nothing short of grotesque. He had wiry red hair and a putty-white face from which sweat copiously poured, despite the air conditioning; to call his features rough-hewn would be unfairly to denigrate rocks. Above all, he had that permanent shortness of breath caused by a large girth, which also caused him to waddle.

'Too many potatoes,' as a Vietnamese said to me later by way of explanation of the pachydermatous ungainliness of the Russian technical advisers whom he had just passed.

'And too much Vodka,' I added laughing, though I was uncomfortably aware that in his eyes I was probably only a fraction less grotesque.

We stayed in the Palace Hotel, which had been renamed in Vietnamese the Friendship Hotel, by which name it was known to no one. It was built in the sixties, not perhaps a memorable epoch in the history of architecture, yet the hotel was not wholly without atmosphere, thanks to the history and intrigue it must have seen and to the mild decay it had undergone. From its roof on the fourteenth floor there was a splendid view of Saigon; I was surprised to see that the city did not extend beyond the far bank of the mud-brown river, not more than 400 yards away, from which green rice fields stretched to the distant horizon. In the other direction sprawled a chaos of rusting tin-roofed buildings, occasional skyscrapers, lesser edifices of darkly-stained concrete, palm trees, godowns, factories and even a church spire or two. By no stretch of the imagination could the scene have been called beautiful; but for me at least it was not without charm. By night, the dim lights of the city glimmered feebly, a testimony to the economic situation; but along the curve of the river the ships were illuminated brilliantly by their own lights, and all through the night one could hear the metallic rhythm of ships' repairs.

We noticed a small and curious refinement in the Palace (or Friendship,) Hotel that had lasted since American days: every morning, afternoon and evening without fail the rugs in the lift were changed. They were frayed and uncleaned since the 'liberation', but the words 'Good Morning', 'Good Afternoon' and 'Good Evening' were still legible on them. The latter in particular conjured in my mind images of quiet Americans, scrubbed and cleaned, leaving the hotel after a hard day's clandestine political activity for a night on the disreputable town.

Nearby the hotel was a secondhand bookshop. It dealt in books left behind by the departing Americans, with a sideline in English grammar texts and language tapes. One of the latter was playing from a cassette recorder, turned up loud for the benefit of everyone. Two tutorial voices enunciated their words with the clipped, pedantic precision of BBC announcers three decades ago. Here was a world in which even waiters were upper class; but the message, it must be admitted, could scarcely have been more appropriate for a communist country:

Customer; I think I'll have a chocolate ice cream.
Waiter; I'm sorry, sir, there's no more chocolate.
Customer; Then I'll have strawberry.
Waiter; I'm very sorry, sir, we haven't got strawberry either.
Customer; Then what have you got?
Waiter; Nothing, I'm afraid, sir.

As for the books, they had suffered in the humid climate: their covers had curled, their pages yellowed, must had grown into their fabric so that an acrid odour rose and caught in the throat when their pages were turned. The books fell naturally into three or four categories, into which the owner or manager had surprisingly (and discriminatingly) sorted them. There were pulp paperback novels of sex and adventure with which soldiers had no doubt tried to beguile the boredom of the 99 per cent of their tour of duty that was not absolute terror. There were dozens of hardback novels about Vietnam by men who, but for their experience, would never have written, and who hoped that burning sincerity might compensate for lack of talent. There were 'family' books, the adornments of middle America: encyclopaedias, picture books of the wonders of the world, and a volume entitled, with unintended irony, *The Legacy of the West*. Finally, there were the academic theses of political science, many of them *Prop. of the US Army*, over which serious military advisers had pondered long and hard. Such effort so ill-rewarded! For who could read with genuine pleasure long volumes devoted to the foreign policy of Burma or the marriage customs of the hill tribes of Laos? And is there anything so stale as twenty-year-old political science?

Perhaps – my blood runs cold – reportage withers even faster. Nevertheless, I bought two books written by Americans in 1967 and 1968 when a visit to Hanoi was still something of an adventure, Harrison Salisbury's *Behind the Lines: Hanoi* and Mary McCarthy's *Hanoi* both of which – but especially the latter – acted as a kind of Greek chorus as I read them in . . . Hanoi.

The bookshop owner, seeing that I was a serious customer and not just a browser with nothing else to do, sidled up to me and offered me something which, by his manner of a Bangkok pimp on the Sukhumvit Road showing prospective customers snapshots of 'his' girls, should have been salacious at the very least. In fact, it was a booklet printed on pink paper entitled *La Semaine à Saigon du 7 au 13.9.63*.

With what strange emotion does one read of a world that existed within one's own lifetime, and yet is now as irrecoverable as ancient Mesopotamia! Semi-philosophical, even mystical, thoughts are set in train: is not five minutes ago – no, not so much, ten seconds, even one! – as distant as a thousand or a million years?

In 1963, there was still a French influence in Saigon. 'The barber shops, beauty parlours, dressmaking houses, with every modern comfort allow you to get the latest Paris Fashions, because nearly all hairdressers, aestheticians and dressmakers are certificated from Paris.' But where now are the 'smart and attractive' shops with their 'rutilant shop-windows . . . full of everywhere products', and where is Guyonnet, the butcher for whose meat – *délicieux, succulent, délectable, merveilleux* – 'even Madame de Sévigné would not find sufficient words to praise'? What has happened to the Vietnamese radio station in the French language with its seven o'clock '*réveil musculaire*'? Where is *La Niche*, offering *soins et beauté des chiens*? Should you still take *Hépatic* for that most vulnerable of organs, your *foie*?

There is an odd juxtaposition of sophistication and naivety in *La Semaine à Saigon*. Amid the advertisements for bars and nightclubs, all with their 'charming hostesses', 'teen-aged lovely singers', 'graceful waitresses' or 'golden voiced songstresses', accompanied by Poon and his orchestra, Patty Pink and his combo or *l'Orchestre International sous la Direction de BOB*, are interspersed jokes of such innocence that any eight-year-old would now be ashamed to tell them:

> Two African explorers are swimming in a river. Suddenly one of them cries out:
>> 'Pierre, Pierre, a crocodile has just eaten one of my feet!'
>> 'Which one?' asks his friend.
>> 'I don't know,' he replies. 'All crocodiles look the same to me . . .'

And 1963 was an age of innocence, too, with regard to what is now lugubriously known as the environment, which then seemed indestructible.

> In Vietnam boundless forests there is important fauna of about 500 species . . .
> Tigers are numerous in every region, and offer fine target.
> Panthers also are abounding, there are 4 dissimilar species: the biggest one has a black flecked skin; the common panther is smaller, with more numerous black spots, the nebulous panther and the Ounce.

And the big target, dream of numerous hunters: the elephant is not scarce in Vietnam.

Several species of wild oxen are easily offered to the big game hunters: the Gaur or Indian Urus of which the track affords an unforgettable emotion . . .

The Bears are also found in Vietnam's forests, there are 3 species . . .

At last the various kinds of deer, very numerous. Among the same game, we cannot here enumerate their numerous kinds and names: from the fair 'Dwarf Deer' to the full flavoured porcupine; from the peacock to the partridge, this small game will offer at every moment, various targets, either to make delicious roast, or to get a scarce specie for your hunting bag.

For $22, you could buy a *Licence D*, 'good only for killing wild and harmfuls beasts such as tigers, leopards'.

Still, an ominous note is not altogether lacking. Above an advertisement for a hotel offering UNSURPASSED . . . SERVICE AND HOSPITALITY! YET, MODERATE CHARGE! appears a little notice:

The declaration of the State of Siege in Vietnam will inevitably bring certain technical and editorial difficulties to the production of our magazine . . . We apologise in advance to our readers and advertisers.

So much for the world we had lost. What of the world we had won?

Out in the street, people offered us old coins and banknotes, guided tours, women, trinkets, Vietnamese *dong* for dollars, all with rare desperation. There were not a few beggars with their hands upstretched from the ground, and young children followed us with melodramatic expressions and gestures of hunger and misery, until they ran away laughing as they clutched the 200 *dong* we gave them (about 5 cents). I soon grew weary of this: either they told other children about us, or our 'generosity' was noticed by them. At any rate, we were rarely without a penumbra of demanding children. Ingo was more patient than I: he just accepted that one had to keep a supply of small denomination notes to pay the children. His patience was born of sympathy, for when he was a child in Weimar just after the war, he too had pestered American soldiers (before Weimar was transferred to the Russian zone) for cigarettes and chocolate which were then the *true* currency of Germany.

We walked towards the river, past the burnt out shell of one of Saigon's buildings, the state import and export company. The upper floors were charred and covered in soot. I suspected that the cause of the fire was fraud about to be uncovered: I was reminded of my time in Africa in the mid-eighties when a fire in the Bank of Tanzania destroyed – not inconveniently – all records of foreign currency dealings.

As we reached the river, a short, wiry figure approached us. He wore a military-style jacket and on his crushed cap I was surprised to see a brass badge of the American eagle clutching arrows in its talons. His name was Nguyen and he spoke English with an American accent and a grammatical error every three words. He wanted us to take a ride in his *cyclo*, a pedicab of old French design with the pedals at the rear.

We were reluctant at first to accept. Was not the image of Europeans riding in vehicles powered by (oriental) human effort one of the icons of anti-colonialism? That one man should ride while another pulled or pushed or pedalled, especially in the broiling heat, seemed repugnant to our newly-tender occidental sensibilities. But Nguyen was insistent: there was no doubting the sincerity of his desire to convey us wherever we wanted to go. And looking around, we saw Vietnamese ride unselfconsciously in *cyclos*. Recalling Dr Johnson's defence of riches – that they gave employment to the poor – we swallowed Nguyen's pride and acceded to his pleadings.

He lost little time in letting us know what he thought of communism. It had impoverished everyone except a few top Party leaders. It was tyrannous, corrupt and unjust. No one in the South wanted it, he said.

Nguyen had been a sub-lieutenant in the South Vietnamese army, three times wounded (when he discovered I was a doctor, I thought he was going to show me the scars of his wounds, but he never did). I wondered, though I did not ask, whether in those days he had been quite so opposed to corruption as he was now. After the 'liberation' he was sent to re-education camp for four years, where they tried 'to clean the brains'. It hadn't worked, not for him and not for anybody else; but outwardly he had conformed to secure his freedom.

Relative freedom, that was, for at the time no one in Vietnam had been free – the whole country was a prison camp. Nguyen found work as a teacher but when, after three years, the headmaster discovered he had been to re-education camp, he was dismissed, since when he had pedalled a *cyclo*. He did not own his contraption: he hired it every day from a man who owned five of them, for 2000 dong (50 cents) a day. When he was lucky, Nguyen made a profit of 15,000 dong ($3.75); when he was unlucky, nothing at all.

As we rode towards the children's hospital, the name of whose doctor I had been given as a contact, a few people called out to us in almost insulting fashion. Nguyen said they were asking whether we were Russian, and I soon learnt to call back *Anh!* (English in Vietnamese). This produced a wreath of smiles and upturned thumbs – anything, so long as we were not Russian. I had encountered this reaction before, in Ethiopia for example, and I was rather saddened by it: not out of sympathy for communism, of course, but out of sympathy for individual Russians, despised as they are everywhere for their poverty and the sins of their leaders, yet who are no worse than any other people, and have strengths and virtues too.

The hospital was French colonial, a series of yellow stucco pavilions open to the breeze, set in the shade of huge, shaggy tropical trees, and surrounded by gardens. Whatever the crimes of the colonialists, they learnt to build for the climate and not to rely for comfort on the vagaries of an uncertain electricity supply. And their buildings were charming, *civilised*, though it undoubtedly took barbarity to build them.

Was this charm for western eyes only? Were the Vietnamese indifferent to the fact that everything constructed after the departure of the French was ugly, functional, tasteless, decaying without the bittersweetness of decay: in short, a mess? No; we never found a Vietnamese – heirs, after all, to a very refined aesthetic tradition – who did not appreciate the virtues of colonial building.

The doctor for whom I was searching was away in France at a conference and would not be back until after we left Saigon. Disappointed, we strolled round the hospital. I wanted to see inside the wards, but had not the courage of my prurience. As we were strolling, a man with a self-important manner came up to us and started to question Nguyen in a decidedly unfriendly, almost threatening way. It was clear he was some kind of security official trying to find out who we were and what we were doing, and so I assumed that expression of absent-minded and idiotic innocence that had helped me in such situations before. (A saintly determination not to understand the significance of what one is being asked will eventually exasperate any petty secret policeman beyond endurance.) The man's questions to Nguyen were sharp; I smiled at him sweetly. Eventually, bowing, I thanked him very much, and satisfied at last that we were a visiting delegation of European subnormals he let us continue.

Outside the hospital, Nguyen complained that only people who worked for the government received free medical care; everyone else had to pay. And medicine was expensive, if it were to be had at all.

Again I wondered how it had been in the old days; and whether he had complained quite so vociferously then.

I arranged to meet Nguyen again a few days later. He was always at the same place by the riverbank, he said; it was risky for him to ply his trade outside the hotels where the foreigners stayed, for the police spies were there. I suppose he knew what he was talking about; but if so, the police spies in Vietnam were not the bone-headed, pebble-suited variety that haunted Eastern European hotels, but people who knew how to melt unobtrusively into the background and quietly observe.

Nguyen was waiting for me as arranged. He promised to show me areas of Saigon no visitor would see unless in the company of a native. His companion pedicyclist was disappointed that Ingo did not come: he had been hoping for a fare, and looked so downcast I thought he was going to cry.

'He says he not lucky today,' said Nguyen. 'He no have customer for four days.'

It was not just a sob story, I thought. I gave him some money, but he cheered up only a little. He had his dignity, and he wanted to *earn* money. But there was nothing else I could do, and so Nguyen and I went on our way.

We followed a road by the river, pausing to look at people who lived under a concrete bridge. Squalid shacks overhung the creeks leading to the Saigon River, the kind of sight that would give you typhoid, if bacilli could enter through the eyes on wings of light. Nguyen said that everything was worse, poorer, dirtier than before – before always meaning before 'liberation'.

Still, these visions of Saigon did not depress me as the frigid, sterile concrete grandeur of Pyongyang had depressed me. 'You won't see signs of poverty in Pyongyang like in other Asian cities,' a sympathiser with North Korea had told me proudly before I went. He did not mention that I would see no signs of life either; whereas in Saigon, for all its squalor, there was activity, movement, laughter, argument.

The Vietnamese government had changed its policy since the Sixth Party Congress in 1987. Whether from conviction or under Soviet pressure to reform, the Politburo had decided to free the economy a little. The land was returned to the peasants on long leasehold and they were allowed to sell their produce to whomever they pleased at whatever price they could get, after a certain delivery quota to the government. At the same time, smuggling across the Thai and Chinese borders was ignored if not encouraged by the government, and the smuggled consumer goods were traded in markets by private traders. Small scale private enterprise was now permitted, with family businesses allowed to employ up to ten people. The economic effects of this relaxation were immediate and dramatic. Rice, which until then had been rationed and in such short supply that people had trekked into Thailand in search of it, was now plentiful. Vietnam had become almost overnight one of the largest exporters of rice in the world. The peasants were prepared to work and produce, because there was some chance now of due reward.

But the effects of the reforms were not only economic. As Marx, who did not underestimate the influence of economic organisation on human affairs, might have expected, the economic changes in Vietnam had brought in their wake great social changes, apparent immediately to anyone who had travelled to unregenerate socialist lands. The people were recalled to life. *Pace* intellectual snobs, the market is not just a soulless economic mechanism; it is a spiritual phenomenon as well, without which there can be no personal freedom, at least in modern societies.

The very success of the reforms, however, posed a serious problem for the Vietnamese government; for the success of the reforms was a complete refutation of everything the government had said and done for the last forty years. Yet the government was also tied to the doctrines of apostolic succession and Caesaropapal infallibility. It was omniscient or it was nothing.

I picked up a little volume of the recent speeches of Nguyen Van Linh, General Secretary of the Central Committee of the Communist Party of Vietnam (ie the Pope). It was called *Vietnam: Urgent Problems*. Following the title page was a photograph of the General Secretary: I knew at once I was not in for an exciting read. The first paragraph was unencouraging:

> After several days of diligent and active work with a high sense of responsibility to the Party and people, today the 6th Congress of the Communist Party of Vietnam has come to fruition.

Although the book was only 147 pages long, I could not help but recall Lord Macaulay's review of a two volume biography of Lord Burghley:

> Compared with the labour of reading these volumes, all other labour, the labour of thieves on the treadmill, the labour of children in the mines, the labour of slaves on the plantation, is but a pleasant recreation.

Nevertheless, I read on. It was my duty: I had to know what the official mind was thinking.

Couched in the stiffest of stiff *langue de bois*, the General Secretary does most of his thinking and writing on autopilot, as befits a man who became a communist at the age of fourteen, sixty years ago, and has remained one ever since. In a talk at 'an informal meeting with artists and cultural activists', entitled 'Art and Cultural Workers Should Contribute to the Party's Renovation Work', the General Secretary said 'I am not a specialist in literature and the arts . . . But as a lover of literature and the arts, I fully agree with the idea that fighters on the cultural and art front need not only sharp knives to remove the bad . . . You are engineers of the soul. You must contribute to building the new-type man.' Not exactly original: there's nothing there with which Stalin or Mao or Enver Hoxha or Ceausescu or Kim Il Sung might disagree.

Yet from time to time the faint glimmer of an idea emerges, reluctantly, from the General Secretary's pages. One has the feeling of a man wrestling with uncomfortable facts, a man whose powers of expression are stunted and arthritic, and whose ideas rattle around like a dried pea in a small bottle. He acknowledges the 'big and instant impact' on the supply of rice effected by the removal of restrictions on private trade, but is unable to draw the obvious general conclusion from this salutary experience. He excoriates what he calls 'bureaucratic centralism', yet defends to the death 'democratic centralism', describing Party and national unanimity as 'the apple of our eye'. But it is in his closing speech 'Delivered at the 2nd Plenum of the Party Central Committee' that the General Secretary reveals his originality and genius. There he says:

> . . . the State's selling of agricultural tools to and buying of paddy from peasants [must be] according to the principle of mutual agreement and price parity . . .

In other words, peasants must be paid: a lesson he had learnt after fifty years of political experience. That something so obvious should have taken half a century to learn *is*, after all, a form of originality.

'He's a good guy,' said Nguyen the *cyclo* driver, referring to Nguyen the General Secretary. He meant, of course, good by comparison with the others in the Politburo. Before he came to power, it was dangerous for a Vietnamese to talk to a foreigner, even for a minute, even to an East German. To do so was to risk arrest and interrogation. His fellow *cyclo* drivers had often been apprehended and questioned about their foreign fares by the police. The advent of Nguyen had led to an immediate easing in the all-pervasive atmosphere of terror. None of this, however, prevented him from telling a political joke against the General Secretary.

'Nguyen and his deputy are flying from Hanoi to Saigon. Nguyen says, "Do you realise that if I threw a 5000 *dong* note out of the window, I'd make someone happy?" His deputy says, "But if I threw five 1000 *dong* notes out, I'd make five people happy." "So what?" says the pilot. "If I threw you both out, I'd make 65 million people happy." '

On the way to where Nguyen lived, we stopped at a little tea shop, where he came to console himself when there were no fares to be had. There he drank a livid red liquid poured over dirty crushed ice while I, usually immune to concerns over the amoeboid dangers of unboiled water, providently chose tea, which arrived lukewarm with a sugary sludge, in a glass of quite spectacular uncleanliness.

Nguyen lived down a teeming alleyway, no wider than an armspan. I should not have ventured down it without him, uncertain as to what my reception as a foreigner might be. I needn't have worried, however: I was received like a returning hero. Children rushed out of cramped front rooms that opened on to the alleyway to shout and laugh and hold my hand. Unlike the children who hung about the hotels, they wanted nothing from me; and the adults bade me welcome with their greetings.

Nguyen lived in a lean-to with walls made of planks and a corrugated tin roof, a single room with a concrete floor, bereft of any furniture except two shelves on which he had stored empty soft drink cans and cigarette packets, the latter stacked like books. They were the only decorations he could afford. There was a large jar of water and a wooden box that contained the clothes he did not stand up in.

'I own nothing,' Nguyen said, prodding his two spare shirts and a pair of trousers. 'Nothing.'

It was true. Until recently, Nguyen had lived here with his wife, but she left him because they argued about the long hours he worked. He went out at six in the morning and returned at eleven at night; she assumed another woman was involved, and never realised that pedalling a *cyclo* was not an easy way to make a living. Arguments had led to fights – physical, not metaphorical. Nguyen had hit her. One day she left taking their son with her, returning to her village 250 miles away. Nguyen missed his son but could not afford the fare to see him.

'When you have money, a woman can love you,' he said. 'When you no have money, she cannot love you.'

He showed me a few pictures of the old days when he was a lieutenant earning $100 a month. He and his wife smiled into the camera, knowing nothing of the trials to come.

When it was hot, Nguyen could not sleep in the stuffy lean-to. Then he went out into the street to sleep. When it rained, the roof leaked, so sleep was impossible then too. All the while he told me this I wondered about sanitary facilities, but did not ask. I could imagine them vividly enough.

Across the alleyway lived his mother and several brothers and sisters. They shared two rooms, one of which opened onto the alley. This room had a large picture of the Virgin and child: Nguyen and his family were Catholics. One of his younger brothers joined us there for tea. He was learning English, Nguyen said, but was too shy to speak it. English was the language of freedom and emigration to the United States and everyone in Vietnam was learning it, to judge from the manuals on sale everywhere. Nguyen's brother showed me his: slightly tattered, it contained as reading practice a story about three children who, during the Russian Revolution, heard that Lenin was going hungry and gave him their lunchtime portion of bread which, despite his own need, he distributed to other children. There was also a story set in an American maternity hospital, in which a nurse, emerging from the delivery room, asked a group of waiting fathers-to-be, 'Comrades, which of you is Mr White?'

Nguyen's brother then showed me a book in Vietnamese that I had seen in many shop windows and on stalls, and which he was reading with great care. It was a translation of Mark H. McCormack's *What They Don't Teach You at Harvard Business School*, and it was the most popular book in Southern Vietnam. (I wondered whether Mr McCormack received his royalties in *dong*.) One of the things which presumably even this book didn't teach you was how to obtain a motorbike in Vietnam. Nguyen's brother was quite frank and un-ashamed about this: he worked for a government organisation where he was so obstructive that people eventually bribed him to do what he was supposed to do anyway.

'Government people get 20 litres of gas a month free,' said Nguyen, taking me for a spin on his brother's Honda. I had the impression that Nguyen was not altogether glad of his brother's good fortune.

Before we left, Nguyen's brother asked me how many teeth I had.

The usual number, I replied, and asked why he wanted to know. Because, he said, he had heard that to meet someone with 36 or 40 teeth was lucky (and obviously a foreigner was more likely to be deformed). Luck in his case, as in so many others, meant emigration to the United States: alas, my dentition could not help him achieve his ambition.

In the afternoon, Nguyen and I went to a football match between a visiting team from the Philippines (representing the San Miguel brewery, whose pennants fluttered around the stadium) and a local team. Before the match begun, Nguyen read the newspaper, a single sheet folded into four and printed as though it were a clandestine publication emanating from a distant cave during a civil war and smuggled at great danger into the city. Strange, then, to read in it of the knighthood of Rex Harrison. Next to this item was a blurred, inky photograph of a woman: Mary McCarthy. She had just died, and though there was an obituary of 500 words or more, her book *Hanoi* was not mentioned. Perhaps even the Vietnamese government found it embarrassing now.

Even Nguyen had heard of our British football hooligans.

'Yes,' I said, 'our hooligans are the best hooligans in the world.'

The match was not a very serious one. A couple of the Filipinos were overweight and their team played without a great deal of passion. They lost 3–0, but did not seem put out by it. This, I thought, was sport as it ought to be: mildly diverting but nothing to riot about.

I was predisposed in favour of the young Filipinos. I had seen them earlier in the week at Saigon's War Museum. There they had clambered laughing over the detritus of war, the tanks and artillery nothing more to them than suitable backgrounds for snapshots to show families back home. Of the tragedy implied by these artifacts they seemed to know nothing, despite the violence of their own land: an ignorance which I hoped would never be enlightened by their personal experience.

Within a week, a violent, though unsuccessful, coup had broken out in Manila.

The war is everywhere in Vietnam, inescapable, not in what you see but in your thoughts. A visitor to the country who knew nothing of its recent history would not conclude it had emerged only a few years ago from four decades of international and civil war. The only obvious evidence is the presence in every town of a War Museum, with mangled helicopters, jets, tanks and howitzers exhibited outside. And – to adapt slightly Spiro T. Agnew's dictum about American slums – once you have seen one Vietnamese war museum, you have seen them all.

Triumphalist propaganda is now rare in Vietnam, at least by comparison with other communist states. I wondered why, and several possible explanations came to mind. First that the Vietnamese are naturally a modest people. Second that such propaganda would inflame a population tired of war and exasperated by the impoverishing economic mismanagement that followed it. (However, sensitivity of this kind is not usually characteristic of communist parties in power.) Third that triumphalist propaganda is paraded in inverse proportion to genuine triumph. The military victory of the Vietnamese was real enough for it not to require absurd embellishment. Whatever the reason, there is little outward gloating or self-glorification in Vietnam, and this is very pleasing.

Of course, the War Museums have their propaganda purpose and children in large groups are dutifully taken round them by teachers. As in most communist propaganda museums, however, I never saw anyone visit them apart from foreigners and children; as institutions, they were as dormant or extinct as churches in England.

They were not without interest, though. When one glimpses the power and sophistication of the weaponry the Americans deployed (a different type of bomb for every military eventuality), one wonders how they could possibly have failed to achieve their end. There were bombs that fragmented over huge distances, killing every living being in their path; bombs that set fire to the uninflammable; bombs weighing four tons that shook the ground as in an earthquake to destroy all subterranean installations; and bombs that defoliated whole forests. The weight, the mass of these things seemed disproportionate to the fragility of what was being attacked, a sledgehammer to crack a nut, an elephant to crush a flea. But the nut remained uncracked, the flea uncrushed.

In the Saigon museum there are terrible pictures. One of them shows a soldier, a presumed American, holding up the head of a decapitated Vietcong guerrilla with a long tatter of skin hanging where the neck should be. According to a guidebook to Vietnam that we bought in England, the American is laughing, though the photograph is indistinct and his laughter could just as well be a grimace of disgust or horror. Another photograph shows an American soldier with a large knife about to cut out the liver of a prisoner: that, at any rate, is the guidebook's interpretation, which presumes the soldier is American, his victim is alive and that the knife wielded is about to cut out the liver.

I resisted the guidebook's interpretation. Though I knew that all nations are capable of bestiality, I was reluctant to admit that people so culturally akin to me could behave in this way, at least as a matter of policy: for if they could, perhaps I could, too. And even if these photographs showed what they purported to show, how representative were they of American behaviour? It does not take a war, after all, to uncover instances of bestial behaviour among half a million men. And by what right, I continued, did the followers of General Giap, who once said 'Every minute, hundreds of thousands of people die on this earth. The life or death of a hundred, a thousand, tens of thousands of human beings, even our compatriots, means little' – by what right did the adherents of such a philosophy display photographs whose meaning derived solely from the preciousness of individual human life?

Still I trembled to look at them.

We went afterwards to visit the tunnels of Cu Chi, about forty miles from Saigon. This system of underground chambers and connecting passages, over 150 miles long, served as the headquarters of the Vietcong. The forested area in which it was contructed was completely defoliated during the war, but now, fifteen years later, scrubby trees had reappeared. A former colonel in the Vietcong gave us a brief lecture on the tunnels – how they had been hand-dug by peasants, their arrangement in three levels, the efforts of the Americans to destroy them – and then another officer took over to show us into the tunnels themselves.

We walked for a while in the scrub. Then the officer challenged us to find a nearby entrance to the tunnels. We looked around, tried a few tussocks unsuccessfully, and then gave up. Triumphantly, the officer showed us a trap door by our very feet, so well camouflaged that even after he had pointed it out we had difficulty in seeing it. He took us to underground kitchens with smokeless ovens, their exhaust vents so long that smoke was dissipated along them, imperceptible even to infra-red sensors; he took us to underground conference chambers where commanders had planned offensives and dormitories where the guerrillas slept, each with escape hatches to deeper, safer levels of the tunnels. He showed us booby traps for intruders into the tunnels, disguised pits furnished with *pungi* sticks, sharpened stakes on which they impaled themselves; he described how the guerrillas had dressed in American clothes and washed with American soap to confuse the alsatian dogs sent to track them down; he described the ways in which the guerrillas had combated the gas and water that the Americans pumped into the tunnels. And then he took us into the tunnels themselves, first assuring himself that we wanted to go and were not cardiac invalids.

They were not more than three and a half or four feet high, so that I moved along them by a method halfway between a crawl and a stoop. Although we were only in the upper level, the heat was stifling; every few yards I sank to my knees for rest. The tunnels were pitch dark, of course, and our torch beam revealed bats flying swiftly and silently towards us, so that it seemed a collision was inevitable. But the bats swerved, with miraculous infallibility, and at the last moment turned without losing speed in the direction from which they had come. After a few of the most strenuous minutes of my life – I am sure I should exaggerate if I were to estimate how many – we emerged into the bright sunlight which scorched my eyes, only a hundred yards or so from where we had entered the tunnels. 150 miles! My knees were weak, I poured sweat like a wrung sponge.

We bought drinks for the colonel and his junior – Coca-Cola smuggled from Singapore (the Americans maintain a complete embargo that forbids foreign subsidiaries of US companies to trade with Vietnam). They, like many others, had spent years in the tunnels. I duly expressed wonderment, and said that I could never, under any conceivable circumstances, emulate them.

'You could,' said the colonel, 'if your country were in danger.'

No, I could not. I could envisage myself fighting in the streets against a foreign invader, so enraged for a time that I was indifferent to danger and my own death. I could be part of a *canaille*, I could throw bricks in a riot, I could hunt for a victim with a lynch mob: but I could not live in those tunnels for years on end, a soldier-termite, taking orders unquestioningly for the achievement of far-distant ends.

I was awe-struck. Awe, however, does not necessarily imply approval or agreement. One can admire the Pyramids without subscribing to the religious beliefs of the Pharaohs. It was self-evident that terror exercised by the Vietcong over the peasantry could not alone explain the construction of this eighth wonder of the world, or that anything other than unshakeable conviction could explain the resilience of the guerrillas who lived in the tunnels for years; but the tunnels struck me nevertheless as a monument to unreason, or at least to delusion, to the capacity of false (or at the very least dubious) ideas to take hold of human minds and exact savage sacrifices. Insincerity in human affairs is always a vice, but sincerity is not always a virtue.

A question – perhaps *the* question – went through my mind like a refrain, as a snatch of tune that, though unloved, will not go away: was it worth it? Later, in Hanoi, I received an unequivocal answer.

There we met Binh, a chemical engineer. He was in his late thirties, and had spent ten years in the North Vietnamese army, some of them guarding American prisoners of war in bamboo prisons in the jungle. He spoke without bitterness of those years; neither, of course, was he nostalgic. He talked of the Americans with a faint twinkle of amusement in his eye. He did not hate or despise them, he was far too intelligent for that; he thought of them rather as people who, in Vietnam, had been out of their natural element and therefore had floundered.

They had not been good soldiers, for obvious reasons. Most of them were conscripts, anxious only to survive their year in Vietnam and return home safely. When they went on patrol in the jungle, they sprayed their gunfire indiscriminately to exhaust their ammunition as quickly as possible, returning afterwards to base. The guerrillas, by contrast, had only a few bullets each, and they never fired without careful aim. The Americans were loaded down with equipment and supplies, reducing their manoeuvrability. The Vietnamese, other than their weapons, carried only a handful of rice. And it seemed that the Americans, used to a high standard of living, could not live without certain comforts and even luxuries. Binh had seen helicopters hovering over platoons of American soldiers, spraying them with water for showers. The Vietnamese, a fastidious people about personal cleanliness, had made do with whatever they could find in the jungle. The hard life they had endured since birth made them tough and adaptable. A life of abundance does not make good soldiers.

I asked why the Vietnamese – why he – had fought so hard and so long?

'We believed,' replied Binh.

For years the Vietnamese were told by their leaders that they had only to defeat their enemies, both external and internal, to become free and prosperous. They believed what they were told because they had no knowledge from any other source. They knew nothing of the true history of the Soviet Union; they knew nothing of life in western countries. And the bombs seemed to confirm what the leaders said.

Well, belief was a thing of the past. Fifteen years later, they were not free and they were not prosperous, despite two further wars. The people of Vietnam had drawn their own conclusions.

As we spoke, we walked together through the huge and echoingly empty Revolutionary Museum. We paused for a time at an enlarged copy of a document in French: the respectful submission of Ho Chi Minh to the Versailles peace conference in 1919. It asked for untramelled freedom of the press, freedom of association, freedom to travel and the same protection under the law for Vietnamese as for French citizens. These requests were, of course, arrogantly turned down, or worse still, ignored: had they been acceded to with a good grace, the history of the world might have been different. I translated Ho Chi Minh's requests for Binh – knowledge of French is dying out now in Vietnam – and then I asked him how many of these desiderata had been achieved in the intervening seventy years. He laughed, this time with a certain bitterness.

Binh had once been sent to Belgium for three months on a training course. It was not only techniques in chemistry he learnt there: he also learnt what it was to be free.

'They tell us you are oppressed,' he said. 'But we see that you are the only free people in the world, the only people who go where they like and do what they like. So only the oppressed are free!'

Unlike many intellectuals in the west, Binh had no doubts about the reality of our freedom. He would have found the mental contortions of philosophers and others to prove that in reality the citizens of liberal democracies were no freer than those of communist dictatorships bizarre, and quite possibly obscene. Of the existence of intellectual fashions – ideas worn and then discarded like clothes – he probably knew nothing.

'Do you think, then,' I asked *sotto voce*, as if about to utter a blasphemy in the inner sanctum of a religious cult, 'that Ho Chi Minh deceived you?'

'Yes.'

'And do many Vietnamese think this?'

'Yes.'

Coming from a man who was not an unthinking opponent of Ho Chi Minh's cause, but rather from one who had devoted ten years of his life to fighting for it, these conclusions were not without a certain impact. They had been bought, so to speak, exceedingly dear.

On the Sunday after our arrival, local government elections were held throughout Vietnam. A few red banners were slung across the streets in Saigon, one or two vans were fitted up with loudspeakers and went round the city pretending to electioneer, and posters appeared with pictures of the candidates. Since they were all chosen by the Party and two thirds of them were certain to be 'elected', excitement on the day was at less than fever pitch. The polling stations were in public buildings, turned for the occasion into secular shrines, draped in red, with large plaster busts of Ho Chi Minh presiding over this farcical similacrum of democracy. Not only was there no choice of candidates, but the electorate had no choice as to whether to exercise its lack of choice: voting, if that is the word, was compulsory.

Nothing could better have illustrated the pathological dishonesty of communists. While they decried the illusory nature of bourgeois democracy, they copied its forms (down to the secret ballot) but deprived them of all content, at the same time claiming to have created a more perfect, 'truer' democracy. And yet they knew all along that democracy and communism are quite incompatible. When Harrison Salisbury went to Hanoi in 1966, the North Vietnamese convinced him that their aim was not the forcible reunification of the country under communist dictatorship. When Salisbury had suggested such a thing to the then Prime Minister, Pham Van Dong, he 'displayed one of the few signs of anger which marked his lengthy discussion', and he said that no one in the North had this 'stupid, criminal idea' in mind. And Le Duan, then First Secretary of the North Vietnamese Communist Party, made a speech to army cadets (but almost certainly for Salisbury's willing consumption) in which he said that when the war ended there would be 'Socialism in the North, democracy in the South'.

Democracy and socialism – opposites, not synonyms.

The elections in Saigon were a sublime irrelevance. Not a single person gave them a moment's thought, and as soon as they were over all trace of them disappeared from the streets, the red drapes and busts of Ho put away until the next electoral charade, intellectually and emotionally as satisfying and authentic as Marie Antoinette playing shepherdess in the gardens of Versailles. Life after the elections did not return to normal for the simple reason that it had never been disturbed by them.

Saigon's Chinatown, where perhaps half a million people lived, was indistinguishable from any bustling, if poor, South East Asian city with a large Chinese community. The old covered market, built by a rich Chinese merchant during the colonial era, was once more the focus of life. The triumphant communists, with their mandarin disdain of trade, had pulled down the statue of the merchant that once adorned the centre of the market, and reduced the market itself to secondary importance by the simple expedient of encouraging shortages and introducing rationing; but the belated recognition that there might, after all, be something to be said for the virtues of free exchange had returned the market to 'normal' – at least for the time being. This qualification is necessary because the Secretary General of the Party has emphasised that under socialism, the object of trade is *not* profit: rather, its purpose is to facilitate the construction of 'large-scale socialist industry' at some time in the future. As an example of what he meant, he cited Lenin's New Economic Policy: a historical example that might not bring much comfort to the market traders, if they stopped to think about it.

Not that they appeared to be sparing much thought for the morrow: sufficient unto the day were the profits thereof. A happy buzz of bargaining, gossip and laughter rose ceaselessly up to the roof. In the market was displayed a variety of produce bewildering to people unschooled in Chinese cookery and medicine; our fascination with what for them were everyday things greatly amused the stallholders. Butchers sold every last part of the carcasses of beasts: was goat's trachea a delicacy, a sovereign remedy, a love potion, or merely the meat of the poor? There were pyramids of spices and vats of sticky preserves; there were little restaurants where people concentrated with seemingly fierce intensity upon consuming their noodle soup, their chorus of slurps a sharp reminder of the cultural relativity of table manners. And then there were stalls with imported toiletries: Thai forgeries, or imitations, of famous brands, such as Colligate, Cammay and Luxx.

Not a hundred yards from the market we visited a Chinese temple, on a street filled with a seemingly random ferment of rickshaws and carts, bicycles and pedicabs. The temple was an island of calm where all agitation ceased in the tapering smoke of incense. From time to time, when someone offered up some money, the gong was struck, and a soothing *basso profundo* growl moved slowly and with dignity through the red-columned halls of the temple. Old ladies in black pyjamas came to make their obeisances to their ancestors and to the goddess of the sea, whose temple it was: she was the deity worshipped by the Saigon Chinese, for she had protected their ancestors on their journey four centuries before when they migrated from south China to Vietnam. This was a religion whose entrails I could never enter: syncretic, with a shifting doctrine, half-philosophy, half-superstition, a way of life more than a dogma. Shut out from its meaning, I could only observe a few of its externals.

The temple guardian asked us to sign the visitors' book and append our comments. What a rich source such books will one day provide for future historians with an interest in social psychology! One wonders what will they make, for example, of the American visitor who said of the temple that it was very beautiful, and wished that Americans had something to be as proud of (as if Manhattan, San Francisco, Harvard, the Library of Congress, the Constitution, were nothing). Will they understand the complex dynamics of guilt and ignorance that underlie this remark? And what will they make of the Frenchman who wrote that the temple was very pleasant to visit, but it was a shame about the conditions in which its turtle (symbolic of long life) was kept, adding a sketch of a turtle enclosed by prison bars? Will they regard this as an instance of terminal hypersensibility, complicated by fulminating moral absolutism? I should have liked to gather further philosophical gems from the visitors' book, but the guardian grew impatient: he wanted me to write something, not read what others had written.

As an author, I decided on succinctness. 'Very nice', I wrote.

The market and the temple reminded us that not everything in life is political. But it was not possible to escape politics for long: we were taken by a guide to see the presidential palace of what is invariably known as 'the former regime'.

It stands empty in a large park in the centre of the city, a decaying and charmless monument to the modernity of the sixties, when it was built to replace its French predecessor, destroyed by fire. Large without grandeur, its concrete, glass, stone and steel structure is entirely angular, as though curves imply weakness. Its architect – a Vietnamese, the guide told us, though whether with pride or shame I couldn't quite tell – had obviously been concerned only that his palace should be considered utterly up to date, forgetting as all avant-gardists do that modernity without beauty is the most ephemeral and worthless of all virtues. The furnishings of the palace were more or less intact, though a little musty, untouched since the day the North Vietnamese tanks crashed through the gates of the park and the last president of South Vietnam, General Duong Van Minh, surrendered. The gates themselves were not directly in front of the main entrance to the palace but slightly to the side, such an arrangement (according to Chinese superstition) impeding the entry of evil spirits. Also impeding the entry of these spirits – though not the tanks – was a small pond, whose stagnant waters were now fishless. The furniture in the palace was largely of Scandinavian inspiration, the decorations Chinese. This extreme uncertainty of taste seemed to symbolise other, more serious uncertainties: but of course, I was touring the palace with the benefit of hindsight.

We peered in at the cabinet room. To judge from the number of seats, South Vietnam was never short of ministers. The cabinet table, said the guide, was the one that General Maxwell Taylor, the American ambassador, used to pound with his fist in his frustration with America's 'puppets'. The room was now unused, silent; I imagined the general, furious, imbued with a sense of historical destiny and of his own place in it, raging intemperately, going red in the face, and I reflected on the folly of passion. No, henceforth I should always have the transitoriness of all sublunary things firmly and equably in sight, and never again lose my temper – at least, not until the next time.

We passed from the 'public' areas of the palace – the reception and banqueting halls, ministerial committee rooms, and so forth – to the private apartments of the presidential family. Considering their reputation for unbridled corruption, the presidents of South Vietnam lived, at least in the palace itself, on a scale that was modest enough. Built around a small open courtyard covered with grenade-proof netting, their bed and dining rooms were no larger than those of an ordinarily prosperous European family. The private apartments did, it is true, contain a discotheque and games room in the very worst taste of the time, which no doubt indicates the presidents were frivolous vulgarians; but the architecture was not that of megalomania, only of profound mediocrity. The staircases, for example, would not have been out of place in a provincial office of the Department of Health and Social Security.

We had the opportunity to compare these living quarters with those of Ho Chi Minh in Hanoi, preserved as a national shrine. There can be no doubt, at least in the negative sense, about Ho's motives in struggling for power for so many years: he did not wish to dwell in marble halls. He refused, for example, to move into the old Governor-General's palace when the French departed for good and all. Rather, he had a wooden pavilion of great simplicity and no great size built in the grounds, overlooking an ornamental lake whose enormous goldfish he used to feed. This pavilion, built on two floors, is elegant, the wood very fine; the upper floor has Ho's two private rooms, a little study with simple but refined wooden furniture and a bookcase with volumes of Lenin and a photograph of the master, and a bedroom with mosquito screens and net. Downstairs is the room in which Ho used to receive the other leaders, the books, all political, in English, French and Russian (he spoke Chinese fluently too), that he was reading at his death still piled reverently on the table before his seat.

What does one make of the difference between the way Ho Chi Minh and the presidents of South Vietnam lived? At every point of comparison, of course, Ho emerges immeasurably the superior. Intelligent, knowledgeable, experienced, incorruptible, a brilliant linguist: he was, indeed, everything a philosopher-king should be. By contrast, the presidents of South Vietnam were shabby place-seekers, nepotistic, cowardly, avaricious and unprincipled.

Yet when it came to votes with the feet, who received more of them? Who created a country from which scores, or hundreds, of thousands have fled in boats, on rafts, on anything that will float for a time, through shark and pirate infested waters, in desperate search of somewhere better?

For all Ho's virtues and talents, his personal honesty, bravery and devotion, one feels a shudder as one inspects his little house. There is something not quite human about it: in a country where family life is so important, there is not the faintest indication of an emotional tie to another human being. I prefer my saints to live in caves and not to try to impose their standards on the world: for singlemindedness is a cold virtue. Chernyshevsky, Lenin's hero, wrote (approvingly) that 'A man with an ardent love of goodness cannot but be a sombre monster.'

Ho was not always thus, far from it: he went through a dandy stage in Paris in the twenties. He even danced and went to the opera. It might therefore be said by way of extenuation that he eventually reacted against the intransigent arrogance of the French colonialism that so cruelly humiliated his ancient, proud and civilized people. But this is at best an explanation, and a partial one at that, not an exculpation. After all, he had observed at first hand the unprecedented tyranny of Stalinism: if he mistook it for freedom he was foolish, if he admired it he was evil. People who love freedom do not drink at the fount of despotism to become despots themselves.

If I had seen the discotheque in the 'Puppet Presidential Palace' after rather than before I visited Ho Chi Minh's house, perhaps I should have thought of it not as a tasteless excrescence but as a welcome sign of human frailty: the very quality that explains why votes with the feet favour the frail.

To escape politics once more we took a boat with a dragon prow on the tea-brown Mekong and visited an island in the river. It was ten kilometres long and I should have said it was a paradise had I not heard a mother shrilly scolding her fourteen-year-old son for spending the whole day in a tea-house with a pool table instead of studying hard at school and getting a good job with the government. The island was irrigated throughout by beautifully cut canals crossed by bridges of bamboo, and everywhere there were exotic fruit trees (exotic, that is, to *us*), coconut palms, bamboo groves, hibiscus hedges and flower gardens.

Five thousand people lived on the island; they owned their land, they fished, and many of their homes were two centuries old, displaying a refinement of taste I might have called aristocratic had not the people been peasants and fishermen. The houses were open to the breeze; their roofs were tiled and their eaves curved gently upwards in the Chinese fashion. There was little in the way of outer walls and so the rooms were almost open spaces. Each house had a shrine to the ancestors and the magnificent old wooden pillars and rafters of the house had gilded Chinese characters carved into them. It was tempting to imagine the island as an undisturbed remnant of some golden age, a pre-communist, pre-colonial Vietnam that might one day revive. Like all visions of a perfect past, mine was a chimera: the island had been bombed and shelled in the war, having been a suspected guerrilla stronghold. But all that seemed long ago and supremely irrelevant now.

In Hue, the old imperial capital four hundred miles north of Saigon, we again escaped into a vision of the past. What remains of Hue is for the most part not very ancient, but it tells of a high culture that has now been liquidated. Its last adept was the emperor Bao Dai, deposed by Ho in 1945, but still living (in Paris). Bao Dai was an intelligent man, but - having been reduced all his life to an ornament of someone else's power – not a serious one: and nothing could better have illustrated the refined frivolity of his court than a palace game in which he became expert. The game entailed bouncing a stick on its end on the ground and getting it to enter a vase with a tiny aperture standing at some distance. This was not conspicuous consumption: it was conspicuous uselessness, the end product of a futile feudalism. Bao Dai was the last scion of a lineage of scholar-emperors who fought vainly to preserve their independence and the Confucian heritage of Vietnam. When he left Vietnam and took initial refuge in Hong Kong, he went to the movies every afternoon: his favourite actress was Jeanette MacDonald.

If Vietnam had had a different history, Hue would now be full of tourists. As it was, the hotel was empty – one walked through it as though one had come to the wrong place – and the fact that another hotel was under construction next door, in preparation for a hoped-for influx of foreigners, seemed as much a work of faith as any medieval cathedral, though of somewhat lesser aesthetic appeal. On the back of my bedroom door were fire instructions, information about laundry services and checkout times, in English, French and Russian. The Russian notice had been almost entirely scratched off. By whom, I wondered? By French or American visitors, humiliated by this evidence of the extension of Soviet power and influence, made possible by their own military defeats? Or by Vietnamese staff of the hotel, angered by the poverty and meanness of the new colonists, who spent what little money they had buying up electronic goods in Vietnamese markets for sale at huge profit at home?

Alas, war and economic devastation can bring certain small advantages to travellers who visit monuments. They are not overrun by vulgar tourists (so unlike themselves), who crave drinks and other refreshments at every step, who want souvenirs of what they scarcely bestow a glance upon, and who take snapshots of Bill with his arms around Buddha. And so we were able to contemplate the tombs of the emperors – Bao Dai's ancestors – in a tranquility that mere peace could never have brought.

The tombs are in a vast area of forested hills reserved for them. One of the most beautiful is that of Tu Duc, the last truly independent emperor, who opposed the French but in the end surrendered to them. At a time when his position looked hopeless, he published a poignant *cri de coeur*:

> Never has an era seen such sadness, never a year more anguish. Above me, I fear the edicts of heaven. Below, the tribulations of the people trouble my days and nights. Deep in my heart I tremble and blush, finding neither words nor actions to help my subjects . . .

Later, during a respite in the French advance, he put to death thousands of Vietnamese Catholics because they had helped or favoured the French. By those who supported colonialism he was portrayed as a bloodthirsty monster; by others, as an essentially gentle man brought to this pass by the terrible logic of his situation. Perhaps there are historical analogies here.

Yet if the tomb of Tu Duc is anything to go by, he was a gentle, not a vicious, man. He spent many days there before he died in 1858, fishing from the small pavilion beside the lotus pond that confers such transcendent calm upon the scene. Apparently sterile, he frolicked there with his concubines, who made him jasmine tea using only the dew that formed on lotus leaves, infusing it overnight in their blossoms. As for the tomb itself, through a deserted courtyard with frangipani trees and stone elephants, it does not contain the emperor's body, which is buried in an unknown place somewhere in the surrounding hills to prevent robbery and desecration of the imperial finery.

If one can compare their lives, why not the tombs of Tu Duc and Ho Chi Minh? There is, of course, a slight unfairness here: Tu Duc endorsed his own tomb, while Ho Chi Minh expressly forbad any memorialisation of himself. In his will, in which he anticipated joining 'Karl Marx, Lenin and other revolutionary elders' (where, one is tempted to ask?), he requested that 'my remains be incinerated . . . Not only is [cremation] good for the living from the point of view of hygiene, it also saves land. When we have a plentiful supply of electricity, "electric cremation" will be even better.'

Who now can say that communism, unlike religion, offers no consolation for the fact of death? Who is so philistine that the prospect of a hygienic electric cremation, power cuts permitting, will not compensate for an eternity of non-being?

Anyway, Uncle Ho did not get what he said he wanted. Instead, *Mavsolexport*, the giant Soviet mausoleum construction, maintenance and export company, which specialises in granite review stands, the embalming of national heroes and goosestep training, was called in. The company constructed a masterpiece of the genre, turning a little bit of Hanoi into Red Square. Inside the tomb lie the waxen remains of Ho. Unfortunately, we could not see them because the tomb was closed for two months' annual maintenance. Even when it is not under repair, however, the tomb of the great egalitarian is not easy for ordinary Vietnamese to penetrate; harder, in fact, than the tomb of the feudal Tu Duc, for no fewer than four separate permissions, each available only from a different office, are required.

One of history's small ironies, perhaps. But my sympathy for Ho is somewhat limited: for I have never wholly believed disavowals by dictators of the personality cults of which they were the object.

By common consent, the most beautiful of the emperors' tombs in Hue is that of Minh Mang, in whose reign the first American set foot in Vietnam, in 1820. The tomb was on the other bank of the Perfumed River, which we crossed in a boat hired at a small and grindingly poor riverside market where, a trifle optimistically, we were offered pieces of freshly slaughtered pig for sale.

The tomb was exquisite. It was in just that state of decay that induces reflection on the transitoriness of earthly existence, without at all obscuring the original design. The first buildings of the tomb to which we came were undistinguished, simple outhouses with crumbling plasterwork, in whose shelter a poor family lived, its firewood stacked against a wall. We wondered whether the beauty of the tomb had not perhaps been exaggerated, but we were soon to be convinced that no words existed with which to do it. For in the centre of a square lotus pond, reached by four stone pathways, was a decorated wooden pavilion in the most perfect of perfect taste. Around the pavilion were formal gardens, and the whole tomb complex was in the shadow of hills covered in pine forest, so that the refined and artificial was united seamlessly with the wild and natural.

We climbed to the upper floor of the pavilion. There was silence, except for the birds and the occasional echoing howl of what I took to be a monkey: of our fellow man there was no sign. At once an almost mystical tranquility enveloped us: silence was the only way of expressing it.

All too soon, we had to leave, but the moments of peace I shall always be able to recall.

Alas, it is the fate of intellectuals to leave no experience, however ravishing, to remain in the memory untainted by theorising. I soon began to muse on my own sensibility: on how different my experience of the tomb of Minh Mang might have been had other people – as I imagined them, eating ice cream, dropping litter and uttering loud inanities – been present there. In my innermost heart, then, was I a believer in an aristocracy of feeling, and not a democrat at all? No; in the last analysis, I attached no great significance to my own exquisite emotions. I was merely glad to have had the occasion to experience them.

We left the tombs of Hue by car. We took with us a peasant and her young son who had never been in a car before. They sat in the front seat, transfixed by the novelty, the comfort, the speed. Their emotions were too deep for speech.

Everyone remarks upon the French character of Hanoi. The leafy avenues, the colonial architecture, the opera house – all survived the war intact. During his visit to Hanoi in 1967, Harrison Salisbury was told that the government expected the city to be utterly destroyed by bombing: a prospect they took with what he called 'aplomb' since Hanoi was considered by them an ugly old city that symbolised the French occupation. After the war, they were going to build a new capital of their own, an example, perhaps, of what the Reverend Dr William Sloan Coffin, another American visitor to North Vietnam, called 'passion rekindled by . . . bomb damage'.

Hanoi is *not* an ugly city, quite the contrary, as every citizen I asked now agreed; and I was far from alone in supposing that a capital built by the present government to replace it was unlikely to be an improvement.

We stayed at the Thong Nhat (Reunification) Hotel, once the Metropole. The first person I saw in the lobby was obviously a journalist, though I am not sure how I knew it even before she imperiously demanded a line to London to report the explosions she heard the night before in Phnom Penh. The somewhat glutinous response of the hotel staff further fanned the flame of her self-importance.

The Thong Nhat is large, old and run down. Well-fed rats circumambulate the vast dining room from time to time with the impunity of household pets; one hesitates before turning on a light or a ceiling fan because of the possibility of electric shocks from the switch; and a Belgian worker for *Médecins sans frontières* told me that the two lightbulbs in his room had exploded. As for the staff, they have that special reluctance to oblige, that stony-faced obstructiveness that one learns to love so in communist countries. It was the first and last time we encountered it in Vietnam.

We were told that a French company was soon to renovate the hotel, to bring it up to 'international standards'. For my part, I very much regretted it. I am a connoisseur of seediness, and I particularly liked the enormous baths, big enough to swim in, with their enamel coating furred by skin-scraping deposits from the unsoftened water, and the huge Hungarian boilers that produced seismic rumbling sounds, whistles and occasional spurts of cold water, unpredictably emitting gushes of boiling liquid the colour of rust every forty-eight or seventy-two hours. How dull and predictable by comparison good plumbing will be!

And what of the mattresses, unchanged since colonial times, with their deep concavity, so that one either rolls helplessly towards the centre of the bed or clings to the edge as in a shipwreck? What will there be to say about mattresses that merely allow one a good night's sleep?

The first time we left the hotel, a Vietnamese aged about sixty, dressed in a lumpy suit and an unfashionable broad tie, bowed us through the door before him.

'Everything,' he said in excellent English, 'must be for foreign visitors first.'

He was polite, but his words made me shiver: they had the unpleasant timbre of *langue de bois*. 'After you' would have sufficed; I thought his manner bore the same relationship to friendliness as pornography does to love. Perhaps what the southerners had told us with a shudder about northerners was true after all: they're *communists* up there.

Out in the street, what the southerners said of their northern compatriots seemed at first to be true. The people who streamed past us, both on foot and on bicycles, were silent and unsmiling. Their expressions seemed grim and their clothes were drab. Many of the men wore olive-coloured topees, as though in some deadly serious satire on colonial manners. Or perhaps they had taken to heart Albert Schweitzer's warnings about the deadly effects on the brain of a single beam of tropical light falling, even for a fraction of an instant, directly on to the scalp (though Schweitzer referred only to the brains of whites). There were more men in military uniform than elsewhere in Vietnam, and even civilian clothes, especially for men, tended to the military colours of khaki and camouflage green. We passed a state department store, recognisable as such at once by its shoddy goods stacked in dusty chaos, the immobility of the store assistants, the shuffling gait of the customers and the byzantine method of payment.

I gazed with special attention at the complexions of the people in Hanoi. This was because Mary McCarthy had written in 1968 of her visit to a school:

> The boys were good-looking, some beautiful even, with lustrous hair, shining eyes, soft clear skin – no acne in North Vietnam.

Alas, acne had returned to North Vietnam, possibly with the economic reforms: not in epidemic proportions, but still it was there, as were the red teeth of betel-chewing, also absent during Miss McCarthy's visit.

These observations of hers were not subsequently a source of great pride to Miss McCarthy. Indeed, in the blurb of her novel *Cannibals and Missionaries* she is described as the author of seventeen books, and *Hanoi* is not listed among them – a slight revision of history of her very own. But her book was nevertheless representative of an entire, if small, genre: the miracles of Ho as related by Susan Sontag, assorted clergymen, academics and journalists.

We found a small miracle of our own in Hanoi, though it was not such as to excite the admiration of intellectuals or men of God, quite the reverse. After forty years of virtuous austerity, when the communists took over effective power from the Japanese and the French were unable to re-establish their authority, the inhabitants of Hanoi were discovering pleasure! Our initial impressions notwithstanding, the effects of the economic reforms had reached even here. A large part of the city was given over to an outdoor market, which had sprung up immediately permission was granted, and at night the stalls in street after street were lit with powerful single lightbulbs, creating a dazzling and beautiful effect in a city not otherwise notable for the brightness of its illuminations. Crowds strolled in these streets, admiring what a few months before had been denounced, rejected, scorned, vilified (but not by them). Restaurants had started up, and pavement cafés; there were ice cream stalls and, most surprising of all, dance halls with popular music and coloured lights. Lovers walked arm in arm, their thoughts manifestly not on building socialism, which even Mary McCarthy admits is 'a sometimes zestless affair'. In one of the parks, a party of pleasantly drunk young Vietnamese invited me for a drink and insisted on giving me a cigarette, though I do not smoke. Hanoi proved there is life after death.

How Mary McCarthy and her ilk would have hated it, how their lips would have curled! It was not happiness they were seeking in Hanoi but redemption from sin. No medieval monk ever outdid Miss McCarthy in the luxuriance of his penitential reflections, or in the theological subtlety of his special pleading. As I re-read *Hanoi* in my room in the Thong Nhat, in which incidentally there were no longer any 'sheets of toilet paper laid out on a box in a fan pattern' as in Miss McCarthy's day, I found myself in a strange emotional limbo between rage and laughter, the nearest I have come to what psychiatrists call a mixed affective state.

Followed absolutely everywhere by 'comrades of the Peace Committee', and even to the lavatory by a 'young woman interpreter' who carried a tin helmet for her protection against sudden air-raids, and who, after she had finished in the lavatory, 'softly led [her] back', Mary McCarthy concluded only that everyone in North Vietnam was most solicitous of her welfare. That a none-too-subtle form of surveillance and control was being exerted did not for a single moment occur to her.

If she had been followed to the lavatory in Pinochet's Chile, I imagine she might have written something different.

Nothing troubled her about North Vietnam, however, armour-plated as she was against the urgings of common sense. Remarking on the formulaic dullness and repetitiousness of the news media, she regretted the western writer's 'convention of freshness', capitalist society having made 'originality . . . a sort of fringe benefit'. As for 'the license to criticize', it 'was just another capitalist luxury, a waste product of the system . . . access to information that does not lead to action may actually be unhealthy . . . for a body politic.' And visiting American pilots shot down over Vietnam she commented, 'If these men have been robotized . . . it had been an insensible process starting in grade school and finished off by the army.' (I wondered what the man I met in Saigon's main post office, who had just been released after thirteen years in a re-education camp, would have made of her opinion.) In any case, brain-washing was not really nasty because, unlike in the Free World, where 'to judge by its artifacts, nobody is free to make a decision to be different from what he is', in the un-Free World, 'the opposite is assumed' and they, the North Vietnamese, 'accept change axiomatically as a revolutionary possibility in human conduct – which Western liberals do not' – the explanation of why such liberals are 'tolerant of difference' while the North Vietnamese are not.

But the crucial passage in *Hanoi* is that in which Miss McCarthy recounts her interview with the Prime Minister, Pham Van Dong. The question that preoccupied her was that of the type of society Vietnam would become after the war was over. She was worried lest 'the enemy, capitalism, repulsed by air and foiled by land in the sister South, should creep in the back way . . .'

Pham Van Dong was her man all right. He spoke of material scarcity in Vietnam 'as a piece of good luck'. But what really endeared him to the visiting American, who was brought up in a rich Chicago family and had never quite got round to renouncing worldly wealth, was that 'he spoke of our automobile-TV culture as of something distastefully gross and heavy . . . With a full-lipped contempt . . . he rejected the notion of a socialist consumer society.' To him (as to all the Vietnamese Miss McCarthy met) American life appeared 'not just grotesque, but backward, primitive, pitiably undeveloped, probably because of its quality of infantile dependency.'

The Prime Minister's rejection of a consumer society – on whose

behalf and by what right he was rejecting it she did not think to enquire
– gave rise to the following reflection:

> In Vietnam I perceived – what doubtless I should have known before – that
> the fear of decentralisation and local autonomy evinced by communist
> leaders is not necessarily an abject solicitude for their own continuance in
> power; it is also a fear of human nature as found in their countrymen, on the
> assumption that modern man is 'naturally' a capitalist accumulator, already
> spotted with that first sin in his mother's womb and ceaselesly beset by
> marketing temptations: if you let workers run factories, they will soon be
> manufacturing Cadillacs because 'the consumer wants them'.

There we have it, the *fons et origo* of the appeal to intellectuals of
socialism: snobbery. Left to themselves, people invariably display bad
taste (a crime for which Lukacs, the Hungarian Marxist luminary who
was also a murderer, thought they should be punished). Therefore,
they must not be left to themselves. Philosopher kings – the Pham Van
Dongs and Mary McCarthys – must teach the people what they 'really'
want, and to reject what they merely think they want because they have
been corrupted, deformed and alienated by advertising and other
capitalist techniques. The ideal of socialists is thus not a society of
perfect justice: it is a society where people do not put plaster ducks on
their walls.

But bad taste was returning to Hanoi and the people loved it.

After I left Vietnam, I encountered some of the boat people in camps
and prisons in Hong Kong and Bangkok. They were, of course,
adamantly opposed to returning to their homeland. In Hong Kong they
lived in crowded camps, surrounded by high walls and barbed wire, a
whole family living in a space the size of a large tea-chest. If anything,
conditions in Thailand were worse. Yet many of the people would
rather have stayed in such conditions for years than again face life in
Vietnam.

How would apologists explain this desperate exodus from a country
whose government they so recently applauded? The first wave of boat
people might plausibly be represented as the flight of 'collaborators'
with the old regime. Indeed, in Bangkok I had a long talk with a man
who had worked in the American and Filipino embassies, who had tried
to escape five times before succeeding, who had been denied all work
since 'liberation' and who had been confined to his home district of the
city, having to report to his local committee three times a week. He was
definitely a man of the old type.

But the 50,000 refugees (or economic migrants) in Hong Kong were almost all from the North, where they had known nothing but communism. They left from Haiphong harbour, under the noses of the officials whom they had bribed with their life savings. I saw the boats myself when I visited Haiphong (where Panamanian and other ships were being loaded with scrap metal, including bomb casings, from the war – it is an ill wind that blows no scrap metal merchant any good). The cost of a passage to Hong Kong per refugee was one or two ounces of gold, though sometimes the bribed officials arrested the refugees after taking their gold and put them in prison, from which they had to bribe their way out. And then they had to start again, saving gold for their passages out . . . The British government was trying to bribe Vietnam into taking the refugees back from Hong Kong – paying the equivalent of an ounce or two of gold per refugee. Misery and despair had thus been turned into lucratively traded commodities, as Marx would no doubt have expressed it.

Miss McCarthy almost lost her faith in Vietnam. 'I've several times contemplated writing a real letter to Pham Van Dong (I get a Christmas card from him every year) asking him can't you stop this, how is it possible for men like you to permit what's going on?'

It never ocurred to her, of course, that her original judgment of him was grotesquely wrong ('magnetic allure . . . fiery, but also melancholy . . . emotional, impressionable . . . at the same time highly intellectual'). Or that the ideas she espoused inevitably had unpleasant consequences. No, somewhere there was a purer, better form of socialism, 'with a human face', living under which 'would require quite an adjustment, but it would be so exciting that I hope one would be willing to sacrifice the comforts of life that one has become extremely used to.'

In the meantime, the Vietnamese would have to content themselves with such reforms as were granted. As Nguyen Van Linh put it (his style refreshingly free from the artificial need for originality):

After this plenum, the Party Secretariat and the Standing Committee of the Council of Ministers must quickly organise the implementation of the plenum's resolution. In the spirit of concentrated guidance as in a military campaign we should closely follow the evolution and detect in time any deviation and mistakes, take necessary complementary measures, and review their implementation in each step . . .

CUBA

Havana is like Pompeii, and Castro is its Vesuvius. The lava of his words has poured over the city continuously for thirty years, preserving it from any form of change except decay. This magnificent city, the pearl of centuries of exploitation, is an inhabited ruin; the inhabitants are like a wandering tribe that has found the deserted metropolis of a superior but dead civilisation and decided to make it home.

Fortunately, very little has been built since that day in January 1959 when the *barbudos*, the bearded ones, entered the city in triumph after the flight of the dictator Batista. The little that has been built is not attractive. The holiest of the country's shrines is now the boat in which eighty-two rebels, seventy of whom were soon to die, made their way from Mexican exile back to Cuba to start the revolution. *Granma*, the boat, is encased in a brutally angular glass case, a giant modernist reliquary of the communist mausoleum school. The little park that surrounds it is filled with lesser relics: the red delivery van from which rebels attacked Batista in the National Palace in Havana on March 13th, 1957, a home-made tank painted the colours of the July 26th Movement (red and black, the same anarchist colours as the Sandinista movement), a grey American sedan from the early fifties, a single-engined naval aircraft: all preserved from vandalism or worse by soldiers who exhibit a strange mixture of Latin insouciance and military preparedness, casually leaning against trees and smoking on duty while keeping an eye out, weapons at the ready, for those who approach with grenades in their pockets.

Before the park stands a low stone plinth with an inextinguishable gas flame and an inscription: Eternal glory to . . .

To whom exactly? After a very short time in Havana, one suspects the inscription should read 'Eternal glory to Me', the Me in question being one of the greatest Mes of the twentieth century, the Me without whom nothing moves in Cuba. Three days after my arrival, with little to do in the evening, I turned on the television – *Tele Rebelde*, Rebel TV, which, as one might expect from its name, purveys only the strictest orthodoxy – and there he was, Me, Fidel Castro Ruz, speaking to a congress of scientific workers. He had not expected to be called to speak, he said, with all the bashfulness of a diva who finds herself with repeated curtain calls for the 974th time in her career. And of course, he hesitated to speak to so august an assembly of scientific workers about the theory and practice of science . . .

An hour and forty minutes later, I switched him off in mid-platitude, unable to tolerate a moment more. He was saying that once a new and superior scientific technique had been developed, it should be put into practice at once, that *not a single moment, not a second*, should be wasted, so that the technique's maximum potential should be realised in the construction of socialism. The Maximum Leader was dressed in his Sierra Maestra kit, a little better pressed and tailored perhaps, but still recognisable as the garb of his youth. His hair and beard, however, had turned nearly white, and he was now as much Old Testament prophet as student revolutionary. The tablets he brought down from the mountain were carved jointly by Marx and Lenin and Helen Steiner Rice. Do this, do that, don't do this, don't do that . . . At first, curiosity kept my eyes glued to the screen. Here was an undeniably great man speaking, if greatness in a man is measured by the vicissitudes he had endured and the effects he has wrought on the world. Castro spoke of the *montón de cosas* – the great pile of things – the Revolution had done, especially in the field of health. A vaccine against meningitis had been developed in Cuba and AIDS was under control, unlike in a country not so very far away. All this the Revolution had done . . .

Well, it was certainly true that the people in Cuba looked healthy enough, especially the children, who were well-fed and well-clothed. According to the statistics, Cubans now had a similar life expectancy to that of western Europeans. Yet there was something disturbing about the way the *Comandante en jefe* stressed the health services in Cuba, even if all he said about them were true. It was not only in this speech but on all other possible occasions that he returned to the subject, so that one grew weary of hearing it, even in a very short time. Man does not live by antibiotics alone.

One sensed that concern for the physical well-being of Cubans was not the only motive of Castro's peculiar emphasis on medicine (after all, his disregard for the value of individual human life is by now sufficiently well-documented). Rather, he was hammering home an important lesson: the Revolution brought you health services, and if the Revolution is overthrown there will be no health services, just as there were none before it. And in this lesson there is a subtext, as literary critics might put it; or a hidden agenda, as conspiracy theorists might say. Castro is telling his people that, just as Mrs Gargery brought up Pip, he has brought them up by hand, and it would therefore be an act of the grossest ingratitude on their part if they were in the slightest to rebel. But if they entrust their lives to him, he will take care of them, and they will be saved even from the jaws of death . . .

Opinions about Cuba and its social services have become so ideologised – thanks in no small measure to Castro's style of politics – that is not only difficult to disentangle truth from fiction or wishful thinking, but even to decide what constitutes a relevant fact. Those who admire Castro stress only the universal literacy and life expectancy of Cubans, unique in Latin America or very nearly so, and the gross injustices that existed under Batista; those who detest Castro emphasise only the economic prosperity of Cuba before the revolution, the complete lack of political and artistic freedom after it, and the vast economic subventions from the Soviet Union necessary to produce such improvements as there have been. The mean between two extremes does not *always* yield the truth, for truth is a tyrant that respects no niceties; but in this case, the mean does seem to me to approximate the truth of the matter.

There was widespread illiteracy in Batista's Cuba, but 77 per cent of the population was literate, a high percentage for Latin America at the time (and still not reached by many countries). This implies there were at least *some* schools functioning in Cuba in those dark days. But there is incontestable evidence also that malnourishment existed among children before the Revolution. Yet the life expectancy, which has since improved by thirteen years, was second in Latin America only to Argentina's. And it is necessary to view these figures not statically, but dynamically. There is scarcely a country in Latin America in which such indicators of social welfare have not substantially improved since 1959.

Hence it is fair to say there have been social improvements under Castro's rule; but it is impossible to assert they occurred exclusively *because* of it, or that they could not have occurred without it. And it seems to me that the only real, if still only partial, justification for his dictatorial methods would be if such methods, and they alone, were capable of producing the improvements claimed for them. Costa Rica proves this is not so.

After an hour of the Maximum Leader, I began to wonder how it was that no one in the audience protested against this inhuman prolixity.

The people in the audience were intelligent and educated, they did not need to be told that two and two made four, they did not necessarily know less than he just because they had never fought as guerrillas in the Sierra Maestra. But he continued to tug at his beard, pull his ear, pass his hand over his forehead, and otherwise break the rules of oratory, while delivering himself painfully, as in childbirth, of truisms. Thirty years of sycophantic audiences had rendered him incapable of concision, of saying anything in two words when a hundred would express the same thought. His fascination with his own personality was such that his merest whim was law for him. I began to wonder also how it was that in those thirty years he himself had not become bored with revolving around the same ideas, the same hatreds, the same hopes, in seemingly interminable speeches. If disillusionment ever set in, I thought, it would do so suddenly, and he would undergo a conversion experience (such a man could not live without certainty), taking everyone with him. He had spoken at length recently about religion, and referred with sympathy to the Jesuit teachers of his youth. I distracted myself by imagining the sage of the Sierra Maestra returning in old age to the Jesuits. His new humility, of course, would be inverted pride; he would not be honouring God, God would be honouring him.

At least I could turn the television off. An important foreign visitor I met in Havana, who was a member of a delegation that had not long before had lunch with Fidel, was not so fortunate. Fidel had spoken at the lunch for seven hours, almost without stopping. He had his generals and cabinet ministers, including his brother Raul, Number Two in Cuba, around him, but the only time they spoke was while Fidel was actually chewing his food, which was not for long because he is ascetic and eats lightly.

This, of course, proves that a true revolutionary does not speak with his mouth full.

By all accounts, however, Castro was a worried man, and occasionally it showed in a gesture or a sigh. The changes in Eastern Europe were not at all to his taste, they presaged no good for his absolute power, and he had not yet worked out how to present these changes to his compatriots. A plot, perhaps, by Enemies of the People? But Enemies of the People should be relatively few, at most counted in thousands, not millions, and certainly not the overwhelming majority of the population as in Romania. The trouble was that Cubans were too well-informed to believe so outright a lie.

The example of Romania was particularly worrying, of course, because, like Cuba, it was a family affair. A Czechoslovak journalist had recently achieved the distinction of being the first journalist from a Warsaw Pact country to be expelled from Cuba, precisely for having drawn an analogy between the *Lider Máximo* and the *Conducator*. The comparison was not quite apt: I never detected in Cuba the burning, all-consuming hatred for Castro that I detected in Romania for Ceausescu, even among those who otherwise had no good to say of him. He was no mere apparatchik with a Lady Macbeth for a wife; he had made a revolution himself, he retained his credentials as a nationalist, and he was still able to appeal to the visceral anti-Yankee feeling of many Cubans. Still, the comparison with Ceausescu was uncomfortable enough to warrant the expulsion of the man who made it.

Nor was this all Castro had to worry about. With the change in the Soviet Union, the supply ships were not arriving with their accustomed regularity and food stores, never exactly a cornucopia, were running short. Before I left Cuba, the prices of eggs and bread, both rationed, were raised by 50 per cent. (It was over a quarter of a century since Cubans were told that food rationing was a temporary measure.) In Santiago, a man invited me to his home next day for lunch, only to cancel because he had been unable to procure extra rations for me to eat. We went instead to a restaurant for Cubans in Cayo Granma, just outside the city, where they served the meal that I ate in every restaurant outside Havana: *cristianos y moros*, Christians and Moors, rice and beans, with the identical, centrally planned meat stew as relish – no vegetables or salad.   Every time I was served this less than delicious meal I regarded myself as extremely fortunate, first I had been permitted to enter the restaurant at all and second that I was actually served with something to eat (by no means synonymous in these circumstances with sitting at a table – my Cuban companion of the moment always making it clear to the waiter or waitress that it would be less trouble for him or her to serve us than not to serve us, obstreperousness being the first rule of behaviour in such restaurants, where those who do not make themselves objectionable tend to go hungry, and a new evolutionary principal is at work, the survival of the rudest).

Cuba's citrus crop was rotting in the orchards for lack of transport and foreign customers. The country's biggest source of hard currency was crude oil sold at a concessionary rate by the Soviet Union, refined in Cuba and re-sold on the world market; and the Soviet Union had cut the supply of crude the previous year by as much as a half. And the sugar agreement with the Soviet Union came to an end in 1991. Although not easy to estimate, it was generally considered that the price the Soviets had been paying for Cuban sugar was well above the world price, sometimes five or six times above it (though they paid mostly in goods unsaleable elsewhere). When the time came to negotiate a new agreement, the Soviet Union – which still needed the sugar – was in a position to impose a much lower price. Altogether, the economic prospects for Cuba were not good.

Castro reacted to the crisis in his usual way. He is a man who, early, in his life, overcame so many overwhelming difficulties that he does not believe there is any problem in the world he cannot solve, any situation he cannot master. When the bodies of the Cuban soldiers killed in Angola during the performance of their 'internationalist duty' were brought back to Cuba, Castro used the occasion to attack the desertion of Eastern Europe from the ranks of the righteous:

> They are not exactly talking of the anti-imperialist struggle or the principles of internationalism in the majority of these countries. The words are not even mentioned in the press. The concepts have been virtually rubbed out of the political dictionary. By contrast, the values of capitalism are regaining unusual strength in these societies . . . The systematic destruction of socialist values, the sapping carried on by imperialism, combined with the mistakes committed, have accelerated the process of destabilisation of the Eastern European socialist countries . . . Imperialism and the capitalist powers cannot hide their euphoria at the events. They are convinced, not without reason, that the socialist camp has now almost ceased to exist. In some of these countries of Eastern Europe they now have complete teams of advisers of the US President, programming capitalist development . . .

This was before the destruction of the Ceausescu regime. Since then, he has remained silent on the subject. Presumably he considered 'the mistakes committed' a sufficient explanation of why millions of people took to the streets of Bucharest and other cities and, unarmed, faced machine guns.

In the same speech, he gave an indirect warning to the Soviet Union (if they were not careful, he would withdraw his seal of approval from it):

> Devastating wars, that cost millions of lives and the destruction of the immense majority of the accumulated means of production, were unleashed against the first socialist state. Like a phoenix, it had more than once to rise

from the ashes and lend services to humanity such as the defeat of fascism
and the decisive support to liberation movements of still colonised
countries. They like to forget this today.

It is repugnant that many in the Soviet Union itself dedicate themselves to
denying or destroying the historic feats and extraordinary merits of this
heroic people. This is not the way to rectify and overcome the unquestionable mistakes committed in a revolution born in the bowels of
tsarist authoritarianism, in an immense, poor and backward country . . .

Therefore we have not hesitated to prevent the circulation of certain
Soviet publications which are loaded with poison against the Soviet Union
itself and socialism. One perceives behind them the hand of imperialism,
reaction and counterrevolution. Already some of these publications have
begun to demand the end of the type of equitable and just commercial
relations that have been created between the USSR and Cuba . . .

Thus the publication in the Soviet Union of the discoveries of mass
graves containing fifty, a hundred, two hundred thousand corpses, all
people shot behind the ear, meant nothing to the *Comandante en jefe*,
the defender of the poor and humble of the world, except a slight
ideological embarrassment. The now-acknowledged murder of twenty
million people is for him nothing but an 'unquestionable mistake', a
mistake for which he grants his absolution.

What is the solution to the crisis? His speech gives a clue:

It has been said that socialism must perfect itself. No one can be opposed to
this principle, which is inherent in and of constant application to all human
work. But is it . . . by abandoning the most elementary principles of
Marxism-Leninism that one can perfect socialism? Why have the so-called
reforms to go in a capitalist direction? If these ideas had a revolutionary
character, as some claim, why have they received the unanimous and
fervent support of the leaders of imperialism?

Never in history would a truly revolutionary idea have received the
enthusiastic support of the most powerful, aggressive and voracious empire
humanity has known . . .

In practice, all of the above can be reduced to a single word, at least by
those accustomed to sifting his speeches for their true meaning as a
clairvoyant gazes into tea-leaves. And that word is not one to bring
comfort to the hearts of many Cubans: belt-tightening.

Belt-tightening! The belts already seemed tight enough to me.
Walking through the streets of Old Havana I came across a notice which
signified how few notches there were to go. It informed the inhabitants

of the city block to which it was affixed how they should apply for beer which, like everything else, was in desperately short supply. It was available only for weddings and the fifteenth birthday celebrations of daughters, one bottle per guest; the applicant should present his residence certificate, his marriage or birth certificate, and various other documents, to the appropriate official. Even a visit to a ministry was called for.

Of course, turning the purchase of beer into a complex bureaucratic procedure has its political advantages. It infantilises people, makes them beholden to an authority which they dare not offend for fear of losing small priviliges. To humiliate people in this way makes them docile, apathetic – at least for a time, until collectively they lose their temper. An economy of shortages is better suited to the purposes of totalitarianism than one of abundance. Perpetual queueing for the bare necessities of life is the best guarantee against subversion.

What else does one see walking through Havana? Nothing can equal the melancholy beauty of the Malecón, the magnificent road that sweeps along beside the sea. On one side the deep blue waves crash against the low sea wall, forming a fine white spume; on the other, grand buildings crumble slowly into dust. I peered into these vestiges of former prosperity: their marble halls are now partitioned into living spaces by plywood, so many square metres per family unit. The entrances to the buildings are dark and neglected; great cracks have appeared in the walls, the paint has turned black, the plaster has flaked away, the marble is chipped, the wood rotten. The buildings belong to everyone: that is to say, to no one.

It is admitted officially that half the population of Havana (that is, a tenth of the population of Cuba) lives in substandard housing. And standards are not high.

At one end of the Malecón, which was made for pleasure but is now deserted except for a few idlers who move in and out of shadows with saurian lethargy, there are still some advertisements left over from prerevolutionary days, for movies – Vivien Leigh and David Niven – and for soft drinks. A single painted sign for Coca Cola adorns the walls on the corner of the Calle Cárcel. I wondered whether these signs remained by oversight or policy. Throughout the city one finds the names of corporations that once had businesses in Cuba: Westinghouse, National City Bank, Philips, Western Union. Even where the metal lettering has been removed from their former offices, the names have remained visibly imprinted on the concrete or the stone below, like an ineradicable scar. One day, one suspects, these businesses or their successors will reclaim their property.

The streets of Havana were utterly bereft of commercial activity. Occasionally a queue would form and ice-cream was for sale – any colour you liked, so long as it was white. The only itinerant salesmen were hawking newspapers, principally *Granma*, the official organ of the Central Committee of the Party which, despite its somewhat eccentric title, sets new standards in journalistic tedium. (The headlines on my first two days in Cuba were: *The Future, the Economy and the Health of the Country Depend on Science*, and, the following day, *At This Moment Science Can Become a Decisive Factor for the Country*.) Also on sale were the trade union newspaper *Trabajadores* (Workers), the official organ of the Revolutionary Armed Forces, *Bastion*, and *Juventud Rebelde* (Rebel Youth), a title stunning in its mendacity, since it competes with the other newspapers only in the abjectness of its sycophancy and comformity to the government line of the moment.

Such shops as there were possessed little stock; they were called only by the products they sold, or would have sold had there been any: Shoes, Fish, Stationery. Clothes shops had dummies from the fifties in their dusty windows, wearing the drabbest garments imaginable. Once more I found this extinction of the aesthetic impulse profoundly depressing.

To compensate for the lack of goods there was a wealth of exhortatory slogans. Noticeboards on every block reminded people of an organisation called SUERC – *El Sistema Único de la Exploración de la Republica de Cuba*. Despite its name, this is an organisation devoted not to geographical research but to civil defence, counter-espionage and internal repression. One reports to SUERC if one has encountered an earthquake, a volcanic eruption, or a neighbour carrying a suspicious parcel. The officers of SUERC are ready to receive denunciations at any time of the day or night. It must be admitted, however, that the notices concerning SUERC are faded and do not carry conviction, rather like those next to them extolling Che Guevara and his ideas.

Fidel, of course, is frequently quoted on walls:

There is no type of force, either internal or external, and no difficulty objective or subjective, that will be able to prevent our victorious and definitive march to the future.

The same, I suppose, can be said for us all, until a physicist invents a method for halting time's arrow.

But Fidel, Maximum Leader as he may be, is not quoted nearly so much as the *Heroe Nacional*, the National Hero, a title bestowed on José Martí, poet, journalist, intriguer, founder of the *Partido Cubano Revolucionario* and, best of all from the point of view of his reputation, martyr in the cause of Cuban independence from Spain. He wrote so prolifically until his death in 1895 that Cuban politicians of every stripe mine his works to prove that they are more *martiano* than the next man. A bust of Martí stands before every school in Cuba, next to the flag; innumerable streets and squares have been named after him: there is an institute devoted to the study of his life and works, or rather to proving that the present government stands in apostolic succession to him; stores otherwise denuded of goods have an endless supply of miniature busts of him; every bookshop has his complete works, as well as anthologies and booklets by him; his words are everywhere; one soon grows sick of him, or of the use to which he is put.

Indeed, one rapidly falls prey to an ambition to throw stones at every icon of the National Hero that one sees – a dangerous proceeding, for in Cuba it would be considered akin to blasphemy. Coming as I did from a society that derides political idolatry, the cult of Martí seemed to me alternately absurd and sinister. The Argentinian writer Alberdi wrote: 'The War of Independence endowed us with a ridiculous and disgraceful mania for the heroic.' This is even more true of Cuba than of Argentina. How I came to hate those little quotations everywhere: *To create is to be victorious* in the post office, where the clerks behind the counter moved resentfully as though struggling through glue; *Men come in two types, those who love and construct and those who hate and destroy* on the crumbling walls of delapidated buildings; *Art is life itself, art knows nothing of death* in the entrance to an art gallery so little visited that it had the atmosphere of a morgue.

Poor Martí, to be used thus! He really was a poet, he really was a hero (he was sentenced to hard labour at sixteen), and yet the visitor to Cuba soon begins to feel as a force-fed *foie gras* goose must feel. The cult would be funny if its intent were not so manifestly to preclude rational thought and to keep minds in thrall to a few slogans and visceral emotions. When I returned to Havana from my tour of the island I stayed at the Hotel Inglaterra, a splendidly restored grand hotel in whose brilliantly tiled dining room the great poet Rubén Darío once dined. In the square before the hotel, among the palm trees, stood a statue of the National Hero. On the 137th anniversary of his birth in 1853 I watched children of five and six lay wreaths at the statue; some of them had been coached to make piping, grandiloquent speeches at the Hero's feet while others stood to attention beside him, bursting with pride that they had been thus selected. I could not long bear to watch or listen. It seemed to me that to foster ardent nationalism, which always involves both self-adulation and hatred of others, in minds so young, at the behest of a far from disinterested government, was nothing short of criminal. The children were well fed and clothed, as all children are in Cuba; their faces were full of innocent happiness, and their minds were being filled with convenient hatred.

Meanwhile, facing the statue, a platform was being erected for a *fiesta* the following day. And in the colonnade next to the hotel, students were painting a vast hoarding, some twenty feet high and fifty long, to adorn the building. It quoted the National Hero himself: 'My sling is that of David.' There are no doubts in Cuba about who is the local Goliath. The same day, the newspaper of the armed forces, *Bastion*, carried Martí's words in bold print:

> Two useful truths for Our America: the crude, unequal and decadent character of the United States, and the continued existence there of all the violence, discord, immorality and disorder of which the Spanish American people are accused.

Actually, Martí's attitude to the Colossus of the North was considerably more nuanced than the above would suggest. He was too intelligent to suppose that the most vigorous and powerful country in the world (as it was even then) could be nothing but a sink of iniquity. But that is how it is now presented, *ad nauseam*, to the Cuban people.

The propaganda takes full advantage of the Latin American tradition of contrasting the material success but spiritual vacuity of *Their* (Anglo-Saxon) America with the material failure but spiritual grandeur of *Our* (Hispanic) America. This contrast is, of course, a common and comforting response by impotence to power, by backwardness to modernity. The Russians responded thus to western Europe; the Muslims to Christendom; and western Europe to America. But when such a response becomes part of an official and unquestionable philosophy, it does great harm, for it prevents proper enquiry as to the sources of power and powerlessness, and promotes instead an attitude both of resentment and self-congratulation, which is emotionally gratifying but worse than useless for stimulating practical improvement.

By the time I left Cuba I was tired of hearing about the crime, unemployment and drug addiction in the United States: never had I been so pro-American. My feeling was reinforced when I visited the Galería Centro Provincial de Arte, to see an exhibition of portraits of Martí by contemporary painters to celebrate his 137th birthday. The artists possessed more visual flair than in any other communist country I had visited, but this only made the intellectual content the more pitiful. One portrait was entitled *Profecía en America*, Prophecy in America, and it was a map with a picture of Martí growing out of the island of Cuba. South of the Río Grande all was verdant, happy jungle, punctuated by pretty little whitewashed and tiled villages, full of dancing villagers; north of the Río Grande, the land flared with the orange flames of Hell, over which flew an evil black bird of prey with the Stars and Stripes in its beak. I should have been less disturbed by this nonsense if the painter had been without talent: but talent in the service of centrally ordained lies is a terrible thing.

Worse still than this dishonesty was a small pen and ink drawing of the Hero attached to words allegedly written in her school exercise book by a ten-year-old child who, in the way that young girls in other parts of the world have visions of the Virgin, apparently heard Martí speaking:

> . . . he was very happy and satisfied with what was happening in his country over the process of rectification and on the campaign to make more with less and over the response that our people have given to the world crisis of socialism, and he sent a greeting to all Cuban revolutionaries and especially to our commander in chief and finally he said socialism or death and that we should remain firm. That's what he said.

On the night of the *fiesta* a small crowd gathered in the plaza and a rock band set itself up on the platform. The glittering foyer of the Hotel Inglaterra filled with more plain-clothes policemen than usual (there were always *some* around), to prevent unauthorised Cubans from entering that paradise. Walkie-talkie in hand, they demanded to see identification papers before letting anyone through. The newspaper had announced the day before that, to celebrate the revolutionary disappearance of all distinction between police and people in Cuba, many of the former would mingle joyfully with the latter at the *fiesta*.

From my balcony overlooking the plaza, I watched the arrival of a torchlit procession. At first I thought it was vast, half the population of Havana, but it turned out to be quite small, at most a few thousand people. As they arrived, floodlit streams of paper were released from the buildings surrounding the plaza, each little rectangle of paper printed with a slogan: *I am an anti-imperialist, I am 100% Cuban, I am David.* From the balcony next to mine, cameramen from *Tele Rebelde* filmed the scene.

I went down among the crowd. The torchlit procession had been greeted with a buzz of expectation, but it had died down by the time I reached the plaza and a strange indifference reigned. The music was loud and inescapable, but people had turned their backs on it. Some sat around the bases of palm trees, quietly chatting among themselves; others stared into the blackness beyond the floodlights. Yet others drifted away from the plaza down the Prado, where some of the residents were on their balconies, dancing to their own music. All along the Prado were stone benches; and there, night after tropical night, the local people sat, waiting patiently for time to pass. The night of the *fiesta* was no different for them.

The political speeches began. What they lacked in originality, they made up in emphasis. It was clear that there was a claque of enthusiasts near the platform, whose *Vivas!* were caught by the microphones and magnified into a simulacrum of popular enthusiasm. In the suburbs of the crowd, however, boredom was all too evident. They did not applaud, they did not echo the slogans, I suspect they did not even *hear* the speeches.

I had been asked by the *Daily Telegraph* to write one of a series of short articles about secondhand bookshops. I was given £25 to buy three books, which I was to review in 250 words. I thought it would be interesting to find such a bookshop in Havana.

On the corner of the *calles* Obispo and Bernaza I found the Librería Cervantes. Its stock was not large, and that part of it which did not consist of somewhat dated textbooks of technical subjects was divided into two main categories: books in English left over from the library of the pre- and no doubt anti-revolutionary Havana Women's Club and slightly soiled political paperbacks in Spanish from the Castro era. Among the latter were some volumes that will one day, perhaps, become collector's items, though most of them were still available as new books, at no extra cost, in the Nueva Poesía (New Poetry) bookshop across the road: *The Memoirs of Leonid Brezhnev, The Speeches of Konstantin Chernenko, The Speeches of Todor Zhivkov.* There was also an anthology, _Bulgarian Journalists on the Path of Leninism_, and a special study of the development of an exemplar of the New Man, _El joven Erich_, the Young Erich, Erich being Honecker, of course. Most touching of all was a children's book, _Felix significa feliz_, Felix Means Happy, Felix being none other than Dzherzhinsky, the first chief of the Soviet secret police, of whom the Poles ask why he was the greatest Pole who ever lived, to which the answer is that he killed more Russians than any other. A nice bedtime story for children.

The volumes from the Women's Club filled me with a different kind of gloom. First they had suffered the physical deterioration that books generally suffer in the tropics, unless especially cared for: mould in the bindings and the nibbling of creatures from several phyla, from arthropods to reptiles and mammals, and the deposition of squashed and mummified insects and the excrement of geckos, leaving dark brown stains upon the pages. Second, they were either impossibly earnest, the diversion of embittered wives with intellectual aspirations –_The Comparative Archaeology of Early Mesopotamia_ – or they sank to the level of magazine gossip – _Group Captain Peter Townsend, the Real Story_. Somewhat incongruously, I discovered among them a Soviet manual of boxing, which, like the two previous books, I declined to review. After much thought, I alighted on three books, which cost in total $3.60 or 60 cents, depending on whether one converted at the official or black market rate of exchange.

Of the books in Spanish I chose _Guantanamo Bay_, by Rigoberto Cruz Diaz. This was a series of interviews by the author with people from a village, Caimanera, near the United States naval base, in which they recounted their experiences of life before the revolution. Naturally, they had not a good word to say for the Americans (or if they had, it was edited out), whom they sometimes described as animals, and whose language they derided as being no more than the roaring or barking of beasts. Indeed, the hatred was so intemperate, with so many racial slurs, that I doubt such a volume could have been published in the liberal democracies that proclaim the virtues of freedom of speech. Many of the interviewed were formerly prostitutes, saved from vice by the revolution. I should have found the indignation over prostitution more convincing had I not been approached quite so many times in Old Havana by young men who knew a young _morena_ who was willing . . . if I bought the young men a pair of shoes at the foreign currency shop. This, I thought, was an even less dignified transaction than prostitution normally is, insofar as it implied an insult to the national currency.

Of the books from the Women's Club, I selected *The Great Mistake* by John Knox and *The Battle of Basinghall Street* by E. Phillips Oppenheim. The great mistake was Herbert Hoover, exposed by the author in 1930 – too late. E. Phillips Oppenheim is a name known to all habitués of cheap secondhand bookshops. He was once the most popular of English novelists, the Jeffrey Archer of his day. Published in 1935, *The Battle of Basinghall Street* concerns the struggle between Lord Marsom, a clever, ruthless Jewish financier who is chairman of Woolito Limited (Woolito being a patented synthetic wool of gorgeous colour), and Lord Sandbrook, a handsome English aristocrat who rides well and spends his time attending the social events of the season. The struggle between sordid commercial professionalism and languid aristocratic amateurishness is unequal: amateurishness wins all the way.

I detected a strange convergence between the values expressed in this fictional pabulum and those of Fidel Castro and Che Guevara. Like Lord Sandbrook, they had never earnt their living in any conventional way; they disdained to do it. Like Lord Sandbrook, their approach to life was moralising and aesthetic. If people had to work, it should not be for personal gain, for filthy lucre, but only for beauty or justice. Commerce was sordid, untouchable, defiling. Lord Sandbrook, indeed, was a Man of the New Type, whose thoughts never descended to securing personal advantage. And like Lord Sandbrook, Castro and Che were aristocrats: from the first moment of their self-consciousness they knew they were not as other men were, they would not melt anonymously into no crowd, their destinies were great. It was the middle classes they hated, despised and feared.

Che, the perfect gentle knight of socialism, exemplifies more clearly than almost any other twentieth century revolutionary the unstable alloy of abnegation and arrogance that is the hallmark of the breed. The son of a freewheeling Argentine businessman with radical political ideas and a mother who espoused Marxism early, his childhood was unconventional. He was encouraged to roam and find his own way in the world. His severe asthma soon put iron in his soul: becoming a sportsman against considerable odds, he learnt the value of willpower. He succeeded academically despite the irregularities of his upbringing.

After qualifying as a doctor, he wandered throughout Latin America, seeing and experiencing for himself the hardships of the majority of the people. He met Castro for the first time in 1955, parting from him ten years later, by which time he had become a world figure. He gave up his high positions in the revolutionary government to resume the life of a guerrilla, and he died – wretchedly – in the Bolivian jungles in 1967, attempting to bring to Bolivia what he had helped bring to Cuba.

No one has ever suggested that Guevara pursued his idiosyncratic course in life for personal gain – as personal gain is usually understood. He did not die a rich man, nor did he live a life of opulence once he reached power (even though the simple food he favoured – steak, lettuce and tomato salad, Spanish cognac – has been rendered luxurious by the economic system he created). He dressed simply, too, and worked extremely hard; he was by all accounts rather shy in personal relations. None of this prevented him from having an ego of immeasurable proportions. His opinions, which he formed very early in his life and upon which he acted, were of quite staggering arrogance.

In his arrogance he was a true follower of Marx and Lenin. He considered that until Lenin's revolution in Russia, men had never acted fully consciously, were still in the realm of prehistory, and were not therefore to be considered human in the full sense.

> With revolution of October 1917 . . . man acquired a new consciousness. The men of the French revolution, who told humanity so many beautiful things . . . were nevertheless simple instruments of history.

Until Fidel and Che came along, with their superior, indeed total, understanding, Cubans were but the blind and unconscious instruments of history, mere feathers on the wind of economic circumstance. Their ideas, their aspirations, their likes and dislikes were the automatic reflection of the (rotten) society in which they lived.

Consequently, according to Guevara, the New Man had to be built – yes, *built*, a word he used many times in this connection. 'A socialist economy without communist morals does not interest me,' Guevara once said, revealing in that short sentence the depth of his lust for power. '. . . One of the fundamental aims of Marxism is to eliminate material interest, the factor of "individual self-interest" and profit from man's psychological motivations.' He might have added, 'The world must become like me.'

He was not, however, being unorthodox from a Marxist perspective. In *The German Ideology*, Marx and Engels wrote:

> Both for the production on a mass scale of this communist consciousness, and for the success of the cause itself, the alteration of men on a mass scale is

necessary . . . not only because the ruling class cannot be overthrown in any other way, but also because the class overthrowing it can only in a revolution succeed in ridding itself of all the muck of ages and become fitted to found society anew.

You, reader, your children, your parents, your friends, virtually everyone you know or have ever met, I, the author of this book, are full of the muck of ages, muck from which we must be liberated – by force, of course – before we achieve true humanity. Not Mozart or Michaelangelo, not Shakespeare or Dickens, not Galileo or Pasteur, achieved this grandeur: only Che and Fidel, Stalin and Vyshinsky, Ulbricht and Ceausescu. What respect for human rights might one expect from anyone who believed such a thing?

But Guevara was capable of believing nonsense even more arrant, the kind of nonsense to which only intelligent people can give their assent, since it requires a vast and intricate intellectual edifice to do so. To him, Marx's description of the world after the revolution was as real as Father Christmas to a credulous child:

In a higher phase of communist society – wrote Marx – when the enslaving subordination of the individual to the division of labour, and therewith also the antithesis between mental and physical labour, has vanished; when labour has become not only a means of keeping alive but has itself become a vital need; when the productive forces have also increased with the all-round development of the individual, and all the springs of co-operative wealth flow more abundantly . . .

I repeat, one queues for an hour to buy an ice cream in Havana in the evening.

Guevara hated the market with a passionate hatred. In part, this could be ascribed to the poverty and misery he saw on his wanderings through South America which, not surprisingly, he ascribed to the reigning economic system. But the real wellsprings of his hatred were quite other: an infinite distrust of human beings as they are (covered up by strenuous protestations of faith in their glorious future), and an insensate urge to control the lives of others. He detested the possibility – no, the certainty – that, given a choice, people would fail to choose what he considered 'socially rational', that they might prefer marzipan pigs to a balanced diet, beer and football to vitamins and higher mathematics. Democracy had for him no connection with choice; he saw nothing democratic about the marketplace. And, alleged deep thinker and theoretician as his admirers would have us believe him, it never occurred to him that his ideal of a fully computerised, centralised economy with only a handful of bureaucrats to run it was a blueprint for the most abject and unreformable of dictatorships – or if it did occur to him, he did not mind, since he was going to be the dictator in question.

Both Guevara and Castro were adolescents denied the opportunity to mature by their early success against a corrupt and brutal dictatorship, a success which fixated their personalities once and for all. Surrounded thereafter by admirers and sycophants, they never had to learn that the world was bigger even than their egos.

But the market, like the whirligig of time, brings in its revenges. I am not thinking of the markets I saw in provincial towns in Cuba – more wretched, less lively, than any I have seen anywhere else in the world except in famine conditions, selling only cabbages with blackened leaves or a few tiny carrots or spring onions, for the sake of which people were obliged to jostle and push as though fleeing before an advancing plague. No, I am thinking rather of the foreign currency shops, whose role in Cuban life belies their calm and hidden exteriors. Many were the Cubans who asked me to buy something for them in these stores, usually entrusting me with their few crumpled dollars which they have stashed away against the day they find a foreigner willing to make illegal purchases for them. For they are not allowed themselves to enter these temples of delight, lest they be corrupted by what they see there, nor are they allowed to possess dollars in the first place: possessing dollars in Cuba is like possessing cocaine in Miami, normal but forbidden.

'Do not buy anything with a Cuban label,' they say with an urgency worthy of true revolutionaries. 'Make sure what you buy is foreign. Spend everything, every dollar, every cent.'

The foreign currency stores are found in the hotels where foreigners stay, and at certain other locations. They advertise themselves as offering 'easy shopping'; otherwise, shopping in Cuba is an activity fraught with difficulties and bureaucratic complications. Cubans dare not approach such stores in the company of foreigners: they are always under close surveillance by secret police. One parts company from Cubans at some distance from their doors; even taxis (other than the special, dollar-charging ones for tourists) dare not approach the hotels.

Focus as they are for so much longing, these stores are disorganised and ill-stocked, their staff indifferent and their goods not infrequently shop-soiled. The clothes are imported from Panama, and of such poor quality that no European or Canadian tourist would buy them for themselves. It is obvious that they are intended for diversion on to the home market, to satisfy a demand that otherwise could not be met, and to mop up the dollars that find their way into private hands. And since such trade is illegal, it also has the advantage of giving the police an instrument of blackmail, as in Romania: for almost everyone in Cuba, at least in the towns, has taken advantage of the trade and wears at least one item of imported clothing.

Cuba's relations with Panama were somewhat murky. The American invasion in 1989 to depose General Noriega had brought forth a rash of posters, already fading or peeling from the walls: Yankee Claws Off Panama! and Panama, We Are With You. The flow of cheap consumer goods had been interrupted, temporarily at least. And Castro had found himself in the uncomfortable position of defending a man who was an acknowledged CIA agent and a drug-trafficking thug, on the principle that my enemy's enemy is my friend.

Perhaps there was more to it than that. Rumours were rife that Castro was deeply implicated in Noriega's drug dealings. In 1989, General Ochoa, the commander-in-chief of the Cuban forces in Angola and hitherto a national hero, was shot after a summary military trial for having allowed Cuba to be used as a staging post for cocaine *en route* for Florida. Castro protested his innocence, of course, but the episode came as a shock and few people seemed to believe the official version. At the very least they believed Castro knew more about Ochoa's activities than he admitted. 'After all,' said a young man to me, 'he knows about everything else that goes on in Cuba. How did he not know about Ochoa?'

I heard another rumour from a man who claimed to have been a member of the revolutionary army in Escambray and once to have met Castro personally. In the early days he had believed Castro's promises – Castro spoke then with what seemed like burning sincerity – but he had long since realised that the Maximum Leader's most important characteristic was a pathological inability to tell the truth (so convinced was he of this that I had great difficulty in persuading him that some of what Castro said about the rest of Latin America – that there was hunger and poverty there, for instance – was indeed the truth). Ochoa, he said, had been a popular commander, and therefore the Castros, Raúl and Fidel, feared him. And the economy of Cuba was in such a mess that a military coup seemed the only answer. Therefore, to discredit Ochoa and to give them the excuse to rid themselves of him, they ordered him to start drug-running operations. It was a trap: they had him tried and shot.

There was no good evidence in favour of his interpretation of events, though given Castro's long history of violent political intrigue it did not seem to me intrinsically impossible; my informant spoke as we drove past the huge Boniato prison, on whose sinister barracks we looked down from the hills outside Santiago de Cuba (Castro was held prisoner there for two and a half months when he was captured after the attack on the Moncada barracks, but the experience did not make him any less inclined to imprison others). My companion claimed to have been an inmate of Boniato in which 5000 prisoners, mainly political, were held, in conditions that defied description. I asked him whether he had read Armando Valladares's book (I can't imagine how I thought he would have got hold of a copy in Cuba). He had not read it, but he said that every detail in it was true. This struck me as a rather cavalier attitude to truth, but hatred is not the midwife of caution or accuracy. Several times he lifted the bottom of his trouser leg to show me he had no socks. No socks! Even under Batista there had been socks!

In Cienfuegos, a port city the stucco of whose once grandiloquent buildings was crumbling like the icing of a stale Christmas cake, I met on a Saturday morning three young black carpenters. They were sitting on the pavement with their feet in the gutter; they had nothing to do and when I said I was on my way to Playa Giron, the scene of the defeat of the Cuban counter-revolutionary expedition of 1961, they asked to come with me.

It is a delight to drive in Cuba because, as in all communist countries, there is no traffic. The roads in the cities are less busy than those of the countryside in Europe. Outside the cities, the roads are empty, except for very occasional lumbering fifties American saloons, bright red or sky blue, with enormous tail fins and acres of chromium plating, or Soviet-made trucks whose gears seem permanently clashing. Effectively, there is no speed limit: the warm air rushes in at the open window and the *salsa* music from the radio urges the foot to press down on the accelerator. What joy – hard currency joy!

I asked the three carpenters why they wanted to go to Playa Giron. They didn't, particularly; there was nothing for them to do there, they said, there was no easy means of returning home to Cienfuegos, and the journey was not without its dangers from the police. But they were tired of the pavement and gutter where they spent most of their leisure time; a journey to nowhere was preferable. A metaphor for life in general, I asked myself? Certainly I was glad there was so much wrong with the world to write about, or else I should have had to face the essential meaninglessness of existence.

I turned to *Radio Martí*, the anti-Castro station beamed from Florida and paid for by the US government. It was sometimes said that the adoption of Martí's name was what really infuriated the Cuban government about it. I do not believe it. The Cuban government – that is to say, Castro – is infuriated by any contradiction, especially from a source that cannot be silenced. But on the south side of the island, coming through the electromagnetic equivalent of a fog, *Radio Martí* was indistinct. I asked my companions whether they ever listened to it.

'Sometimes,' they said, with no very great enthusiasm.

And did they want one day to visit the United States?

To my surprise they said no; there was too much crime there, too much racial feeling, too much violence. France was their beacon, their acme of civilisation.

Their answer impressed me. Though not highly educated – perhaps *because* they were not highly educated – they had retained their independence of mind and had formed their own judgment of things. Knowing most of what they were told to be lies, they had not come to the easy and obvious conclusion that the exact opposite must be the truth. Only one of them had ever been to Havana, none had been as far away as Santiago. Their opinions were the result of slight information and common sense reflection, but were not therefore shallow. They were not socialists, yet they knew the reintroduction of capitalism in Cuba would not be without its problems, and that such as they might suffer from it. I do not think I could easily have had a similar conversation with three young carpenters in England or the United States.

They were disaffected, but not violently so. They did not like the Castros – especially the *General del Ejército*, General of the Army, Raúl Castro – but their detestation fell far short of that excited by Ceausescu in Romania. Like everyone else, they assumed *los dirigentes* – the leaders, the bureaucrats, the generals – were living off the fat of the land, eating not beans and rice but lobster mayonnaise. And they were fully conversant with some of the less attractive aspects of the dictatorship of the proletariat, as Castro is pleased to call his rule. For example, whenever they held parties the police would arrive at midnight to break them up, using truncheons and even dogs. They were subjected to arbitrary police checks; and as for elections, they were simply non-existent in Cuba. They spoke of the absence of elections with a bitterness I found surprising, considering how often in Cuban history elections had been fraudulent: but even fraudulent elections of the old type were an acknowledgement of what should happen, a bow in the direction of popular sovereignty – and furthermore a diversion from the daily round, a factor not to be underestimated where boredom is as crushing as in Cuba.

We reached Playa Giron, near the Bay of Pigs. The coastline was flat, the bush dense with shrubs that thrived in saline soil. The settlement itself consisted of neat cabins and a large hotel. Well before we reached the hotel, where I intended to have lunch, my three companions asked me to set them down. They were not allowed inside even if I were prepared to pay for their meal in dollars. The policemen at the door of the hotel would prevent any infringement of the rules. My companions said they would wait for me a few hundred yards away, in shadows. Before alighting from the car, they looked around to check that no one was watching.

To my surprise, the hotel was full of Cubans, who paid in otherwise valueless *pesos*. On a platform by the swimming pool were four leggy blacks in swimsuits, performing what was obviously supposed to be a folk dance to the beat of a drum. Their expressions were eloquent of a boredom more profound, transcendental, than that of a schoolboy parsing Latin words. They performed the dance perfunctorily, as though it had been laid down in a five year plan. No one watched them, there was no applause between dances.

In the dining hall there was a buffet, spread with delicacies such as tinned fish, lettuce and tomatoes. Here was luxury! I did not enjoy it, however, because of my three companions who were waiting for me outside, segregated from the vanguard of the proletariat within.

Before leaving Playa Giron, I decided to visit the commemorative museum there. Outside was a Sea Fury, a naval aircraft of British manufacture that blew up the *Río Escondido*, the invaders' main supply ship, and thus played an important part in their defeat. My companions did not want to come to the museum, either because they were bored with the whole story, which they had already heard time out of number, or because it was not safe to be seen in my company. At any rate, I was the only visitor to the museum that afternoon.

Cuban museums are like speeches by Castro: over-inclusive, rhetorical, self-justifying. Concision, evidently, is not a Cuban gift, even when it comes to selecting photographs. Nevertheless, the small possessions of those who died in the fighting (on the revolution's side) were eloquent testimony to bravery and belief. The cause of the counter-revolutionaries was not noble; some of the participants were extremely unsavoury, psychopathic murderers from Batista's time, who were to be given the task in the new government of dealing with the opposition. Those who claim to fight for freedom are not infrequently fighting for power, which is a rather different matter.

It was during the Bay of Pigs invasion that Castro first announced that the revolution was socialist. 'This is the Socialist and Democratic Revolution,' he said, 'of the humble, with the humble, for the humble . . .'

My three carpenters were waiting for me, but they gave no sign of recognising me. Before they got into the car they checked again that no one was looking. We were on our way to Playa Larga, from which it would be even more difficult for them to return, and where there was nothing for them to do. Boredom, however, has its imperatives, and they came.

The coast was unspoilt, not much different from when Columbus landed, except for the road. There is definitely something to be said against economic development and mass tourism. All thoughts of primeval innocence were dispelled, however, as we reached Playa Larga. A policeman on a motorcycle stopped us and spoke sharply to the three carpenters. Where were they going, why were they with me? They mumbled something about a lift and the policeman looked at me, the naive tourist, debating whether to carry the matter further. Deciding against doing so, he bestowed a last hostile glare on the three traitors and rode away on his motorcycle. As soon as he was out of sight, the three young carpenters scurried off into the bush and I did not see them again.

Playa Larga is little more than a hotel on a long, tranquil tropical beach. Tourism is the great white hope of the Cuban economy, for Cuba has an equable climate, a beautiful coast, historical monuments of great interest, and an agreeable people. Indeed, there are very few economic hopes beside: its agriculture is as dominated by sugar, a crop without an export future except to countries that cannot pay for it, as ever it was, and its industry is inefficient and likely to remain so. In short, Cuba faces the inherent problems which can only be overcome by agile pragmatism, not adolescent dogmatism. Dogmatism, however, claims to settle all problems in advance, and is therefore more attractive to egocentric young intellectuals than is slow and piecemeal improvement.

Tourism, of course, would destroy the very beauty it intended to exploit. There is a coastline west of Santiago, where the Sierra Maestra comes down to the sea, of such stunning beauty – long, deserted black sand beaches, palm fringed shores, and an azure sea – that only communism could have preserved it from the tombstone slab hotels that ruin coasts the world over. But preservation from ruination is not a positive achievement of regimes such as Castro's, the result of solicitude for the glories of nature. On the contrary, there is no pollution in the world like communist pollution; there are factories in the communist world that seem to produce nothing else. The very iconography of communism extols pollution: splendid landscapes never appear in its posters without a factory belching smoke in the background, smoke itself having become a symbol of progress.

There *is* tourism in Cuba, however, and very unattractive it is. I spent a night in a resort a few miles from Cienfuegos, where parties of holidaymakers from Canada stayed. They had come to Cuba for the sea, the sun and the sand. They were not interested in the country itself, and it did not worry them that they were carefully segregated from Cuban reality, that there were policemen at the door of their hotel to ensure it did not enter. On the contrary, they were too busy escaping their own reality to be concerned with anyone else's. And who could blame them? Not I, who had almost forgotten the rigours of routine, whose work consisted of doing whatever caught my interest.

But still I found Cuban tourism disturbing, as I had once found Haitian tourism disturbing. It was not just that many of the tourists appeared like beached whales, or that ladies who would have been regarded as plump even by Rubens squeezed their puckered, ageing flesh into exiguous lime-green vests and tight lemon yellow shorts (after all, had they not a right to do so if they so chose?) Rather it was that I sensed a hysteria in their laughter, as if they were laughing not because something was funny, but to persuade themselves and others that they were enjoying themselves. And as they gathered in the bar and restaurant, their Cuban guides, exuding *bonhomie* as gigolos exude charm, moved among them explaining what was on the programme for tomorrow, and what entertainments there were for the rest of this evening, as though to leave them for a moment to their own devices were to court disaster. They had to be kept amused, like children, not only for their own sakes, but also to prevent them from developing any idle curiosity about Cuba.

Tourism is unlikely to develop in Cuba, however, while waiters treat customers as class enemies and the food is so wretched. As in most communist countries, waiters are kings, they can give or withhold, permit or deny; their jobs are amongst the most desirable in the land, for they work where sometimes there are onions and tomatoes. These aristocrats of the lettuce leaf, however, find it difficult to enter imaginitively into the world of their foreign clients, where waiters are not demigods or tyrants of the tables, but ordinary men and women doing a job of no extraordinary status. And one day, if ever tourism is to develop in Cuba, receptionists, shop assistants, porters, waiters and the rest will have to lose that extraordinary habit of theirs, common to their brothers and sisters in Eastern Europe, of ignoring someone even though he is right in front of their face and there is nobody else in sight and they have nothing whatever to do. This disregard is not just discourtesy such as may be encountered in almost any society; rather, the rudeness is ontological, it speaks of a hatred of the world as it is. In private life perhaps they are charming, passionate lovers, devoted parents, reciters of lyric verse; but the face they turn to the world is of granite chilled by cold winds.

At Playa Larga there was a power cut just as I was about to order a drink (no beer, only rum, take it or leave it). The barman closed the bar with indecent haste. He guessed, I suppose, there was to be no more power that night; and though I am certain this power cut was not the first the hotel had ever suffered, there were neither candles nor oil lamps to subsitute for electricity. Even in Zairean villages in the jungle I had found candles.

I visited several more of the holy places of the revolution (I never found a church open in Cuba, but I was told that the Cubans were the least Catholic of Latin American nations, even before the revolution). The tiny hamlet of La Plata was the site of the first successful military action by the July 26th Movement – so called after the date of Castro's quixotic attack on the barracks in Santiago. La Plata is on the fringes of the Sierra Maestra. On the way there, I noticed a propaganda hoarding that obviously had long remained unfinished. The slogan read: *Sólo trabajando y* – Only by working and . . . And what? Only by working and by struggling against the imperialists can we complete this hoarding, perhaps?

One day in 1957, Castro's men descended on La Plata's little garrison of sixteen soldiers and killed several of them (Che Guevara's account is a little vague on this point). Unimportant in itself from a purely military point of view, the Battle of La Plata – in Latin America, clashes between sixteen men on the one hand and twelve on the other are frequently dignified as 'battles' – announced to the world that the rebels were still alive after Batista had pronounced them dead and increased their morale. They also doubled their supply of ammunition and two of the captured soldiers joined their little army. Later, after taking power, Castro returned there to sign a land reform decree, thus demonstrating his flair for publicity.

At La Plata there is a little museum. I had seen most of the photographs it contained several times before (indeed, *ad nauseam*), but with the mountains of the Sierra Maestra looming up behind, the pictures of Castro and his few followers took on a new meaning. One cannot deny grandeur to a man who, giving up the chance of a luxurious life and a successful conventional career, took to the hills and an existence of the utmost discomfort, to say nothing of danger, with little to propel him but his faith in his own future.

Beyond La Plata we reached a settlement along a dusty, uneven road (I was with a Cuban who had bribed his boss at his place of work to mark him down as present while he spent the day with me). We were lost and asked the way back to La Plata of an old peasant who was sitting by his hut, round which a small black pig rooted and chickens pecked for sustenance. Apart from the fact that there was now an electricity line to his hut, I doubted whether much had changed for him in the two or three decades. His wife, bent by age and toil, brought us low, rough-hewn chairs to sit on with the simple courtesy typical of peasants. They apologised for having nothing to give us.

It emerged that the old man had been one of the first to aid the rebels. (Was this, though, not a claim that everyone in the district might think it prudent to make?) He remembered Castro then, a simple man who spoke clearly. The peasant was shrivelled, almost desiccated, but he had never been tall, and I wondered whether Castro's height – more than six feet – had not impressed him almost as much as his words. At any rate, some of the peasants gave him and his followers food and information about the movement of the *rurales*, the brutal armed force in the pocket of the landowners. This was a dangerous thing to do, and a brave one since victory was by no means certain; and once the *rurales* suspected the old man was on the rebels' side, he had had to flee into the mountains.

He spoke of the past with neither bitterness nor enthusiasm. What had happened had happened. He did not say whether it was for the good or the bad: perhaps the habitually powerless eventually cease to think in moral categories. In any case, he had lived all his life in conditions in which to express an opinion was dangerous, possibly deadly, and one does not lose the caution of a lifetime just because a stranger comes along and would like to ask a few questions. But when my companion offered to buy his pig, he refused very firmly indeed. What value was money to him, what could he buy with it? The answer, of course, was nothing: he was living in a demonetarised society. There was a drought, there was no seed to plant, no fertiliser, he said. The pig was all he had. Things were bad. Again, he blamed no one – disaster was like the weather, unavoidable.

My companion asked him about Castro. Had he ever returned to vist his former helpers in the Sierra? No, the old man replied; obviously he was too busy as president. But he had once seen Raúl drive by in a convoy of vehicles. Raúl had not stopped. The old peasant related this with a face drained of expression, as though everything had been as he expected.

The peasants, I was told by a resident of Havana, were Castro's reserve of support. The life of a peasant in Cuba was preferable to that of a peasant elsewhere in Latin America. And certainly one does not see the destitution in the countryside there that one sees elsewhere; the children are all healthy and well-fed, and they go to school, not to the hillsides miles from their home to gather bundles of firewood or to pick coffee under whose weight they return bent double.

I was not long enough in Cuba to form even the slightest estimate of Castro's popularity among the peasants. I gave lifts to many, but they were *callado* – tight-lipped. Only one spoke expansively, and he was drunk. I picked him up in the hills above Trinidad, an old colonial town of great charm. The hills were forested, and suddenly, unexpectedly, there was a clearing with a large brown modern building without anything to indicate what it was, no sign or notice to the public. In the surrounding forest I saw people walking or jogging, all in the same wine-coloured tracksuits. The building, apparently, was a sanitarium, perhaps an excellent institution: but the atmosphere was sinister, a scene from a novel by a tropical Kafka.

The drunken peasant insisted I have some of his rum. He put his arm round me as I was negotiating a hairpin bend and swore eternal friendship. I have received many such protestations before, all round the world, and try not to show that I find them tiresome, or how much I dislike the stale warm fumes of alcohol breathed into my face point blank, least of all on hairpin bends.

'How do you like Cuba?' he asked.

'Very pretty,' I replied.

'Aren't we freer than you?' he asked.

'No, on the contrary.'

He was puzzled. My words worked slowly through his alcohol befuddled brain. Perhaps the only foreigners he had met before were internationalists, the diminishing band of camp followers from Europe and America, who only praised and flattered.

'What do you mean?' he asked. 'We are free, completely free . . . Not like before.'

'I can come to Cuba,' I said. 'But can you come to my country?'

My question bothered him. I doubt he was much in the habit of abstract argument.

'Yes,' he said, choosing the lie as a method of extracting himself from an awkward situation. 'This year you come to Cuba, next year I go to London.'

I decided against pursuing the point further. There was a silence, which he broke.

'How are the police in your country?' he asked.

'How are they in yours?' I retorted.

'No problem,' he replied. 'We have no problem with the police.'

Swallowing my not inconsiderable reservations about our own force, I said that in our country the police carried no arms.

'What?' asked my passenger.

'Our police are not armed,' I repeated.

My passenger uttered what sounded like a cry of pain.

'I don't understand! I don't understand!'

I could not explain further. What was there to explain, what had he failed to understand? The difference between what I had said and what he had been told about the rest of the world? Was his concept of himself as a free man so fragile, so brittle, that the faintest contradiction threatened to shatter it? If this was not so, why his expression of pain?

It has been said that no man is as unfree as the slave who imagines himself at liberty. Here was a man, too young to remember the Batista years, who was free neither to buy nor sell, to travel, to speak, to read, to think, and yet considered himself free. What was this concept of liberty, I wondered?

It was sad that his untruth about the police in Cuba, whether intentional or not, had called forth from me less than the whole truth about the police in my own country. But if I had given him a truer, more complex account, what would he have remembered but those things that confirmed what he already thought he knew? Here is the logic of wars of propaganda, of half-truths in the service of higher Truth.

It is remarkable what such logic can do. It can obscure the most obvious truths. In the New Poetry bookshop in Havana I bought a slim volume entitled *Delitos contra la seguridad del estado* – Crimes Against the Security of the State. It was was written by Abel Enrique Hart Santamaría, son of the Minister of Culture, Armando Hart, a man of a somewhat opportunistic ideological trajectory (believing at one time that the Communist Party should not be allowed to function legally after the revolution), and Haydée Santamaría, an early follower of Castro who took part in the assault on the Moncada barracks and whose brother, Abel Santamaría was tortured to death in captivity after-wards, as was her then boyfriend, Boris Santa Coloma.

Thus Abel Enrique (named Enrique either after his paternal grandfather who was the first post-revolutionary chief justice of the Supreme Court of Cuba, or after his paternal uncle, who was killed while manufacturing a bomb during the revolution, or after both) is decidedly an aristocrat – of the new, revolutionary kind. He dedicated his slim volume to (among others) 'all the revolutionaries of the world who have suffered the torment of political imprisonment, which was for Marti more real and painful than Dante's Hell.' A man of sensibility, then, who sympathises deeply with the plight of those incarcerated for their beliefs . . .

Alas, no. His no doubt peculiar upbringing endowed him with the soul of a lackey, and with a mind less suited to explaining phenomena than to explaining them away. The main conclusion of his book, which is based on his graduation thesis at the faculty of law of Havana University, is the following:

> The fundamental cause of political crime is the existence of the exploitation of man by man. This cause disappears with the growth of the Socialist state, and with the disappearance of political crime there is the appearance of the counter-revolutionary crime . . .

In other words, if there is no political crime, there can be no political prisoners. This is doubtless what Castro means when he says there are no political prisoners in Cuba.

In this peculiar conception, political prisoners are those who are imprisoned in the course of trying to bring about superior, more 'progressive', social and political arrangements. Anyone who indulges in oppositional activity under socialism is clearly trying to bring about a reversion to a backward condition. 'Counter-revolutionary crime,' writes Abel Enrique, 'arises from the logical resistance of the overthrown classes who try to recover their former privileges.' They should be locked up.

I drove to Santa Clara, the city east of Havana where one of the last battles of the revolutionary war took place. Batista sent the flower of his remaining army in an armoured train towards the Sierra Maestra, a last desperate throw. The train was ambushed and derailed by Che Guevara, who had led his column of men 420 miles from Oriente province, during which march they had eaten only fifteen times, or once every twenty-eight miles. Three hundred men – some of the officers were scarcely more than boys – defeated 3,000. The war was over.

Some of the armoured trucks of the train now form a monument, repainted and cleaned up, but perched at angles on the rails to denote their derailment. I went in the company of a schoolteacher who took me also to his school, a styleless modern building which, though completed only the previous year, had the atomosphere of terminal tropical decay about it. His school was attended by many pupils from Angola and Mozambique, who came to it after several years on the Isle of Youth (formerly the Isle of Pines). He introduced me to a Mozambican who had been in Cuba since the age of ten, and whose main interest was in dealing in goods from the foreign currency shops. He was learning to be a mechanic at the school, which was vocational rather than academic: he told me his father owned several fishing vessels in Maputo. From this and his prolonged residence in Cuba, I concluded that his father was a man of considerable importance in FRELIMO.

In Santa Clara there is a large monument to Che, brightly floodlit at night, so that it glows over the otherwise dully illuminated city. The statue of Guevara is of craggy black metal and gives the impression he was slightly malformed. He appears to be stooping like a hunchback, and his shoulders are too broad for his height. In front of the statue is a reviewing stand of whitish stone and a large parade ground of the same material, all floodlit. That there was more light in this eerily deserted place than in the rest of the city put together seemed to me unsurprising.

The most important of the revolutionary shrines I visited was the Moncada Barracks in Santiago de Cuba. It was here that in 1953 Castro and about 130 followers, some of whom were allegedly under the impression they were going for target practise, attacked the second largest barracks in the country. The assault came at five-thirty am on the morning following the night of carnival, when many of the soldiers and officers were expected to be suffering from hangovers and thus to be incapable of resistance. The purpose of the assault was not really clear; perhaps it was to spark an uprising in Santiago, perhaps it was merely propaganda of the deed (the flag of the movement was in the colours of the anarchists, black and red).

A debate rages about the nature of Castro's ideas in 1953 – whether he was already a communist or not – but one thing is clear, that he was hell-bent on power and he wanted to achieve it by violence. His unquiet spirit, which manifested itself early in his life, could always find some pretext for violence. Though his published political programme was radical, it was not unprecedentedly so; he later claimed that it did not represent his true beliefs, but was moderated in order to draw as many people into his movement as possible. In other words, he claimed that even in 1953 he deceived his followers in order to bend them to his will. Such is the moral *milieu* in which he has lived his entire adult life that he is actually proud of his dissimulation; he is incapable of seeing that there is anything distasteful about it, and would no doubt dismiss such scruples as contemptible weakness.

Sixteen soldiers were killed in the assualt on Moncada, including the officer of the day. *They* of course are not memorialised anywhere – into the dustbin of history with them. But the assault was badly planned and executed, and it failed. Many of those captured immediately afterwards were brutally tortured and killed, initially for the sake of revenge (unsurprising in the circumstances), but later as a matter of policy. The brutality of the response to the assault turned the Cuban public against Batista and obscured the dubious nature of Castro's enterprise. The participants who were captured later – including Castro himself – were treated more leniently. Sentenced to fifteen years' imprisonment, Castro actually served less than two: not an excessive punishment for having occasioned the deaths of sixteen men. That they were in the service of a dictatorship seems to me to make little difference: Castro had displayed a taste for the genre of violence even while Cuba was still a democracy (however imperfect). One of the lessons he drew from the whole experience was never to show mercy to opponents. Mercy can rebound on those who show it.

Moncada, is a long, low building painted yellow. Most of it has since been converted into a school, an intelligent if cynical piece of propaganda, implying that the revolution has beaten swords into ploughshares. There are more schools, it is true; but there are also more guns, and certainly less butter, than ever there were before.

The bullet holes in the stucco facade have been carefully preserved (they are floodlit at night), and I shouldn't have been surprised to find peasants approaching them to touch them reverently and pray for the recovery of their sick pig. There is a museum in the barracks whose entrance is in the most pockmarked part of the wall, and there is a plaque calling eternal glory down on to the martyrs of Moncada (eternal glory having long since been incorporated into the panoply of Marxist-Leninist concepts). The contents of the museum were drearily familiar, the incarnation of half-truth and distortion in the service of lies. One does not read, for example, of the long co-operation between Batista and the communists, or of the latter's rejection of the assault on Moncada:

> We repudiate the Putschist methods, peculiar to bourgeois factions, of the action in Santiago de Cuba . . . an adventurist attempt to capture . . . military headquarters. The heroism displayed by the participants in this action is false and sterile . . .

On the contrary, the view of history presented in the museum is that presented in a book called *As We See Moncada*, a compilation of paintings by children between the ages of four and twelve, with text also by them, published by the New People publishing house in 1975. The first chapter is called *Martí, intellectual author*. The first picture is by a ninety-year-old called Isaura Costas. It is of a simple yellow house with three blue windows and a red door – the house in which Martí was born. The caption reads:

> Martí was born on Paula Street on January 28. His parents were people of modest means. He was very fond of children, and he wrote a book for us called *La Edad de Oro*; for us he is the apostle, and also the intellectual author of Moncada.

Next comes a portrait of Martí, drawn with a purple face and a pink shirt by Drago Stoyanovich, aged twelve. The caption reads:

> When we say poet, journalist and revolutionary intellectual, we think of José Martí who, by his meritorious example, helped the Cubans to figth [sic] for freedom.

Three pages on, little Jorge Cazola aged ten has painted the barracks blue, and in the red background are the flags of Cuba and of the July 26th Movement, and a portrait of Martí, also in blue. The caption reads:

> We say that Martí was the intellectual author of Moncada because, based on his revolutionary ideas, he was determined to free Cuba from Yankee imperialism – to bring her the liberty she has today.

There follows an account in pictures of the escapade, then the triumph of the revolution, and finally the conversion of Moncada into a school. The last picture, by Idelka Pedroso aged six, shows the barracks (also painted blue) flying the Cuban and July 26th Movement flags and a schoolgirl, taller than the building itself, standing beside it. The caption reads:

> The former Moncada garrison is a school now and like the other garrisons, has been transformed into a school by the Revolution because we don't want to have any sign of illiteracy in Cuba, and because we want all the children to have schools, and to put an end to the past, when the schools were only for the children of rich people. The Revolution let us put an end to this injustice.

To put an end to the past: to begin again, the dream of adolescent revolutionaries everywhere. When I read of such aspirations, I think of Goya's picture of Saturn devouring his children.

How does one escape in Cuba from the world of slogans demanding Socialism or Death, Marxism-Leninism or Death? I found solace in the Academy of Sciences, in the Calle Amargura. It contains a museum dedicated to Carlos J. Finlay, the Cuban who in 1881 demonstrated the transmission of yellow fever by mosquito. His father was a Scotsman, his mother a white Trinidadian; he studied in Paris, Madrid and Philadelphia, and was fluent in four languages. His house still stands along the Prado, a commemorative plaque affixed to its crumbling walls. Inside, the rooms have been partitioned with plywood or cardboard: the Revolution considers the rooms too large to remain in use as they were built.

The Academy of Sciences has a splendid, dark, and restful if somewhat grandiloquent interior, full of busts and paintings of historic moments in science, bookcases with leather-bound volumes, marble halls, and a lecture theatre that contains the very lectern from which

Finlay first communicated his truly great discovery to the world. How civilised the Academy seemed, uninvaded by the intellectual brutalism of the world outside. The charming lady who showed me round did not mention politics or ideology once. Nevertheless, it transpired I had chosen a bad time to come and my visit was regretfully cut short: it was Martí's birthday and the Academy was soon to close so that the staff could attend a meeting in homage to him.

What would Finlay, Cuba's greatest scientist, have made of all this? Perhaps he would have laughed. Somewhat embarrassingly for the official, state-propagated historiography, Finlay never supported the nationalists against the Spanish, though he lived through all three wars of independence. Science and medicine, not politics, were his *métier*; and one cannot help feeling he was the better man for it.

Nevertheless, a nationalist use has been found for Finlay, over and above the understandable pride in his discovery (what a fine leap of the imagination to conceive that an insect might through its bite spread the invisible agent of disease, and what intelligent dedication to prove it!) I found a book entitled *Alas amarillas* – Yellow Wings, by Sergio Amaro Mendez – devoted to the discovery and its persistent denial by the Americans, who believe to this day that their man, Walter Reed, after whom the great army hospital in Washington is named, discovered the transmission of yellow fever by mosquito. (For example, the two volume work, *Principles and Practice of Infectious Diseases*, by Mandell, Douglas and Bennett, published in 1979, states that 'The Yellow Fever Commission under Dr. Walter Reed, proved that the mosquito was the vector of yellow fever.') This refusal to recognise Finlay at his true worth is taken as just one more example of the arrogant depreciation of anything Latin American by the *anglosajones*, and much as I detest strident nationalism, whosoever it might be, I admit that as I read of Reed's dishonest treatment of Finlay, my blood began to boil on behalf of the Cubans.

Reed treated Finlay in Cuba very much as Best treated Paulescu in Romania. Both Reed and Best were hard on the heels of a great discovery, but failed to make it themselves; both therefore denigrated, misread or underestimated the work of their predecessors, either consciously or unconsciously, in order to claim priority for their own work; both probably believed that no truly important discoveries could emanate from such scientifically backward insignificant countries as Romania and Cuba.

It is humiliating enough to belong to a nation dominated politically by its neighbours; but when its culture, art and scientific achievements are also despised, the insult is complete. Imagine, then, the rage of having the greatest scientific discovery of one's nation unscrupulously appropriated by foreigners who are already replete with every kind of glory! Yes, nationalism in these circumstances is understandable; but still it is an evil, and men manipulate it for evil ends.

There are still a few foreign philo-Fidelistas living in Cuba, though their number is almost certainly dwindling. I visited one of them, an Englishwoman whose name I had been given in England, who lived in El Vedado, a section of the Harana where the former bourgeoisie built their villas with engaging rodomontade, the architectural equivalent of a Castro speech, grand Corinthian or Ionic columns (sometimes both) adorning even the most modest of constructions. They knew how to build for the climate, however: high ceilings, stone floors, verandahs, tall shuttered windows to admit the breeze or exclude the glare. They planted trees for shade and altogether succeeded in creating one of the least dispiriting suburbs I have seen anywhere in the world.

Of course, the Corinthian columns are crumbling now and perhaps one day they will collapse altogether, bringing down their *portes cochères* with them. It won't matter, of course; who needs a *porte cochère* in the new Cuba? And I must admit once more that decay has its charms, and Vedado would not have been the same for me without its atmosphere of an era irrevocably past.

The Englishwoman lived in a grand house which, however, had suffered the fate of grand houses unmaintained for thirty years. The appliances in the bathroom, for example, did not work any longer, water being distributed from a red plastic bucket. The house was dark and cool, and in a state of terminal dinginess. Personally, I shouldn't have minded living there.

When two English meet they listen carefully to the way the other speaks. They do this whether they want to or not, whether consciously or not; they would do it even if they were two survivors in a lifeboat in the middle of the ocean. The presence or absence of the glottal stop is enough to establish friendship or antagonism. Some adopt the glottal stop for political reasons: it means they identify with the under-privileged of the world. Though of humble origin, my speech contains no such stops, which makes me suspect in the eyes, or should I say the ears, of many of my fellow-countrymen.

The Englishwoman was the daughter of diplomats, and thus not a daughter of the proletariat. She had come to Cuba to visit them fifteen years ago and had stayed ever since. She worked as a translator and lived in what had been the servants' quarters, surprisingly well-built and comfortable. The basic mistrust between us prevented me from asking any of the interesting questions that naturally occurred to me. Still, it was clear enough she was a sympathiser, and described in glowing terms the new type of family doctors who not only cured but visited their elderly patients once a week to ensure they were not doing anything unhealthy. This filled me with as much gloom as it filled her with enthusiasm: the prospect of reaching 75 years of age to be hectored by young doctors was sufficient to make me wish for early death. It was Dostoyevsky who remarked that even if authority were constituted solely for our own good, we should wish to disobey it, just to assert our personalities. He was right.

She spoke, too, of the enduring enthusiasm of the crowds for Fidel. Could it be that she had failed to notice the dissolution in Cuba of the distinction between what was voluntary and what was compulsory, one of the hallmarks of a totalitarian dictatorship? Or was I merely assuming that my distaste for such regimes must be shared by a majority of Cubans?

In my hotel I met two British newspaper correspondents. They were sitting at a table for two in the restaurant and I joined them, bringing my chair over to their table. One of them, who knew Cuba well, said that the transfer of customers from one table to another was generally not allowed in Cuban restaurants, and called down the anathema of the waiters on anyone who tried it. This time, however, it passed off peacefully.

The one who knew Cuba well had just written a story about the Pan-American Games, which were due to be held in Cuba the following year. The bowling event had been cancelled because of the United States' embargo on sales to Cuba. In his article he had called the sport nine-pin bowling, and his editor had questioned whether it should not have been the ten-pin variety. He had thus spent the morning trying to find out whether the cancelled event was nine- or ten-pin bowling. The correspondent's life seems a glamorous one, but like any other it has its drudgery.

We talked of Cuba, and of how long Castro would last. They said that the lot of the Cuban peasant was better than that, say, of the Mexican peasant. In Cuba, the existence of a malnourished child would be news. Yes, I remarked, but one would have been able to say the same thing ten years ago, and if Castro survived, one might be able to say the same

thing ten years hence (though even this was doubtful). The achievements of the revolution were at best static, its drawbacks growing by the
hour. Cuba's problem was that it had been steered up a blind alley
without a reverse gear.

Many had predicted, they said, that Cuba would have difficulty
reintegrating the 50,000 soldiers brought home from the African wars
where they had defended the Marxist regimes of Angola and Ethiopia.
It had been predicted there would be unemployment and social unrest
on a large scale. But this only showed a fundamental lack of
understanding of how societies such as Cuba's functioned. There being
no market in labour, there was simply no imperative for a job to
correspond to any work that actually had to be done. Thus, instead of
unemployment, Cuba had low wages; instead of inflation, a shortage of
goods and a black market; instead of a housing shortage, universal
decay. Whether this was preferable, said the correspondents, was a
matter of fine judgment.

I pointed out two things. First that the system involved state
supervision of and interference in the details of everyday life, and also
the most absolute censorship, such as the two correspondents would
not tolerate for a moment in their own lives; second, that when refugees
from other countries of the continent voted with their feet or their
boats, they never voted for Cuba. This the correspondents did not
deny.

We talked of racism in Cuba. Racism is claimed by Marxists to be a
disease of capitalism, a form of false consciousness that it generates
among its disadvantaged classes to prevent them from seeing where
their true interests lie. Did racism still exist in Cuba? Yes, but in a
muted fashion. Certainly the United States and other countries had no
right to tax it on this score. But it was significant that most blacks
believed they had been sent in disproportionate numbers to the African
wars. (There might, of course, have been a good military reason for
doing this.) But was their belief true, I asked? One said it was
impossible to tell, but the mere fact that this belief existed among black
Cubans proved they still felt disadvantaged in Cuba. The other replied
that he wouldn't say there had been discrimination against the blacks,
exactly. It was not that more blacks had been chosen for military
service; rather it was that more whites had been exempted from it.

This was the kind of mental contortion that Cuba exacted from free
men of good will striving to be fair; what must it have exacted from the

people who lived there? (Incidentally, when we talked of racism, we did not mention the destruction of Havana's Chinatown, because the Chinese are no longer deemed a victim race.) I left Cuba with an almost physical disgust for politics, and I resolved never to write on a political subject again. I resolved to write about Nature or Art instead, if I wrote at all. But it was a resolution I knew from the start which I should find it difficult to keep.

On the aircraft back to Canada, I read a Saturday edition of *Juventud Rebelde* (Rebel Youth). In its middle pages were the first instalments of accounts by two Cuban journalists of a journey through Mexico to the United States border, obviously intended to be a crescendo of horror as the Monster (as Martí once called the United States) grew nearer. The articles were well-written, and I thought it was a clever idea to let readers see the same journey through the eyes of two different people (though my suspicious mind also thought of other reasons why the journalists should have travelled as a pair – to spy on one another).

Here were two talented young men, who had lived all their lives in Cuba and for whom the Cuban system was as natural as the free market system was to a native, say, of Chicago, suddenly plunged into a world where the rules were different, where everything they had learnt about how to survive in everyday life was irrelevant. In a way, then, they were making my journey in reverse, and I found myself wondering whether my reactions to what I had seen were not as predetermined as theirs. For in Mexico, they saw and felt all that Castro would have wished them to see and feel:

No, no thank you – I say to a child with a squalid body who offers me a magazine. He looks at me with his Indian's eyes and continues imperturbably with his work.

This time, I thought, no one is going to swindle me. In the days before I received my training as a traveller in realities so different from ours, I'd fallen into more than one trap. Images flashed in my memory: in the metro a vendor of peppermints almost succeeded in filling my pockets with them merely because I had paid attention to his sales talk; in the Xochimilco Gardens I was caught in the crossfire between two women, each offering cooked dishes with an eternal litany. Without realising it, I found myself seated at a table with a menu with special prices . . . Another time, at the Hidalgo station, I nearly found myself with an armful of native dolls because I didn't know how to ignore the salesman and wanted to be friendly. Now, only a moment before while getting on to a bus, I had what I swore would be my last setback: a woman with an ageless face offered me a little pillow that I thought was included in the price of the ticket. But it wasn't free . . .

Here is Castro's aristocratic idea of commerce as theft, as intrinsically ignoble and demeaning. Cubans were supposed, no doubt, to be appalled at the vulgarity of what was described. More likely, they would ask their elders what peppermints were.

Later, taking a train to Hermosillo with a Mexican intellectual, the author of the article reverts to an old and familiar Latin American theme:

> [Our] conversation . . . has only one subject, finance . . . Feeling a mistaken shame . . . I mention the poor state of my purse. Afterwards I learnt, in conversations begun in the editorial offices of newspapers and finished in bars . . . that this lack of money was a problem common to all the journalists of the continent. Very few were the journalists of the area who had sufficient income to pay for an investigation into a foreign country. Only the gringos and Europeans – alleged a respected colleague – had enough money to travel through our countries to write about realities they didn't understand. With us, talent is synonymous with little money.

The words *realities they didn't understand* echoed in my brain. Could it be that I had got everything wrong, that I had failed to understand Cuba? Did the slogan 'Defence for production, production for defence' not signify what it appeared to signify? Did the notice in a Havana workshop to the effect that lack of respect for one's superior at work was counter-revolutionary mean other than what I took it to mean? Did the empty shops, the crumbling buildings, the lack of entertainment, the queues, the fear, the uniformity of stated opinion, the lack of elections, the domination of one man over ten million, the universal surveillance, not mean what I took them to mean? Did medical care and a bare sufficiency of rice and beans render freedom superfluous? Was I wrong to conclude from the fact that no refugees ever sought asylum in Cuba that whatever its achievements Cuban socialism was not what anybody wanted if offered a choice? I tried to doubt my own judgment, but in the end I couldn't.

AFTERWORD

Shortly after my return from North Korea, I met a professor of medicine, a man of wide culture and learning, at a party. I described to him the ceaseless, ubiquitous and inescapable propaganda I had encountered there.

'Ah,' he replied, with a faint but knowing smile playing upon his lips (he had never been to North Korea), 'but have you considered how much power Rupert Murdoch wields in this country?'

This was not untypical of the response of liberal intellectuals to my unflattering descriptions of life in the communist countries I had visited. If one were to respond to a description of the horrors of Nazism by remarking on the prevalence in one's own country of domestic violence or of cruelty to animals, one would be regarded (rightly) as a moral idiot; yet when one responds to the horrors of communism by making fatuous comparisons with the imperfections of representative democracy, one can still consider oneself to be, in some unspecified way, on the side of the angels. And this long after the Soviet Union has admitted that what for nearly seventy years it called anti-Soviet propaganda was actually the truth.

It is curious that western intellectuals who have demanded, and generally enjoyed, the utmost freedom for themselves should for so long have felt a sentimental attachment to a form of tyranny more thoroughgoing than any other in history. For decades they blinded themselves to the obvious, and indulged in the kind of convoluted apologetics that required for their elaboration both intelligence and dishonesty. The social and psychological consequences of a system of food rationing controlled by the same power that controls the secret police and all sources of employment and information somehow failed to impinge upon their imagination. They wanted a utopia, but they wanted it elsewhere.

It was never a utopia, of course. The extraordinary deadness of communist countries, detectable even at their airports, is simply the deadness of communist prose transferred to life itself. The schemes of communist dictators to reform the whole of humanity, to eradicate all vestiges of the past, to build a new world with no connection to the old, are not the whims of despots made mad by the exercise of arbitrary power, but the natural outcome of too credulous a belief in a philosophy which is simple, arrogant, vituperative and wrong. When men reach power who believe that freedom is the recognition of necessity, is it any surprise that tyranny ensues?

The creed is dead or dying, at least in Europe. But Europe is not the world, and credulity springs eternal. There are Marxist guerrilla movements in many parts of the world where intellectuals take advantage of the desperation (which they do everything to augment and magnify) of the poor. Everywhere they are fighting to create the New Man and the New Society, as if it had never been tried before, as if the consequences were unknown. After completing my journeys through Albania, North Korea, Romania, Vietnam and Cuba, I visited Peru. By then Romania had had its revolution, Albania was wavering, and cracks had appeared even in North Korea's granite facade. But in Peru, the former Professor of Philosophy at Ayacucho University, Abimael Guzman, led the Shining Path movement, *Sendero Luminoso*, believed by him to be the only truly Marxist movement in the world, the vanguard of the coming universal revolution. In the name of the proletariat, to which Guzman never belonged, children of nine and ten were being taught to cut throats with knives and crush skulls with rocks; and a new device, drawing inspiration from the car-bomb, had been employed to some effect – the *niño-bomba*, the child-bomb. Children were loaded with dynamite and exploded at their target. *Sendero Luminoso* justified the means by the inevitable end:

Fifteen thousand million years of matter in motion are leading
necessarily and inexorably . . . towards a society of Complete Harmony.

INDEX